1982

Don and Mary
from
Joe and Arlene

we hope this will help to identify
any strange birds in your woods!

Enjoying

INDIANA BIRDS

ENJOYING

INDIANA BIRDS

BY

Alfred (Bud) Starling

DRAWINGS BY

Donna L. McCarty

INDIANA UNIVERSITY PRESS

Bloomington and London

Manufactured in the United States of America

Library of Congress Cataloging in Publication Data
Starling, Alfred, 1928–
  Enjoying Indiana birds.
  Bibliography: p. 305
  Includes index.
  1. Birds—Indiana. 2. Bird watching—Indiana.
  I. Title.
QL684.I5S7 598.2′073′09772 78-3247
ISBN 0-253-31956-0   3 4 5 82 81 80 79

In appreciation—

to Catherine J. Hill, friend and co-worker, for all
the help given to me throughout the years, with a
special thanks to Catherine for her help in deciphering
my hieroglyphics and "private" spelling.

and to Cynthia M. Tabbert, for her careful editing
and typing of the text of this book. Without Cynthia's
love of the printed word and constant cajoling of me
to put down in writing my feelings about birds, this
book would have had to be written posthumously!

*and to my wonderful family—*my wife, Norma, and my
children, Wayne, Keith, Scott, and Wendy—who have
always been understanding of my obsession with birds
and have allowed me to spend the necessary time away
from domestic duties to pursue this obsession.

CONTENTS

JULY

AUGUST

SEPTEMBER

OCTOBER

NOVEMBER

December

INTRODUCTION

BIRDS AND MEN have always had a special relationship. People have historically looked at birds in their search for answers to some of life's questions. During Columbus's first venture to the New World, it was a dove carrying a green sprig that told the weary sailors that land was not far off. In Europe it was golden canaries which men took down with them into the mines that signaled whether or not the mines contained fatal gases and whether it was advisable for the miners to continue down or to draw back in their quest for valuable ore. Songbirds dying after the spraying of insecticides prompted Rachel Carson to write a revolutionary book, *Silent Spring*, thus creating a new era of environmental awareness.

History is dotted with examples of men who became intrigued with birds, and then used this interest to change the world. Charles Darwin, after thinking about the behavior of finches on the Galapagos Islands for twenty years, concluded that life was not created instantly, but rather evolved through a long-term, gradual process in which the inhabitants of the world either adapted to their environment or perished.

A birder, naturalist, philosopher, and author, Henry David Thoreau, who crystallized his thoughts while scrutinizing birds and the out-of-doors, changed the political climate of the world with his essay on civil disobedience.

A writer and lover of birds, John Burroughs, taught a man who eventually became President of the United States the romance of birding, and later this man, Theodore Roosevelt, was responsible for the establishment of many of our national parks, parks that are now enjoyed by millions of people each year.

Poets have frequently referred to the "dove of peace" and the "bluebird of happiness"; and our Founding Fathers chose to select a bird, the bald eagle, as our national emblem.

The question is why have birds had this extraordinary influence on people? Why not fish, insects, butterflies, or mammals? Why not ferns, grasses, wildflowers, trees, or anything else that makes up our environment?

An answer to this intriguing question would require an analysis of all of the feelings that man has, for birds are so diverse that they appeal to all the different views and emotions that man is capable of expressing. For those who appreciate beauty, there are warblers—thirty to thirty-five in Indiana alone. They run the gauntlet from the rather plain pine warbler to the spectacularly colored Blackburnian; and their songs range from the high-pitched cadence of the blackpoll (heard only by those with a keen sense of hearing) to the raucous ramblings of the yellow-breasted chat. Those who admire the trait of aggression can look to the hawks and owls for the epitome of this quality; for industriousness, to the many species of birds that possess it in large measure, like wrens and sparrows. Courage, tenacity, devotion to family—these are all qualities evident in the world of birds.

The birds that I've chosen to include in this book are not the only birds that can be found in the state of Indiana; actually, well over two hundred different species of birds either nest or pass through Indiana each year. Also, the birds covered in this book can be seen in most of the states east of the Mississippi River. With a few exceptions I've avoided writing about rare or exotic birds and have concentrated instead on the birds that the average person with an active (or latent) interest in birds can see by putting forth a reasonable effort.

Among the birds which I have not included in this book but which do occur in this region and which could be found by anyone putting forth a moderate amount of effort are the following: horned grebe, snow goose, black duck, gadwall, shoveler, both greater and lesser scaup, ruddy duck, common and red-breasted merganser, broad-winged hawk, ruffed grouse, and Virginia rail.

Shorebirds which might have been included are semipalmated plover, American golden plover, solitary sandpiper, both greater and lesser yellowlegs, least sandpiper, short-billed dowitcher, and semipalmated sandpiper. Among the gulls and terns there would be herring gull, Bonaparte's gull, Forster's tern, common tern, and Caspian tern. Flycatchers not included are least, willow, and wood pewee. The swallows omitted are tree, rough-winged, and barn. Both the long- and short-billed marsh wrens were excluded.

The vireos and warblers omitted here but which are found in Indiana each year are the following: yellow-throated vireo, solitary vireo, warbling vireo, blue-winged warbler, Tennessee, Nashville, parula, magnolia, Cape May, cerulean, Blackburnian, yellow-throated, chestnut-sided, prairie, palm, Kentucky, and Canada warblers. Also excluded are the ovenbird and Louisiana and northern waterthrushes. Lastly, the following sparrows are not included here: savannah, grasshopper, vesper, chipping, and swamp.

In my judgment, all of the above-named birds, plus the ones included in this volume, could make up a personal list of birds seen in Indiana in your lifetime. (Experienced birders call this a "life list.") If you are interested in pursuing this challenge, you need to follow these four steps:

1. Purchase a pair of fairly good binoculars. I recommend seven-power, with a 35 millimeter front lens, at a cost of $25 to $400. Approximate cost for a good pair, $100.
2. Buy a reliable field guide. I would recommend *A Field Guide to the Birds: Eastern Land and Water Birds* by Roger Tory Peterson (cost, about $8). First written in the middle 1930s, it has been revised a number of times since. This book is considered to be the birders' "bible."
My second choice would be *Birds of North America* by Chandler Robbins, Bertel Bruun, and Herbert S. Zim, published by Golden Press at a price of about $5 to $8, paperback or hardback.
3. Discipline yourself to spend a few hours each week getting out to a park or woods or large body of water (reservoirs, lakes, or rivers). The important thing is to get out regularly, perhaps weekly.
4. Be patient in trying to learn all the birds. It can't be done all in one year. In fact, you should guard against getting discouraged the first year. Consider—many of the warblers and shorebirds are here only for a week or two in spring and fall. In addition, many birds require such specialized habitat that a birder must search out widely diverse and distant areas.

Time spent the first year should be considered as a learning experience, a whetting of your appetite for the next year. In the second year, you should feel more confident of your ability to identify fifty to one hundred different birds. By your third year, seeing all of the birds included in this book would be a good possibility. In your fourth year, you should have the satisfaction of knowing that you are a participant in an activity that has been called America's most popular pastime. It can be a worthwhile adjunct to anyone's lifestyle, or one that can become an all-consuming passion.

Birding can involve as little exertion as watching birds from your kitchen window, or as much as climbing a mountain in search of an eagle's or a hawk's nest. It can be a hobby, a sport, or a science, depending on each person's interest and personality. It can be pursued as a youngster or as a retiree. It can be nearly cost-free (one of the best birders I ever met never owned a decent pair of binoculars), or it can require considerable expenditure for telescopes, photographic equipment, books, recording devices, and trips to exotic and faraway places. Birding can be followed singly, in pairs, or in groups—as a personal endeavor or as an organized activity.

The National Audubon Society now numbers around 500,000 members, with chapters in all states, including Hawaii and Alaska. There are at least fourteen chapters in Indiana. I recommend attending a meeting of the chapter closest to your home or, better yet, a field trip with an Audubon group near you. Association with experienced birders can be an enormous learning help.

Each month of the year offers a special menu of birding fare. Most people like spring and fall birding. But some claim that there is nothing to equal birding in the winter or summer. Some of my most exciting birding experiences have occurred during a torrential rain or during a severe snowstorm.

This book has been arranged as a month-by-month chronicle of birds found throughout the year, rather than as a compilation in an alphabetical or a scientific order, with the hope that a reader may become interested in a bird described and be impelled to leave his easy chair and go out to see the live bird. In all cases I've personally seen the birds during the month in which they are included here, and it is possible for you to see them, also. Granted, a trip to a wooded swamp to find some birds, like the prothonotary, may be required. On the other hand, in order to see other birds, like the cardinal, you may only be required to look out the window.

Birds included here were placed in particular months for specific reasons. For instance, I chose to place the cardinal in the February section because it is during the frequently drab days of this month that the cheerful, bright-red cardinal stands out most. It may be an author's whim, but I recommend that a reader turn to the January section of this book to read about the birds normally seen in one of our coldest months on a sultry, hot August afternoon spent on a porch swing.

It is not necessary to have a Ph.D. in ornithology to contribute to man's knowledge of birds or to go on a safari to Africa to learn about birds. There are a great many different birds in your own neighborhood, county, and state. My purpose in writing this book is to acquaint you better with the birds right at hand and, perhaps, to kindle an interest that will bring as much lifelong enjoyment to you as I have found.

ALFRED (BUD) STARLING

Indianapolis, Indiana

Enjoying

INDIANA BIRDS

JANUARY

JANUARY IS NOT A MONTH that is generally associated with birds. In fact, there are fewer species present in Indiana in the months of December, January, and February than during any other time of the year; but if I were to select one month to begin to learn the birds of Indiana, it would be the month of January.

The fact that there are fewer birds enables a person to concentrate on the birds that are here. It is one thing to say that you have seen a downy woodpecker and a hairy woodpecker, but it is quite another thing to be able to say say that you know intimately these two similar woodpeckers, know how the two differ in their feeding habits, their flight, their call notes, their mannerisms, and how their call notes and habits change as the year progresses.

Birding in January offers the opportunity to know in depth the birds of an area. The deciduous trees are without leaves, making it easier to see birds, the woods are quiet, few people are about, and there is a still sereneness throughout the landscape that is not duplicated at any other time.

1

Each January presents questions that beg for answers. Will the winter finches build up, or will they mysteriously disperse? Will it be a good year for the goshawk and rough-legged hawk? Will the "half-hardies" (brown thrasher, hermit thrush, robin, and phoebe) survive the harshness of winter? These questions and others must be examined and answered each year. You don't need to consult a scholarly, scientific journal or a research ornithologist to find answers to these questions; with a little time and effort, you can decide the answers yourself. The reward of knowing that you have added, however minutely, to the bank of knowledge of birds can be a satisfying experience.

January is also the ideal time to start a bird list. Bird listing has become a very popular activity; just about all birders—people who regularly study birds—maintain a list of some sort. A bird list can be as simple or as complex as you wish to make it. Some of the possible lists that you may want to consider are the following:

> *A life list.* Birds seen during your lifetime comprise this list. It can be divided into birds seen in the United States and birds seen in the world. The top birders in the U. S. have more than 700 birds on their U. S. life lists; and anything over 600 birds is considered outstanding. A world list of over 2,000 would put you in the major league of birders.
>
> *A state list.* A number of less demanding lists may be worthwhile for you to consider, for example, either a yearly or a lifetime list of birds sighted in your state. A figure of 200 different species for a yearly list or 250 for a life state list would be considered outstanding.
>
> *An area list.* You might want to consider a year's list for a specific park or area in Indiana where you spend leisure hours. If you can turn up 200 different birds in a park or other area, you can be satisfied that you have done a thorough job.
>
> *Your home list.* Another list that you might want to consider is a yearly list of birds seen on your own property. This list will vary considerably, depending on the specific size and type of land involved. Any list of over seventy-five birds found during the year without leaving your own backyard is a good score. In addition, many people keep track of the spring arrival dates of their backyard birds.

Listing can be fun, but starting the year with a goal of becoming familiar with the birds that you will encounter during the rest of the year is the important object, and there is no better time to start than January.

SIZE: *L. 28–36" (71–91 cm). W. 58" (1.47 m).* COLORING: *In breeding plumage and in summer, head and neck black with a white collar. Back has a distinctive white and black pattern. In winter plumage appears as a grayish bird with lighter underparts. Has prominent bill.* HABITAT: *Ponds, lakes, reservoirs, oceans.* NESTING: *Substantial mass of vegetation in or near water, frequently on an island; 2 eggs.* UNUSUAL MANNERISMS: *The eerie, wild "laugh" and weird, yodeling calls heard in its breeding*

Common Loon

[GAVIA IMMER]

The first weekend of a new year is an appropriate time to become acquainted with the common loon. The loon is the first bird listed in a scientifically written bird reference or catalog of birds. The reason for this is that biologists have determined that the loon, our most primitive bird, has certain physical characteristics that link it to reptiles whence birds are thought to have evolved.

The primitivism doesn't imply that the loon is ill equipped to fill its niche in life—quite the opposite—for it is endowed with a sharp bill and very powerful wings that enable the loon to dive to great depths and pursue fish, its normal diet. Very few fish can avoid the powerful dive and the determination of a loon when it is searching for food. Many years ago, loons were considered "fair game" for hunters because there was statistical evidence that the loon would eat species of fish that were held in high esteem by fishermen. It seems, now, that loons are better appreciated for their great addition to our environment and are seldom hunted.

The loon is a more common bird in Indiana than one might expect. In the fall, it passes through our state in good numbers. It prefers the larger bodies of water; for instance, I have seen more than 100 of these big, diving birds on one reservoir, Eagle Creek, during one month (October). The loon does not, as a rule, winter in the state, although it has been sighted on recent Christmas counts. In the early spring, as the ice starts to leave the lakes and reservoirs, it will again be seen throughout Indiana. The major nesting areas are the lakes of Canada. As Hoosiers who have spent their vacations at fishing camps in Canada can attest, virtually every lake of any size has its pair of nesting loons.

grounds seldom heard in Indiana. One of the most accomplished diving waterfowl, having the ability to stay submerged an amazing length of time. IDENTIFYING HINTS: *Long-bodied, with thick, pointed bill held horizontally. In flight appears hunchbacked.* STATUS IN INDIANA: *Fairly common spring and fall migrant. Uncommon winter resident when there is open water. Does not nest in Indiana.* RANGE: *Breeds from Alaska south to northernmost border of United States. Winters as far north as there is open water, south to the Gulf Coast.*

The common loon is most often seen in Indiana in its non-breeding or winter plumage. In this plumage it appears to be a large, rather long bird with gray head and back, white underparts, and a prominent bill. In the breeding plumage, the common loon has a black head and neck, and the back and sides have a black-and-white checkered look.

It is unfortunate that the loon is seldom heard in Indiana, for the "call of the loon" so often referred to in literature is a unique sound of nature. Once, when it was spring on Lake Ontario and the lake was fog covered, I heard hundreds of loons giving their maniacal laughter. This sound, that early morning, seemed to me to be perfect background music for a scene from Dante's Inferno.

Bald Eagle

[HALIAEETUS LEUCOCEPHALUS]

Americans celebrating their nation's bicentennial in 1976 were encouraged by the fact that their national bird, the American bald eagle, was making a determined comeback.

Ten years ago knowledgeable persons were warning that this great symbol of America would become extinct as a nesting bird in the United States. Nesting sites that had been used by bald eagles for years were being deserted, and those eagles continuing to use these habitual nesting sites were not successful in raising young. There were various

SIZE: *L. 30–31" (76–79 cm). W. 7–8' (2.1–2.4 m).* COLORING: *Blackish-brown in adult plumage, white head and white tail. Immature birds lack the white head and tail.* HABITAT: *Seldom seen away from water—rivers, seacoasts, lakes, marshes.* NESTING: *Mammoth nest of sticks, usually in the top of a tall tree, frequently a dead tree; 1–3 white eggs.* UNUSUAL MANNERISMS: *Male and female reputed to mate for life. Same nest, with addition of materials, used year after year. Eats primarily dead or dying fish.* IDENTIFYING HINTS: *Soars on flattened wings. Immature birds can best be told by large size and a scattering of white in the wing linings.* STATUS IN INDIANA: *Rare migrant, spring and fall. Most frequently it is the immature birds that are seen in November and December.* RANGE: *Breeds primarily in Alaska, Canada, and northwestern states. Winters as far north as there is unfrozen water.*

hypotheses as to the reasons for this dilemma. The most widely accepted theory was that the bald eagle, being primarily a fish eater, was consuming fish that had been contaminated by the insecticide, DDT; and the eagle's reproductive system was being adversely affected.

In 1974 there were signs that the bald eagle decline had slowed, and the next year there were indications that the bald eagle population in the United States was stabilizing and even improving somewhat. The eagle was returning to areas where it had not nested for years, and people who were keeping counts of hawk and eagle migration at some of the famous hawk-watching points in eastern North America commented on the good numbers of immature bald eagles sighted—a sure sign of successful nesting.

Just such a young eagle was sighted in mid-January 1976 perched in a tree overhanging a bank of White River, just east of the Indianapolis Museum of Art grounds. A group of birders there was treated to an unusually close look at the eagle.

It is one thing to cite the vital statistics of the bald eagle—almost three feet tall, weighing around ten pounds, with wingspan measuring up to seven feet—but it is quite another thing to see this grand bird closely enough to watch it laboriously flap its huge wings as its moves away from those who have intruded upon its privacy.

The adult bald eagle is an easy bird to identify. The great size, together with the white head and white tail, cannot be confused with any other bird. Unfortunately, it takes four years for the bald eagle to reach this mature stage of its majestic plumage. The immature bird can be mistaken for the golden eagle. Look for the white markings on the front part of the bald eagle's wing and also for the lack of a black band on the tail. The bald eagle flies with its wings held flat, while the golden eagle's flight is like the flight of the soaring hawks.

The bald eagle is <u>not known to nest in Indiana anymore</u>, although *1978* it is seen occasionally in migration during the spring and fall. There are a number of records of its wintering in Indiana when it can find open water.

Just why this eagle was seen within five miles of Monument Circle in Indianapolis is open to debate. It may be that it had moved south as the lakes and rivers to the north froze solid—or, perhaps, having heard of the bicentennial decorations put on display in the Mile Square area of Indianapolis, it wanted to give encouragement to the citizens who had worked so hard, preparing for our country's two-hundredth birthday.

Downy Woodpecker

[PICOIDES PUBESCENS]

Hairy Woodpecker

[PICOIDES VILLOSUS]

The most common woodpecker in Indiana and in the United States is the downy woodpecker. It is found in almost every woods throughout Indiana and is with us each month of the year.

Perhaps if it were not so common, the downy's admirable qualities would be better appreciated. John James Audubon, over one hundred years ago, summed up his analysis of the downy woodpecker by saying, "It is the hardiest, most industrious and spirited of all the wood-peckers." These characteristics, coupled with the fact that the downy eats large numbers of insects that are detrimental to man's interest, make it a most welcome part of our fauna.

The downy woodpecker has a white breast and white back. The wings are black with a series of white wing bars, and the head and tail are also black. The male and female are identical except that the male has a small red patch at the back of the head which the female lacks. The downy and its close relative, the hairy woodpecker, are the only woodpeckers found in Indiana with white backs.

On one recent January walk, it seemed to me that the male and female downys were beginning to think of the housekeeping duties in which they would be involved in about three months. The male was paying more attention to the female than he had previously, and

DOWNY WOODPECKER

Size: L. 6–7" (15–17 cm). Coloring: *White back and breast, black wings with white markings. Male has red patch on the top of the head which female lacks.* Habitat: *Mixed open woods; suburban backyards, orchards.* Nesting: *Nests in cavity in tree, stump or fencepost; 4–5 white eggs.* Unusual Mannerisms: *Most common woodpecker in eastern North America. Will readily come to a feeder containing suet.* Identifying Hints: *Undulating flight, small bill.* Status in Indiana: *Common year-round resident and nesting bird.* Range: *Breeds from Alaska to southern United States. Winters throughout its range.*

although it may have been my imagination, it seemed to me that the female was inspecting, with a critical eye, trees that might be suitable for raising a brood of young this year. The downy will select a tree or stump and excavate a hole about one inch in diameter and then proceed to dig out a cavity about a foot down from the opening. There, the female will deposit her four or five eggs, and a new generation of downys should take their place in the world by the middle of June.

The hairy woodpecker looks identical to the downy except for being two inches longer. This size difference can be deceiving when the two species are seen separately. A better field mark is the size of the bill. The hairy's bill is about as long as its head and is thick at the base. The downy's bill is much smaller. A good analogy would be a dentist's probe in relation to a carpenter's chisel. The hairy woodpecker is more of a sedentary bird than the downy and is more often seen in the deep woods, although it occasionally will partake of suet in a yard feeder. Downys will outnumber hairys at a feeding station at least twenty to one.

Both the downy and the hairy are superbly equipped to fulfill their roles as extractors of grubs and insects from trees. Their two toes in front and two toes in back enable them to clamp to a tree and position themselves to deliver hammer blows to the tree. Once a hole is made in the bark, both the hairy and downy can make use of their remarkable tongues which can be extended beyond the bill into the cavity of the tree. The tongues then become spear-like and can be used effectively to extract the food the bird is seeking.

It strikes me that the woodpeckers' tongues are used, almost exclusively, to do good in the world—while man frequently uses his to distort truths and inflict hurts upon his fellow inhabitants of the earth.

HAIRY WOODPECKER

SIZE: *L. 8½–10½" (21–26 cm).* COLORING: *White back and breast, black wings with white markings. Large bill.* HABITAT: *Deciduous forests, wooded swamps.* NESTING: *Nests in cavity in trees or dead stub of tree; 4 white eggs.* UNUSUAL MANNERISMS: *More often seen in larger and more mature woods than its close relative, the downy woodpecker.* IDENTIFYING HINTS: *The call note, a single, emphatic, "peek," separates this bird from the downy.* STATUS IN INDIANA: *Fairly common year-round resident and nesting bird.* RANGE: *Breeds from northern Alaska to Central America. Winters throughout its range.*

SIZE: *L. 4–5″ (10–13 cm).* COLORING: *Black cap and bib, white cheeks.* HABITAT: *Edge of deciduous woods, ornamental plantings around suburban backyards.* NESTING: *Normally in a tree cavity, occasionally will accept man-made birdhouses; 6–8 eggs.* UNUSUAL MANNERISMS: *Very tame, has been known to feed out of the hand. Readily patronizes winter feeder supplied with sunflower seed.* IDENTIFYING HINTS: *Quite vocal, calls its own name.* STATUS IN INDIANA: *Year-round resident, is replaced by very similar "black capped" chickadee north of central Indiana.* RANGE: *Extends eastward from New Jersey through states south of Great Lakes west to Oklahoma and south to Texas and Florida.*

Carolina Chickadee

[PARUS CAROLINENSIS]

Just about anyone who feeds wild birds during the winter in Indiana has been visited by a chickadee. In fact, the chickadee is often the favorite bird of those persons who have a bird feeding program. A supply of sunflower seeds and suet will almost surely attract a small band of chickadees—even in the heart of a metropolitan area.

They seem to delight in adverse weather; let there be rain, and the chickadee maintains his cheerful ways. Let there be a raging snowstorm and zero temperatures, and the chickadees continue, undaunted, on their happy ways—looking almost like children frolicking in the snow. They seem to enjoy human activity and company, and with patience, a person can even tempt them to take sunflower seeds from the hand.

There are a number of different species of chickadees in the United States, but only two are found in Indiana, the Carolina chickadee and the black-capped chickadee. The Carolina chickadee is the southern form and is the chickadee found from Indianapolis, south. In the northern parts of the state, the black-capped is the predominant species. The difference between the two is slight; both are small birds with a black cap and bib and a white cheek patch. The differences are reputed to be that the Carolina chickadee is slightly smaller, has less white in the wing, and has a slightly different song. In the Indianapolis area, I've never seen a chickadee that I've felt positively was a black-capped, although I'm sure a few get this far south some winters.

Chickadees nest, normally, in cavities in trees or tree stumps. Although they will use abandoned woodpeckers' holes, they are fully capable of excavating their own nesting sites. They have surprisingly large broods, and it is not unusual for chickadees to raise six or seven young each year.

Although chickadees are year-round residents in Indiana, it is in the winter that they are most in evidence. Their cheerful, oft-repeated song, "chicka-dee-dee-dee," is easily remembered and is familiar to just about everyone who spends any time out of doors.

There is something encouraging about watching chickadees in the winter. No matter how dark and gloomy the day—no matter how bad the weather—the chickadees remain lively and saucy: the bird with the cheerful heart.

Blue Jay

[CYANOCITTA CRISTATA]

"Bailiff, will you please bring in the accused?"

"Yes, Your Honor."

"Mr. Blue Jay, you stand accused of perpetrating crimes against humanity. How do you plead?"

"Not guilty, Your Honor."

"Very well, the court will now hear the prosecuting attorney's case against Blue Jay."

"Your Honor, it is a well-known fact that Blue Jay is very aggressive, that he tends to monopolize the feeding station, that he and his female companion (who, incidentally, looks like him) wear very gaudy attire, and that this shockingly blue garb is topped off by a very prominent crest. Your Honor, we have eye witnesses who have seen Blue Jay stealing eggs from his neighbors' places of habitation. We have other witnesses who will testify that Blue Jay becomes very secretive during the months of May and June and that he is very reluctant to have anyone see where he is raising his family.

"And, Your Honor, another point I would like to stress is that Jay has no regard for the suggestions of Planned Parenthood. Why, 'tis said, they have four or five young ones each year. Now, if all these heinous crimes are not enough to convict this rascal, I can state unequivocally (for I heard it myself just the other day in snow-covered woods not far from my house) that Blue Jay mimics other inhabitants of the woods. Your Honor, I rest my case."

"Will the defense attorney please come forward and summarize why

SIZE: *L. 11–12″ (28–30 cm).* COLORING: *Bright blue above, white below, prominent crest, black facial markings.* HABITAT: *City parks, suburban yards, forests, both deciduous and coniferous.* NESTING: *Bulky nest, usually well-hidden, of twigs and bark, lined with fine roots and pine needles; 4–5 eggs.* UNUSUAL MANNERISMS: *Great mimic. Can mimic the red-shouldered hawk perfectly. Migrates in large numbers in spring and fall.* IDENTIFYING HINTS: *Easily recognized by its familiar "jay, jay" harsh call, as well as its (self-) descriptive, bold cry, "thief, thief, thief!"* STATUS IN INDIANA: *Year-round resident and common nesting bird throughout the state. Most of our nesting jays move south in winter and are replaced by birds which have nested to the north.* RANGE: *Breeds throughout its range, east to the Rocky Mountains from south Canada to the Gulf of Mexico.*

he feels that Blue Jay should be found 'not guilty' of the crimes for which he is accused?"

"Thank you, Your Honor. It will be a pleasure to speak in defense of Blue Jay. Allow me to discuss, point by point, the accusations that my worthy opponent has brought up. Aggressive? Yes, Blue Jay is aggressive, but since when is that a crime? Much of the work of the world would not get done if it weren't for aggression. Extreme dress? I would suggest that Blue Jay is a style setter. The blue of his attire is one of the most beautiful colors in the world. I prefer it to the blue of the bluebird, which is held in high esteem. As for Blue Jay's crest—why, to my eyes, it is more attractive than the crest of Cardinal. Secrecy around the homestead? Yes, but that is because Blue Jay is a good provider and protector of his family. Certainly THAT is no crime!

"My worthy opponent brought up a question as to Blue Jay's diet, in that Blue Jay was seen taking an egg. Your Honor, I happen to know that he is very cholesterol-conscious, and eggs make up an infinitesimal percentage of his diet. As a matter of fact, I have some carefully gathered statistics which show that over seventy-five percent of Blue Jay's diet consists of grains, nuts, and berries. A mimic? Yes, Blue Jay IS a mimic, but is it not true that we all mimic sounds or actions that we have heard or seen? If this be a crime, we all are guilty! In conclusion, Your Honor, I would like to say that Blue Jay adds dash, color, and exuberance to our community; and the world would lose some of its sparkle if Blue Jay weren't around."

"Ladies and gentlemen of the jury, you have heard the evidence. Let me admonish you to consider only the facts and not to be influenced by hearsay evidence."

Now, what say *you*? Is Blue Jay innocent—or guilty?

Long-eared Owl

[A s i o   o t u s]

One of the more uncommon owls found in Indiana is the long-eared owl. Just how uncommon is open to conjecture. Both Amos W. Butler's studies at the beginning of this century and more recent studies indicate that the long-eared owl is a nesting bird in Indiana which can also be found here during the winter months.

The difficulty in determining the proper status of this bird, not only in Indiana, but also in other states, is that it frequently goes undetected. Very nocturnal, it is seldom active during the day. It is silent except during the mating season, in March and April. It can be confused with its more common relative, the great-horned owl. The long-eared owl is quite safe from detection because of its ability to blend with its surroundings. Often it will roost on a limb, close to the trunk of a tree, and won't flush until the tree is pounded on. This is especially true if the female is setting on eggs or has young birds in the nest.

The long-eared owl is a crow-sized, grayish-brown bird with an orangish-brown face. Its eyes are a piercing yellow. The ear tufts, which aren't really ears, are positioned close to the center of the head. The streaking on the breast tends to be vertical, rather than horizontal, as is the streaking on the great-horned owl.

The long-eared owl is said to be one of our most beneficial birds of prey. More than eighty percent of its food is made up of mice, rats, moles, and other members of the rodent family. An analysis of the long-eared owl's pellets (regurgitation of bones and fur) taken from a roosting area, shows that very few birds are eaten by this owl and that its food is, primarily, other nocturnal creatures.

One cold January morning when a long-eared owl was pointed out to me by a young friend, a keen observer, the owl was behaving in a typical manner, quietly perched near the trunk of a large pine tree. The vertical streaking on the breast and the gray-brown coloring made the bird appear to be part of the tree. It could easily have been over-

looked. There are, undoubtedly, other long-eared owls secretly hiding in some of the patches of evergreens that dot the Indiana landscape. The challenge is in trying to find one of these mysterious birds.

SIZE: *L. 13–16" (33–40 cm). W. 39" (1 m).* COLORING: *Gray-brown back, chestnut facial disk, yellow eyes, vertical breast streaking.* HABITAT: *Deciduous and evergreen forests.* NESTING: *Often uses old nests of crows, hawks, or squirrels. Occasionally nests in tree cavities, usually evergreens; 4–5 white eggs.* UNUSUAL MANNERISMS: *Difficult to flush, generally stays close to trunk of the tree. In winter, occasionally gathers in small groups.* IDENTIFYING HINTS: *Chestnut facial disk, yellow eyes. Ear tufts close to center of head. Vertical striping on breast.* STATUS IN INDIANA: *Status somewhat unknown because of its secretive habits; has been known to nest in Indiana in the past. Very uncommon fall, winter, and spring resident.* RANGE: *Breeds from northern Canada to mid-central United States. Winters from southern Canada to Gulf of Mexico.*

Starling

[STURNUS VULGARIS]

The most unpopular bird in America is the starling. Yet, there is good evidence that the starling eats more insects that are detrimental to man's interest than any other bird in the United States. It is generally agreed that the starling was introduced in this country because of its proven appetite for various harmful beetles. However, no one could have predicted, in 1890, that the starling population would reach the giant proportions that it now has attained.

After many unsuccessful attempts to establish the starling in this

SIZE: L. 7½–8½″ (19–21 cm). COLORING: *In spring and summer, black bird with purple and green iridescence, yellow bill. In winter, heavily streaked with white dots, dark bill.* HABITAT: *Cities, parks, suburban areas, farmlands.* NESTING: *Nest located in cavity almost anywhere; 4–6 pale bluish-white eggs.* UNUSUAL MANNERISMS: *Excellent mimic.* IDENTIFYING HINTS: *Gathers in huge flocks in winter. In flight, stubby tails. Yellow billed in summer; dark billed in winter.* STATUS IN INDIANA: *Abundant, year-round resident and nesting bird.* RANGE: *Breeds from southern Canada south to Florida and Gulf of Mexico states. Winters throughout its breeding range.*

country, a relatively small breeding colony took hold in New York City in 1891. The previous year sixty birds had been released in New York City, and this group was augmented by an additional forty birds in the spring of 1891.

This group of one hundred birds began to breed and build up to the point where it became necessary for the birds to move out of the city. By the turn of the century, the starling had been sighted in Connecticut and New Jersey. By 1915 it was being reported in Pennsylvania and Virginia. During the 1920s the starling was reliably reported as far west as Iowa and as far south as Florida and Louisiana. Sometime in the 1940s, the starling had reached California.

In fifty years the original number of one hundred birds had increased to millions of birds, and the huge gatherings of starlings, in the fall, had become a familiar sight to just about everyone living in America. The reason for this phenomenal success has been subject to much debate.

Many factors are involved—abundant food, lack of natural enemies, favorable climate—all of which have worked to the starlings' benefit. Its ability to change its diet from insects (when they are abundant) to fruits and seeds (when they are plentiful) is a decided asset for the starling.

Another asset is that, because of its early arrival at its breeding grounds, the starling can select the most favorable nesting sites. The fact that a pair is often able to raise three successive broods of six birds each year has certainly added to its population growth.

Indiana has its share of starlings. Anyone who has seen the vast hordes of these birds going to roost, each fall evening as the sun goes down, can attest to this fact. In the winter, it is the most common bird to be found in the cities. Recent studies indicate that the starling population has become stabilized and may be decreasing somewhat. For some time, this trend has also been evident for another import, the house sparrow.

The lesson that we should have learned from our experience with the starling is obvious. Our environment is very complex, and we should be extremely careful about introducing unnatural elements into it. How does that television commercial go? "It isn't nice to fool mother nature."

SIZE: *L. 17–19½″ (43–49 cm).* COLORING: *Red crest, black back and belly, white facial markings and neck stripe.* HABITAT: *Substantial woods, both coniferous and deciduous.* NESTING: *Nesting cavity excavated in tree or stump; 3–4 white eggs.* UNUSUAL MANNERISMS: *This species changing its habits; now being seen in suburban areas.* IDENTIFYING HINTS: *Oval-shaped nesting hole, large size of bird, brilliant red crest. Conspicuous white wing lining evident in flight.* STATUS IN INDIANA: *Fairly common year-round resident and nesting bird.* RANGE: *Breeds throughout the eastern half of the United States, southern Canada, and the north parts of the West Coast. Winter resident throughout its range.*

Pileated Woodpecker

[DRYOCOPUS PILEATUS]

My nomination for the most spectacular bird to nest in Indiana is the pileated woodpecker. This crow-sized woodpecker with a flaming red crest has made an excellent comeback during the past twenty years. Some of the earlier ornithological literature predicted that the pileated would become extinct in America as the primeval forests disappeared. This has not happened. The pileated has been able to adapt successfully to its changing environment; while our other large woodpecker, the ivory-billed, has not.

During the past two years, I've been told of three different sets of pileateds feeding at backyard feeding stations within ten miles of the center of Indianapolis. Years ago, this would have been unheard of. Still, its preferred habitat is a large mature forest. Most ornithologists agree that they mate for life and use the same nesting areas for many years. A good clue to their presence in the area is the large oblong holes they hammer into a diseased or dead tree. They raise one brood a year, and three young is a normal hatching. The pileated may return to the same tree, year after year, to nest but always drills a new cavity.

The primary food of the pileated consists of insects that infest standing and fallen timber. It also likes wild berries (who doesn't?) and acorns. I have frequently seen the pileated searching fallen tree trunks for its favorite food, ants. An analysis of the stomach of one pileated revealed 2,500 large, black ants!

Except for man, the pileated seems to have few enemies. Its large size, powerful flight, and formidable bill tend to discourage most of the birds of prey from doing battle with a mature pileated. Early settlers are said to have tried to eat this great woodpecker, but, to quote from Audubon, "Its flesh is tough, of a bluish tint and smells so strongly of worms and insects, that it is extremely unpalatable." Hardly a gourmet's delight!

When seeing the pileated in its normal habitat, one is always encouraged to imagine what our forests were like one hundred years ago. Fortunately, this great bird has learned what Darwin proclaimed, that "to survive and prosper, it is necessary to adjust to changing circumstances." Good advice for anyone!

FEBRUARY

THE MONTH OF FEBRUARY can seem like the longest month of the year, rather than our only month containing just twenty-eight days. The days are short, and seem even shorter because of the frequently drab skies.

It never ceases to impress me, watching birds during this second month of the year, that chickadees, nuthatches, and kinglets appear actually to revel in the most severe weather. Let a blizzard drive the temperatures down to the zero mark, and the chickadees seem to put on a new air of confidence. The kinglets move about the evergreens without a concern for the bleak climatic conditions. The white- and red-breasted nuthatches continually move up and down the trees, stealthily looking for insects that have been overlooked by other birds. Yet none of these birds measures over five inches long or weighs more than two or three ounces. All of them have legs no bigger than a match stick and toes so delicate they can perch on a string or hang upside down from a crevice in the bark of a tree.

While we are confined in draft-free enclosures, listening to our heating systems constantly running, these little mites are spending their fourteen-hour nights in thickets or evergreen trees, serenely content just to get out of the biting wind. True, birds have a high metabolism rate; and, true, they can fluff their feathers to provide a reasonably effective insulation. Science can offer further convincing hypotheses that explain how birds can survive in the North during the winter, but the sight of a chickadee on a cold, February morning never fails to make me think of how much more we have to learn about efficiently utilizing some of the lessons taught by nature in order to better our lot.

Soon after the middle of the month, subtle signs begin to appear, signaling that a change of seasons is approaching, that winter has lost its hold on Indiana, and that spring is moving doggedly forward. Horned larks can be heard calling overhead, and the crows start to become restless and move farther away from their winter's roosting place each day. The big owls, the barred and great horned, are more vocal. They already have selected mates and nesting sites, and the females will soon start incubating their first eggs.

The tree buds have become swollen, and the forest floors seem not quite so brown. Sometime after the twenty-fifth of the month, the first red-winged blackbirds and common grackles will move in, mostly males, noisy and enthusiastic. Then we can all breathe a sigh of relief; the worst of winter is over.

True, there will be some cold weather ahead and some snow and ice during the state high school basketball tournament, but just around the corner lies the long-awaited spring!

Common Crow

[CORVUS BRACHYRHYNCHOS]

It's strange that relatively minor changes in habitat can adversely affect some birds. Other birds cannot tolerate temperature changes. Still other species are totally dependent upon a very narrow choice of food; and when this food is no longer present in the area, the bird must either move to a different location or perish. The common crow has none of these problems. It can eat anything, temperatures seem to have little effect on it, and if a woods where it resides is removed, the crow will soon find another one.

The crow has periodically been subjected to campaigns aimed at reducing the crow population. The hunting of crow is a popular form of recreation in some parts of the country. Yet the crow survives—it more than survives; the crow seems to prosper! It almost seems to be saying, "Do your darndest, but I shall not be ill-affected by your activities." Perhaps behaviorists would be well advised to study more closely the lifestyle of the crow. The crow could be a good example in demonstrating how to prosper in the face of adversity.

The common crow is a year-round resident in the state of Indiana

SIZE: *L. 17–21" (43–53 cm)*. COLORING: *All black*. HABITAT: *Woodlands, farmlands, suburban areas*. NESTING: *Nests in medium to large trees, both deciduous and coniferous. Large nest; 4–6 eggs*. UNUSUAL MANNERISMS: *Gathers in large flocks in late fall and winter. Is very secretive in nesting area*. IDENTIFYING HINTS: *Large size, chunky shape, with fan-shaped tail. Characteristic call, "caw, caw."* STATUS IN INDIANA: *Common year-round resident*. RANGE: *Breeds from Canada to Florida. Common year-round resident throughout the United States.*

and can hardly be confused with any other bird. It nests throughout the state, and its familiar voice is known to everyone.

In the winter, crows congregate in huge evening roosts, seeming to favor areas with large trees, preferably on a hill. I recall being involved in an effort to take a count of one of these roosts a number of years ago. Several of us stationed ourselves at different areas around a large cemetery and started to take count of the crows as they came in to roost for the evening. One difficulty we had in getting an accurate count was that the crows were still coming in after dark. Our tally at the conclusion of the evening showed that more than 10,000 crows occupied this one roost. There have been counts taken in some of the roosts in eastern cities where there were over 100,000 crows counted.

In late February and early March, these winter gatherings break up, and crows pair off and begin to occupy themselves with domestic duties. In spite of the crow's being a common bird, it is no easy task to find a crow's nest, for they are very adept at concealing their nests.

The question of just what a crow eats has been the subject of much study. There are those who say the crow does much damage to farm crops; others say the bird's diet is beneficial to man's interest because the crow eats so many insects and grubs. In any event, there is no question that the crow is a clever and resourceful bird. Henry Ward Beecher once said that if men were birds, few would be clever enough to be a crow.

Horned Lark

[EREMOPHILA ALPESTRIS]

A birder may have one advantage over the non-birder—he has the continuing opportunity to detect subtle signs that the next season is approaching. After a long winter, any indications that spring is coming are encouraging.

The first migrating bird to appear in Indiana, and in much of the East, is the horned lark. True, it is not an obvious migrant like the

SIZE: *L. 7–8″ (17–20 cm).* COLORING: *Brown-backed, yellow face, with black bib and eye crescent. When seen up close, black horns.* HABITAT: *Airports, barren ground, golf courses, athletic fields.* NESTING: *In hollow in the ground, shallow cup of coarse stems and leaves, lined with fine grasses; 3–5 eggs. One of our earliest nesters.* UNUSUAL MANNERISMS: *Our only true lark, song given while in flight, high-pitched series of tinkling notes.* IDENTIFYING HINTS: *This bird walks, instead of hopping. In flight looks to be light-bellied with a dark tail. Folds its wings tightly after each wing beat.* STATUS IN INDIANA: *Nests throughout Indiana. Possible to find each month of the year. A few winter here.* RANGE: *Breeds from the Arctic south to central states. Winters throughout the United States as far south as the Gulf states.*

blackbirds, robins, and bluebirds; but, nevertheless, it is a bird that has spent some time south of us and annually makes its move north. Unfortunately, most people are unaware of the horned lark's presence here. This is understandable, for the horned lark is not a bird that normally can be found in backyards or at feeding stations. They are much more apt to be found in country fields that have little vegetation, like airports, golf courses, and the edges of highways. Generally, during the colder months they are found in groups, rather than singly.

The horned lark is a brown, sparrow-like bird with a yellow throat, a black mark through the eye, and a black ring on the upper breast. It has two black horns on the top of the head. A help in identifying this bird is its manner of moving about when on the ground: it walks, instead of hopping. In flight it shows a light belly and a dark tail. It nests throughout the state of Indiana and is the earliest nester of our songbirds. Nests have been found as early as February, but its regular nesting times are in March and April. Because of its early nesting habit, many nests are destroyed by the March snows and freezing weather. Two broods of four birds, each, would be expected in Indiana. The larks build very simple nests that blend so well with the surroundings that they are perfectly concealed. Meadows, cemeteries, airports, golf courses, and athletic fields are the preferred nesting sites of the horned lark.

The great English poets were deeply inspired by the lark, especially by their lark's song which, I'm told, is similar to the flight song given by our horned lark. Browning joyfully proclaimed that when the lark is on the wing, "all's right with the world." Tennyson claimed that the lark's song lifts the spirit, and Shakespeare prophesied that the lark would sing hymns at heaven's gate.

While our lark, the horned lark, may not have inspired our poets to the heights of the English poets, the return of the lark, so reliable every year, is always most welcome.

Great Horned Owl

[BUBO VIRGINIANUS]

If the lion is king of the beasts, the great horned owl must be designated king of the woods. It is absolutely fearless in defense of its nest and has no hestitation in attacking such formidable prey as the raccoon, domestic dog, and cat, and is one of the few enemies of the skunk. Its normal diet includes a preponderance of birds, rabbits, and rodents.

In recent years, the great horned owl seems to have had at least normal nesting success. In 1975 I found three successful nestings within fifteen miles of Monument Circle in Indianapolis. I wonder how many major cities could boast of this fact! The horned owls usually raise two young a year. Their preferred nesting site here in Indiana is a used hawk's or crow's nest, generally quite high up in the tree. They nest early in the year, in February or March, incubate the eggs for about a month, then feed and care for the young birds for an additional month or so, at which time the young are pretty much on their own.

Crows are usually the first to bring to our attention the presence of great horned owls, for they are mortal enemies, and with good reason! The horned owl will tear into a roosting flock of crows and kill as many as it can catch. The crows, in turn, will harrass the owl whenever they spot one during the day. The chances are 99 out of 100 that if you see a large owl with ear tufts being pursued by crows, you are seeing a great horned owl.

I have always questioned the logic of the claim that animals or birds must perform some service to man before they are of value and that their respective good must outweigh the bad. And that they must conform to a particular pattern that we feel is beneficial. If the same criteria were used to judge human beings, I'm afraid many of us would fall short!

The great horned owl is a nonconformist. He doesn't fit into behavioral patterns that we might prefer. Let us hope that we will always have the wisdom to appreciate the great horned owl for the magnificent creature he is.

SIZE: *L. 20–25" (51–63 cm). W. 55" (1.4 m).* COLORING: *Variable, from dark brown to gray body, brown face mask with yellow eyes and white throat. Horizontal barring on breast.* HABITAT: *Woodlots and larger forests. Occasionally found in city parks.* NESTING: *Most often nests in previously used nest of crow, hawk, or heron; occasionally in tree cavity; 2–3 white eggs.* UNUSUAL MANNERISMS: *Very early nester.* IDENTIFYING HINTS: *Large size, prominent eye tufts, white throat patch.* STATUS IN INDIANA: *Common year-round resident and nester; more common in northern half of Indiana.* RANGE: *Breeds from the Arctic to southern tip of South America. Year-round resident throughout its breeding range.*

White-breasted Nuthatch

[SITTA CAROLINENSIS]

Red-breasted Nuthatch

[SITTA CANADENSIS]

The two species of nuthatches that occur in Indiana are both present from October until May. The *white-breasted nuthatch* is a year-round resident of the state; that is, it is found here each month of the year, breeds here during the summer, and stays with us all winter. It can be told by its bluish back, black head, and white breast and face. In the summer, it retreats to the woods and becomes somewhat secretive, but in the winter it seems to change personalities. Then, it's a friendly, rather tame bird that will readily come to a backyard feeder.

The white-breasted nuthatch and its close relative, the red-breasted nuthatch, are sometimes referred to as the "upside-down birds" because of their manner of feeding. They are frequently seen moving down the trunk of a tree with their heads pointed toward the ground. By feeding this way, they are able to see insects that the woodpeckers and other birds that feed in a normal position have overlooked.

RED-BREASTED NUTHATCH

SIZE: *L. 4½–4¾" (11–12 cm).* COLORING: *Upper parts blue-gray, underparts pale rusty. Black cap, prominent white eye stripe.* HABITAT: *Coniferous woods. In winter prefers evergreens but will accept other wooded areas.* NESTING: *Nest placed in excavated cavity in tree or rotted stump; typically, birds will smear resin around the entrance to the cavity; 5–6 eggs.* UNUSUAL MANNERISMS: *Frequently seen feeding with its head toward the ground.* IDENTIFYING HINTS: *Voice is diagnostic. Has been described as sounding like a toy trumpet—tiny, high-pitched "yank-yank-yank" call. Rusty underparts and white eye-line best field marks.* STATUS IN INDIANA: *Primarily a winter visitor. Some years, quite commonly seen. Present from October through April. Does not nest here.* RANGE: *Breeds from Canada to most northern states. Winters south to Gulf Coast and northern Mexico.*

WHITE-BREASTED NUTHATCH

SIZE: *L. 5–6" (13–15 cm).* COLORING: *Blue-gray above, underparts and face white, crown black.* HABITAT: *Mixed woodlands, suburban yards, orchards.* NESTING: *In natural tree cavities 15–50" above the ground; occasionally will accept man-made nesting box; about 8 eggs.* UNUSUAL MANNERISMS: *Feeds "upside down." Common visitor at winter feeding stations. Known to hide seeds in crevices in the bark of trees.* IDENTIFYING HINTS: *White face with black eye. Song a nasal "yank, yank."* STATUS IN INDIANA: *Common year-round resident and nesting bird.* RANGE: *Breeds from southern Canada south to the Gulf Coast. Permanent resident throughout its breeding range.*

The *red-breasted nuthatch* is primarily a winter visitor to Indiana. Some years, only a few are seen all winter long. Other years, they are quite commonly seen in parks and backyards, even showing up regularly at feeding stations. The red-breasted nuthatch has a chestnut or rose-colored breast and bluish back. The best identifying mark is the black line that runs through the eye and divides the otherwise white face.

There is also a considerable size difference between the two nuthatches. The red-breasted is four inches long, and the white-breasted, six inches in length. The red-breasted's winter song is always a pleasure to hear. It sounds like notes blown from a child's top trumpet.

The red-breasted normally nests north of Indiana in an evergreen forest. It arrives here in September or October and departs in April or early May. I suggest that, in order to attract these two birds, you get a mesh bag (the kind that oranges, potatoes, and onions are packed in) and ask your butcher for five or ten pounds of beef suet. Sometimes the butcher will give it to you, but, if not, the cost of the suet will be very nominal. Place the suet in the bag and hang it on a tree limb—and I'm sure you will have not only nuthatches but other birds as winter boarders as well. The suet feeder, along with a feeder to hold sunflower seeds and perhaps a thistle feeder, is all you will need to start your own "free lunch program" for birds.

The winter feeding of birds will give you many hours of enjoyment. There is something pleasant about looking out from the warm comfort of your kitchen or living room and seeing brightly colored birds, happily partaking of your benevolence. It's rather like the feeling a parent gets when seeing his offspring sleeping, safely tucked in for the night.

Cardinal

[CARDINALIS CARDINALIS]

When a bird expands its population and range, usually some negative results are involved, such as other native birds being displaced or disturbed. Sometimes man's activities are adversely affected. A good example of this would be the introduction of the house sparrow and

SIZE: L. 8–9" (20–23 cm). COLORING: Male, all red, except black area around face. Female, soft brown body, with traces of red in wings and tail. HABITAT: Edges of woods, suburban gardens, parks. NESTING: In small trees, both deciduous and coniferous, dense shrubbery, tangles. Loosely built nest lined with grasses and hair; 3–4 varicolored eggs. UNUSUAL MANNERISMS: Will readily come to backyard feeding stations offering sunflower seeds. IDENTIFYING HINTS: Prominent crest in both sexes. Large, conical bill. Loud, cheerful songs given year round. STATUS IN INDIANA: Common nesting bird. Common year-round resident. RANGE: Permanent resident throughout eastern United States.

starling to this country and their rapid expansion of population and range. There is one striking example, however, of a bird which has increased in numbers and has expanded its breeding area and still pleased everyone. That bird is the cardinal.

Probably no other bird has been more responsible for stimulating an interest in birds than the cardinal. It has many attributes admired by men. It has beauty and an outstanding song. It stays with us the year round and will readily come to a bird feeder. Its feeding habits are entirely beneficial to man's interest. Devotion to family and a "live and let live" philosophy are also characteristics that the cardinal exhibits.

Ancestrally, the cardinal is a bird of the South. During the past seventy-five years, it has gradually become established in the northern states. In Indiana the first successful nesting on which I have found records was in 1883 and in Marion County, 1898. By the 1920s it was firmly established in the state. In 1933 the cardinal was officially designated as our state bird. Indiana is not alone in selecting the cardinal as the state bird; six other states have bestowed this honor on the cardinal.

In the 1920s the cardinal became established in Minnesota, Michigan, northern Ohio, and western New York. During the 1930s it reached the New England states and southern Ontario, Canada. Its range is still expanding today.

Determining just why a bird is successful in range expansion while other birds are not, requires a great deal of study over a long period of time. Some birds increase rapidly and then decrease just as rapidly. Many times the reasons for these changes are subtle. In the case of the cardinal, many factors are involved, among which are the cardinal's ability to vary its diet from insects and berries in the warm weather to seeds in the winter and the fact that the cardinal is very solicitous of its offspring and probably raises a higher percentage of young than do most other birds. Cardinals raise more than one brood a year—sometimes as many as four. This forces the young to move away from the nesting area to find their own place in the sun, and a wider dispersal is the result.

Describing a cardinal almost seems unnecessary. The male is all-red except for black markings on the face. The female is buffy-brown with traces of red in the wings, tail, and crown. Both birds have a prominent crest.

These handsome birds, who are very fond of sunflower seeds, are welcome visitors at our feeding stations all year long.

American Robin

[TURDUS MIGRATORIUS]

Robins frequently attempt to winter in Indiana. Unfortunately, each year some calamity seems to befall them. Especially detrimental to wintering robins are severe ice storms, which seem to occur in Indiana on a regular basis.

In February 1976, for example, an unprecedented number of American robins were reported throughout the central Indiana area. An estimated one thousand were seen adjacent to an Indianapolis shopping center, and hundreds were seen in one backyard. A number of residents of Carmel, Indiana, called to report flocks of robins feeding on bushes and trees that had retained their fruit. They were seen in the hundreds at the Park-Tudor School and in Crown Hill Cemetery. I saw them on Meridian Street in front of the Grain Dealers Mutual Insurance Company and in the park south of the American Legion national headquarters.

It is not unusual for a few robins to winter this far north, but they normally are confined to wooded areas and often seek out evergreen trees for shelter. Just why the robins stayed that year in such large numbers is not known, but my guess is that the following factors were involved: a successful breeding year the previous summer for all the thrushes, a good growing season for berries and fruit (the favorite foods of thrushes), and the previous mild, protracted fall. These factors would explain why so many robins stayed beyond the normal migration period.

What effect the severe ice storm we experienced that year had on the wintering robins will certainly bear watching. Many times the combination of low temperatures and scarce food supplies for two or three days will spell disaster for the members of the thrush family.

Robins hardly need any description—the dark back and chestnut-colored breast of the adult birds are known to virtually everyone. The young birds that we see in the summer and fall have spotted breasts—evidence that they are members of the thrush family.

SIZE: *L. 9–11" (23–28 cm).* COLORING: *Brownish-gray above, brick-red below. Young birds have spotted breasts.* HABITAT: *Cities and suburbs, farmlands, open woods.* NESTING: *Compact, mud-lined, in a tree or on a ledge; 3–5 greenish-blue eggs.* UNUSUAL MANNERISMS: *Often seen on lawns, "listening" for worms.* IDENTIFYING HINTS: *Red breast, melodious song, "cheer-up, cheerily."* STATUS IN INDIANA: *Very common spring and fall migrant, common nesting bird. Uncommon winter resident.* RANGE: *Breeds from northern Alaska south almost to Gulf Coast. Winters primarily in southern United States.*

It is well known that robins have no hesitancy about nesting close to human activity, and this affords us an excellent opportunity to study their family lifestyle. The mud-lined nest and beautiful blue eggs are familiar to almost everyone. Robins generally raise two broods of four each year and frequently will return to the same tree or nesting site year after year.

My advice is that if you do see an American robin in February, do not start taking the storm windows down or let the furnace go out, for the robin ranks about equal to the groundhog as a meteorological forecaster.

Brown-headed Cowbird

[MOLOTHRUS ATER]

The only birds in America that do not build their own nests and raise their own young are the cowbirds. There are two recognized species of cowbirds, the bronzed cowbird, found in the southwestern parts of the United States, and the brown-headed cowbird, a common bird of the lands east of the Mississippi River.

The cowbird can be seen in Indiana every month of the year but is most commonly seen during the months of March to November. A few are found where there is a reliable source of food during December, January, and February. They can occasionally become a nuisance at a winter feeding station, for they tend to dominate the area in which they feed.

Our cowbird, the brown-headed cowbird, is a medium-sized bird, between the size of a robin and a sparrow. The male is the only bird seen here that has the combination of a brown head and a black body. The female is a slate-gray bird without streaking on the breast.

Why the nesting instinct is absent in the cowbird, yet is so overwhelming in other birds, is unknown. One possible reason that has been advanced is that the cowbird, at one time, was very dependent on the American bison. As the bison were continually searching for fresh

SIZE: *L. 7–8" (17–20 cm).* COLORING: *Male, black body, shiny brown head. Female, overall gray, with unstreaked breast.* HABITAT: *Woodlands, farmlands, suburban areas.* NESTING: *Builds no nest; places eggs in nests of songbirds; 4–5 eggs.* UNUSUAL MANNERISMS: *Puts eggs in nests of smaller birds, giving the cowbird young the advantage for survival over host birds' young.* IDENTIFYING HINTS: *Only blackbird with brown head. Voice, high, thin whistle. Walks, rather than hops, when feeding on the ground.* STATUS IN INDIANA: *Very common spring and fall migrant; very common breeding bird. Uncommon winterer.* RANGE: *Breeds from central Canada south to southern United States and northern Mexico, avoiding southeastern coastal areas. Winters primarily in the southern part of its breeding range.*

grazing lands, their constant movement did not allow the cowbird the time necessary to build a nest, incubate the eggs, and feed the newly hatched birds. Consequently, the cowbird became very adept at depositing her eggs in other birds' nests.

Invariably, the recipient of the cowbird's eggs is a smaller and less aggressive bird. Strangely enough, the foster birds will rear the young cowbirds with as much enthusiasm as if they were their own. Last summer I watched a small warbler, a redstart, feeding a young cowbird. The redstart seemed to be almost exhausted, trying to contain the appetite of the cowbird. Feeding a young bird twice its size and not even its own offspring, emphasizes how strong the maternal instinct is in birds.

A number of birds have developed defense mechanisms to avoid hatching cowbird eggs. Some have learned to recognize cowbird eggs and hence desert the nest or remove the eggs. Others will build a new floor over the cowbird eggs. There have been yellow warblers' nests found with four and five floors built over cowbird eggs. But once the eggs have been hatched, it seems that the foster parents are compelled to obey the feeding instinct.

The parasitic habits of the cowbird have created a serious problem of survival for one of the rarest birds, the Kirtland's warblers. The total (world) population of Kirtland's warblers is estimated to be less than one thousand birds. This endangered species has a very restricted breeding range limited to the north-central part of the state of Michigan. Cowbirds have deposited eggs in Kirtland's warblers' nests to such an extent that it has been feared that the limited population of this warbler could not be built up. A major effort has been made to remove cowbirds from the area, and I understand that progress has been made toward stabilizing the population of the Kirtland's warbler.

It strikes me as strange that only the cowbird in America does not build a nest and raise its young; while in Europe it is the cuckoo that does not raise its own young. Perhaps each environment has a void that is filled by the unusual behavior of the cowbird and the cuckoo.

Common Grackle

[QUISCALUS QUISCULA]

By the middle of February, blackbirds will have started to arrive in Indiana. The common grackle is normally the first on the scene, soon to be followed by other members of the blackbird tribe—cowbirds, red-winged blackbirds, and rusty blackbirds. They will arrive in immense flocks, and many people become concerned because of the large numbers of this family of birds that become so evident.

For some reason, great quantities of birds, of any species, have always made man uncomfortable. Before the turn of the century, passenger pigeons darkened the sky of the Midwest with their vast hordes. It was considered, then, that passenger pigeons were an inexhaustible source of food. Virtually tons of passenger pigeons were killed and packed in barrels and shipped to eastern cities. Anyone who suggested that there would come a time when there would be no more passenger pigeons on the earth would be ridiculed. That time did come, however; and in the 1930s the last passenger pigeon died in a zoo in Cincinnati, Ohio.

SIZE: *L. 10–12" (25–30 cm).* COLORING: *Appears black, but is actually iridescent; depending on the light, shows blues, purples, greens, and bronze.* HABITAT: *Suburban lawns, open woodlands, parks, fields, farms.* NESTING: *Bulky nest made primarily of sticks and lined with grass, placed in a spot found all the way from a low bush to tall tree, showing a special preference for evergreens; 5 eggs.* UNUSUAL MANNERISMS: *Perhaps the most common blackbird in Indiana. Gathers in huge flocks in the spring and fall. One of the first birds to arrive in the spring.* IDENTIFYING HINTS: *Bright yellow eyes, rudder-like tail. Loud, squeaky voice.* STATUS IN INDIANA: *Very common spring and fall migrant, common nesting bird throughout the state. A few winter each year.* RANGE: *Breeds from southern Canada to the Gulf states east of the Rocky Mountains. Winters in southeastern United States, occasionally north to Great Lakes area.*

During the past few years, great numbers of blackbirds—red-winged blackbirds, grackles, cowbirds, starlings, and rusty blackbirds—have been killed in various communities in Kentucky and other states. The help of the United States Army has been solicited in this. The position of the National Audubon Society in this dilemma of the eradication of the blackbirds seems to me to be a reasonable one. It is: take just a portion of the monies being spent to kill blackbirds and try to ascertain scientifically if these blackbirds do pose a problem. Are they a health hazard? Do they work a hardship on agricultural activities? We may find these birds are diligently and effectively working to reduce crop pests.

The common grackle is the largest of the blackbird family found in Indiana. The most reliable field marks of the common grackle are the light-colored eyes, the iridescent coloring of the body, and the large, wedge-shaped tail that the grackle seems to use as a rudder when flying. Although a few grackles winter in Indiana, the vast majority of them are absent here during the months of December, January, and February.

I will have to confess I enjoy seeing the grackles and other blackbirds when they arrive prior to the spring equinox, for their appearance is a sure sign that the worst of winter is over. Just around the corner are daffodils and crocuses.

MARCH

For THOSE WHO ENJOY the change of seasons, birding holds a special reward. Not only do you get to enjoy each season of the year—spring, summer, fall, and winter—but you also get to enjoy each season longer than the non-birder. Birds anticipate the seasons; consequently, if your favorite season is spring, as it is for many people, you don't have to wait until the vernal equinox, March 21, to recognize that spring has arrived. For birds have been heralding the arrival of spring from the very beginning of the month. The cardinal has been singing a different song, the song sparrow has shaken off his lethargic ways, and the woodcock has begun his dusktime mating ritual. Blackbirds are everywhere now, and many of them already selecting nesting sites.

The main ornithological feature of the month of March in Indiana is the fine waterfowl migration—true in spite of the fact that Indiana is not blessed with an ocean shore or a large, natural body of water (except for those few northern counties that border Lake Michigan). Yet, twenty-five or thirty species of ducks, grebes, loons, and geese make a stopover in Indiana each March.

Is there anyone whose day isn't different after looking up to find the first flock of Canada geese on a crisp March morning, anyone who doesn't find life's tasks taking on a different hue after hearing those nasal honks and seeing a "V" formation of these large birds as they search out the nearest body of open water?

Open water, at times in March, can contain some of the most colorful birds in the world. The wood duck, the green-winged teal, the American wigeon, the pintail, and the mallard are beautiful birds and, some years, are present in large numbers. Unfortunately, most of them are here only for a short time before they head northward to their breeding grounds.

March is a month of anticipation—anticipation that soon the woods will be alive with birds and the hillsides profuse with wildflowers. All the familiar birds of summer are now on their way. A sage once wrote that the joy of life is in the exhilaration of the climb, that the expectation of fulfillment or happiness is often more satisfying than the attainment of a goal. So it is that March, for the birder, is a joyful time.

Eastern Bluebird

[SIALIA SIALIS]

A harbinger of spring, the Eastern bluebird, is probably the most beloved of all of our native birds. The bluebird has been selected as the official state bird by four states.

Unfortunately, the bluebird is subject to wide population fluctuations and is not as common as we would like it to be. Because the bluebird is primarily an early spring migrant, it frequently falls victim to severe snow and ice storms. This, coupled with the decrease of its favorite nesting habitat, unkempt orchards, has caused the population to fall drastically during the past thirty years. The bluebird is also preempted by other species more successful in competing for suitable nesting cavities, in particular, the starling and the house sparrow. In Indiana, the bluebird can be termed an uncommon nesting bird; however, I feel that it has had a small but appreciable increase in population during the past few years.

It takes many years to rebuild a bird's population, but fortunately, programs have been adopted to help the plight of this gentle bird which is exclusive to the North American continent. Various farm organizations, the Camp Fire Girls, and other concerned individuals have led the campaign to place specially designed bird houses in areas that are suitable for this insect-eating bird. My daughter, Wendy, has taken part in this effort. It seems to me that these "bluebird trails" are bearing fruit, and we owe these groups and individuals a vote of thanks for adding to the beauty of our landscape.

The bluebird's nest is unusual in that the only material used is fine

SIZE: *L. 6–7" (16–17 cm).* COLORING: *Male, blue-backed, chestnut breast and sides with white underparts. Female, similar but considerably paler.* HABITAT: *Likes open farmlands with short weeds, old orchards.* NESTING: *Cavities in dead trees, or will accept man-made houses. Nest of dried weed stems and soft grasses; 3–5 sky-blue eggs.* UNUSUAL MANNERISMS: *Often perches hunched on telephone or fence wires, or in dead trees. Song sounds like "Cheer, cheer, cheerful charmer."* IDENTIFYING HINTS: *Only bird east of the Mississippi with blue back and chestnut front.* STATUS IN INDIANA: *Uncommon nester, with population subject to wide fluctuations. Occasionally winters in small groups of 4 to 5. Population severely decreased in last three decades.* RANGE: *Breeds from south Canada to Florida, east of the Mississippi.*

grasses. The female lays three to five pale blue eggs in the neatly compacted nest. Abandoned woodpecker holes in wooden fence posts or decaying trees make ideal natural nesting sites for this bird. Juvenile bluebirds from the first brood often help feed and train fledglings from the second brood—a characteristic peculiar to this species of bird.

A nature writer once wrote that the bluebird has "the blue of the sky on its back and the brown of the earth on its breast." This pretty much describes the male bluebird, although "rusty," rather than brown, would be a more accurate description of the bluebird's breast color. The females are a paler replica of the male, and the young birds' speckled breasts give credence to the bluebird's membership in the thrush family. I have always found the blue coloration on the back of the bluebird almost impossible to reproduce artificially. It has to be seen in the field to fully appreciate its magnificence.

Bluebirds have a variety of songs that they give at different times of the year, but in springtime they can often be heard giving their best-known song. With a little stretch of the imagination, they seems to be saying, "Cheer, cheer, cheerful charmer!" This warbling sound, when heard on a fresh spring morning, will brighten anyone's day. Perhaps the bluebird is trying to tell us that life isn't always filled with vicissitudes; and if one has patience, better times lie ahead.

Whistling Swan

[OLOR COLUMBIANUS]

A whistling swan was seen in early March at one of our reservoirs—here just one day and sighted by only a few people. Unfortunately, Indiana is not on the normal migration path of the whistling swan, and only a few of these majestic birds are ever seen in the state, and then only in the fall or in the spring. As a rule, they winter off the coast of Maryland, south to North Carolina on the Atlantic coast, and off the California coast on the west.

SIZE: *L. 48–55″ (1.2–1.4m). W. 7′ (2.4m).* COLORING: *All white with black tail.* HABITAT: *In migration, found in large rivers, reservoirs, lakes. In nesting area, found in shallow waters.* NESTING: *Nest is large mass of grass and moss placed on an island or edge of a lake; 4–6 white eggs.* UNUSUAL MANNERISMS: *Long neck held straight up. Very wary.* IDENTIFYING HINTS: *Large size; pure white wings and body.* STATUS IN INDIANA: *Very uncommon spring and fall migrant; does not nest here.* RANGE: *Breeds in Alaska, northern Canada. Winters off both United States coasts, rarely in Great Lakes area.*

In early spring the eastern population moves up the coast, then west through the Great Lakes. They breed in the extreme northern parts of this continent all the way to and beyond the Arctic Circle. Once seen, this magnificent bird is not soon forgotten: pure white except for the black bill and feet, four feet long, erectly held head, long neck, and weighing up to twenty pounds. The whistling swan is the largest water-fowl likely to be encountered in Indiana.

If you see a large, snow-white bird flying with its neck outstretched, you are seeing a swan. It is worth a trip to Lake Ontario or Lake Erie to see these swans when they first move in among the floating clumps of ice. They are extremely wary at these times and are difficult to approach. A flock always seems to have a sentinel posted to warn of potential danger. As in the case of all the large, heavy-bodied waterfowl, swans prefer to face the wind when rising. With this in mind, it is sometimes possible, by proceeding stealthily, to get fairly close to a flock of swans.

Once airborne, they are powerful, swift fliers and have been clocked at speeds up to 100 miles per hour. When intent upon flying a consid-erable distance, they frequently will form a V-shaped wedge similar to the flight of geese.

Swans were formerly held in high esteem by royal families who decreed that only royalty could possess swans. It is easy to see why they admired the swan—the white plumage, great size, stateliness of posture, its tenacity in defending its young—all attributes to be admired.

Ancient poets and writers made many references to the swan. It was called by some, "the bird of Apollo," and it was claimed that when death was imminent the swan sang a beautiful song of joy because it was about to join the gods. Socrates felt that man would be well advised to treat approaching death in the same manner.

Red-winged Blackbird

[AGELAIUS PHOENICEUS]

One of the most welcome scenes of early spring is that of the red-winged blackbirds' return to the marsh. In Indiana the first returning red-wings can be expected sometime during the month of February. These first birds are most often males, and they show an enthusiasm that is lacking in red-wings that have wintered here. There are times during April and May when red-winged blackbirds are the most common birds in Indiana.

Years ago this blackbird was found almost exclusively in cattail marshes. This is no longer true. The red-wing will nest now in dry fields, pastures, hedgerows, and even in ornamental shrubs. Its ability to change nesting requirements is probably the main reason the red-wing has been able to maintain its population.

The red-winged blackbird is a rather controversial bird. In the South, especially where rice is grown, the red-wing does considerable damage by pulling up the young rice plants and eating the grain as it ripens. The red-wing, along with other members of the blackbird family, gathers in huge numbers in the winter, and much time, effort, and money has been spent in trying to disperse these winter roosts. These efforts to reduce the blackbird population have had limited success. Studies indicate that killing literally hundreds of thousands of blackbirds in the winter only temporarily reduces the blackbird population. The birds that survive have less competition on their breeding grounds and are able to raise larger broods successfully, thereby building up to their normal population in a short time. During the summer, the red-winged blackbird is almost totally a beneficial bird. Its food is made up of harmful insects and weed seeds.

The male red-wing is one of our most easily recognized and most familiar birds. It is all black except for the red patch and yellow border at the bend of the wing. The red on the wing is not as evident at other times during the year as it is in springtime. When the males are estab-

Size: *L. 7–9½" (17–24 cm)*. Coloring: *Male, black, with red wing patches. Female, brown with heavily streaked underparts.* Habitat: *Marshes and wet areas preferred, but accepts a wide variety of open fields.* Nesting: *In cattails or small bushes near water; 3–4 pale bluish eggs.* Unusual Mannerisms: *Very aggressive and vocal in defense of nest. Usually among the first migrants to return in the spring.* Identifying Hints: *Red wing patches. Undulating flight. In spring perches on roadside fences.* Status in Indiana: *Common nesting bird throughout Indiana. Very common spring and fall migrant; uncommon winterer.* Range: *Breeds from Canada to Florida. Winters south of the Great Lakes to southernmost states.*

lishing breeding territories in the spring, the wing patch is used both for impressing the female and as a warning to other males to stay away from the area. The female is quite a different-looking bird—brown-backed with heavy streaking on the breast. When she is incubating eggs or tending her young, her brown coloration blends in perfectly with the surroundings.

Debating the assets and liabilities of the red-winged blackbird can be a time-consuming chore that almost never can be concluded to everyone's satisfaction. Aesthetically, there is no question that the red-winged blackbird adds immeasurably to our enjoyment of the out-of-doors. For whose spirits are not lifted by the red-wing singing his lusty "konk-la-reee" on a frosty, spring morning!

Eastern Phoebe

[SAYORNIS PHOEBE]

The coming of spring always signals the return to Indiana of our earliest flycatcher, the eastern phoebe. The rest of the flycatcher tribe won't be on the scene until a month later, but the phoebe, the hardiest of the family, is the first to arrive in the spring and the last to leave in the fall. Sometimes this propensity for arriving on its breeding grounds before the danger of severe weather is past proves disastrous to the phoebe, because ninety percent of its diet consists of insects. When a late snowstorm or ice storm occurs, making insects unavailable, phoebes sometimes perish in large numbers, and a period of many years is required for them to build up to their normal population level.

Aside from being the first flycatcher to arrive in the spring, the phoebe has another "first" to add to its laurels. It was the first species to be banded in America. John James Audubon, when studying a family of phoebes in Pennsylvania in 1803, tied a silver thread on the leg of a young bird, and the next spring the phoebe returned to the same area with the thread still attached to its leg.

SIZE: *L. 6½–7″ (16–17 cm)*. COLORING: *Olive-green above, breast area lighter, no eye-ring or wing-bar.* HABITAT: *Woodland ravines, suburban areas.* NESTING: *Often build nest on shelf-like projections in farm buildings, under bridges and trestles. Compact, lined with mud; 4–5 white eggs.* UNUSUAL MANNERISMS: *Often return to the same bridge or nesting site for many years.* IDENTIFYING HINTS: *Only flycatcher which is a persistent tail wagger.* STATUS IN INDIANA: *Fairly common breeding bird; early migrant, is present in Indiana from March to November; rare winter resident.* RANGE: *Breeds from central Canada to Gulf states. Winters primarily in southern United States.*

Some flycatchers are difficult to identify, but such is not the case with the phoebe. It does not have wing-bars or eye-ring, as most of the flycatchers do, and the bill of the phoebe is dark. The best field mark, however, is the phoebe's habit of wagging its tail! If you see a rather dark bird sitting on an exposed branch of a tree, busily darting out to catch flying insects and returning to the same branch, the odds are good that you are seeing a member of the flycatcher family. If this bird is wagging its tail, it's a phoebe.

As with all birds, learning the call is the best aid in first locating the phoebe. In the spring the phoebe is a persistent singer, repeating its name over and over—"fee-bee, fee-bee."

Phoebes nest throughout the state of Indiana. The most favored nesting sites are underneath small bridges and on the shelves in little-used farm buildings. The eastern phoebe is usually a bird of the suburbs and farms, rather than of the city, although during its spring migration it is possible to find a phoebe in the metropolitan areas. Look for it along the edge of a stream or river.

Early spring is the most exciting time of year for most birders. Each week brings new birds back from the South, and as the season progresses, each day will add more species. I've never heard a birder complain that there is nothing interesting to see or do. The problem is quite the opposite; there is never enough leisure time to see and do all the birding that he wants to do.

Rufous-sided Towhee

[PIPILO ERYTHROPHTHALMUS]

Unseasonably high temperatures and south winds, which sometimes occur in early March, often bring a number of different birds to Indiana well ahead of their normal time schedule. It is sometimes difficult to determine which birds have wintered here and which ones have just arrived from the South, but the enthusiasm with which the birds sing is a helpful clue in identifying the new arrivals. It seems to me that

SIZE: L. 7–8½″ (17–21 cm). COLORING: *Male, black head and upper parts, white underparts, chestnut sides. Female, black of male replaced with brown.* HABITAT: *Hedgerows, brushy fields, thickets, edges of woods.* NESTING: *On or near the ground, usually well concealed; 4–6 white eggs.* UNUSUAL MANNERISMS: *Likes to forage among dead leaves.* IDENTIFYING HINTS: *Learn distinctive song, "drink your tea!" Shows white in tail and wings in flight. Call note, "to-wheé?"* STATUS IN IN-DIANA: *Common spring and fall migrant and summer nester. Uncommon winter resident.* RANGE: *Breeds from southern Canada throughout United States except for Great Plains. Winters primarily in southern part of its range.*

when birds first arrive, they have an exuberance in both behavior and song that is not duplicated at other times of the year. It's almost as if they are saying, "We had a nice time in the South this winter, but it's good to be back in familiar territory."

One bird that frequently comes rather early is the rufous-sided towhee. This handsome ground feeder is usually heard before he is seen. Not only is he a fine vocalist, but he also, frequently, gives away his presence by noisily kicking in the dry leaves when searching for food. When he gives his full spring song, it is an easy call to remember. The song seems to advise, "Drink your tea!" In the spring, the song is repeated from morning till night.

The male rufous-sided towhee is a very attractive bird—black head, chest, and back with a white belly—and, as the name implies, rufous or chestnut sides. The female is similarly colored, except the black is replaced by brown. Both the male and female towhees have prominent white spots in the tail. Towhees are generally shy and retiring and like to feed under shrubs and bushes, making it difficult to see their full plumage. When approached too closely, they fly close to the ground to another tangle, and all that is seen is a flash of white tail spots.

The towhee is a surprisingly common bird in Indiana and is with us from early spring until late fall. Its preferred nesting habitats are brushy fields and hedgerows. The nest is most often built on the ground or in a small tree or bush. As a rule, the towhee will raise two broods of four during the nesting season. Although a few try to winter here each year (especially if they can find reliable backyard feeding stations), most winter in the southern states.

One of the intriguing aspects of birding is the names given to birds by the early ornithologists. The rufous-sided towhee is one of many bird names that is not only pleasant to say but creates a certain, instant image. I think these early namers of birds would have been very successful working for large advertising agencies responsible for creating image-provoking names for breakfast cereals and other foods. Wouldn't a shopping list be more fun if it contained a request for a golden-eye beverage or ringed-neck cornflakes!

American Woodcock

[PHILOHELA MINOR]

One of the first land birds to arrive in Indiana each year is the
woodcock. As the earth begins to thaw in the early spring, woodcocks
begin their move northward. They are absent from Indiana only from
about the middle of November until the end of February. The departure
in the fall and the arrival in the spring varies from year to year, depending upon climatic conditions, but normally the woodcock can be
expected by the first of March. A few will stay in Indiana and nest,
but most of them will nest in the more northern states.

The woodcock is a little larger than a robin and gives the illusion of
having no neck. Its back is brown with light striping, and the breast is
a light, warm chestnut color. The best field marks are the extremely
long bill and prominent dark eye.

Woodcocks, which migrate at night, occasionally become confused
by city lights and end up in unusual places. One such disoriented
woodcock was found in mid-February near Monument Circle in down-
town Indianapolis.

During the months of March and April the woodcocks perform
their well-documented nuptial flights. If you live in a wooded area, it
may be going on in your own neighborhood. Any warm, windless
evening from late February on would be a good time to witness this
intriguing spectacle.

I recall leading a group of about twenty-five persons on a hike a
number of years ago to watch the male woodcocks performing for their
ladyloves. We went to a very fashionable suburban residential area that
had always been favored by the woodcocks in the spring. We were
fortunate in finding three different males performing for the females.
We were unfortunate in that some of the residents of the area became
alarmed at the sight of twenty-five people engrossed in studying the
antics of a brown, robin-sized bird in their front yards and called the
law! It was with some difficulty that I tried to explain to the officer just

SIZE: *L. 10–12" (25–30 cm).* COLORING: *Grayish-brown back, rust-brown belly, black-and-white striped crown. Very long bill.* HABITAT: *Moist woods and thickets near open fields.* NESTING: *Nest built on the ground, usually in dead leaves; 4 eggs.* UNUSUAL MANNERISMS: *Elaborate spring courtship flight. Eyes placed in an unusual position in bird's head, allowing it to feed by probing in the mud while still looking out for danger.* IDENTIFYING HINTS: *Extremely long bill. Appears neck-less.* STATUS IN INDIANA: *Fairly common spring and fall migrant, uncommon summer nester. Rare winterer in southern Indiana.* RANGE: *Breeds from southern Canada to central United States. Winters primarily in southern part of its breeding range.*

what we were doing. It seems that this sort of activity is not covered in law enforcement handbooks.

Once my son, Scott, and I spent an hour looking for woodcock at Eagle Creek Park, in Indianapolis. We found no less than twenty males engaged in their spring ritual. I'm sure there are many areas in Indiana where this spectacular display is duplicated. Rather than being depressed by the six o'clock evening news on television, I recommend that you find a moist, wooded area with an adjacent clearing. Listen for a rather nasal, single call, "peep, peep, peep" (hard to put into words). This sound will continue for thirty or forty seconds, then the male woodcock will erupt perpendicularly from the ground and start his love song as he performs aerial gyrations high in the sky.

Evidently this display is effective, for the woodcock has been able to survive in spite of hunting pressure and decreasing habitat.

Bufflehead

[BUCEPHALA ALBEOLA]

The smallest of the ducks that visit Indiana annually is the bufflehead. It is a member of a group of birds referred to as "divers"; that is, they dive beneath the water's surface in search of food. Like most of the other diving ducks, the bulk of the bufflehead's diet is made up of animal, rather than vegetable material.

In Indiana the bufflehead is present, mainly, in the spring and fall, although it will winter here when it can find open water. It is often found in gravel pits and farmland ponds and will revisit these favored places each year. In the fall, it is a rather late migrant, seldom being seen before the middle of October. In the spring, it is usually late in March and during the month of April that we find this little duck here. It does not nest in Indiana; its major nesting area is in the western prairies of Canada. The bufflehead will search out a hole in a tree, most often a cavity previously used by a flicker or other woodpecker, and there it will lay its eggs and rear its young.

SIZE: *L. 12–14" (30–35 cm). W. 24" (61 cm).* COLORING: *Male, white bird with dark back, dark head with prominent white head patch. Female, dingy gray, with white ear patch.* HABITAT: *Lakes, ponds, reservoirs, gravel pits.* NESTING: *In hollow trees, close to water; usually 10–12 off-white to pale greenish-buff eggs.* UNUSUAL MANNERISMS: *A diver, with elaborate courtship behavior.* IDENTIFYING HINTS: *Small size, with disproportionately large head. Also, white head patch of male.* STATUS IN INDIANA: *Common migrant, seen most often during October to November and March to April.* RANGE: *Nests in northwestern plains. Winters wherever there is open water from the Great Lakes south.*

The male bufflehead—a beautiful bird—has a white body and black back. Its most prominent feature is the large, white head patch. The female lacks the white head patch and white body of the adult male and, in contrast, gives the appearance of a small, dark duck with a disproportionately large head. There is a small, white cheek spot on the otherwise dark head of the female that is a help in identifying this bird. In flight the bufflehead shows large, white wing patches.

During its springtime visit, the bufflehead is often seen acting out its courtship display. The male, proudly showing off his handsome white head, frantically swims around, and dives under, the demure female. It is not unusual to see as many as a dozen pairs of these perky birds, all performing on one small pond. The nature photographers who helped produce the wonderful motion pictures created by the late Walt Disney were much taken by the courtship display of waterfowl, the bufflehead for one.

Literally millions of people have paid admittance fees to movie theaters to see the courtship displays of waterfowl captured on film. It is not necessary to patronize a theater to see this production. It's about ready to begin any mid-March. The admission is free, and it's a live performance!

Ring-billed Gull

[LARUS DELAWARENSIS]

It often comes as a surprise to Hoosiers to see gulls in Indiana. Actually, gulls are not that uncommon here; in fact, in that part of the state which borders Lake Michigan, gulls are a year-round, integral part of the landscape. In the rest of the state, gulls can be seen from October to April, patrolling the major rivers and their tributaries and frequenting the larger reservoirs. There are four species of gulls that come to Indiana on a regular basis: the herring gull, the Franklin gull, the Bonaparte's gull, and the ring-billed gull.

The ring-billed gull is our most common gull and the one that is

SIZE: *L. 18–20″ (45–50 cm)*. COLORING: *Gray-winged with black wing tips, white body, head, and tail. Legs yellowish.* HABITAT: *Lakes and rivers, occasionally can be found feeding in freshly plowed fields, garbage dumps.* NESTING: *Nests usually found on islands in lakes, often in colonies with other gulls and terns. Flimsy nest on the ground in open area; 2–4 eggs.* UNUSUAL MANNERISMS: *Graceful, strong flier. Frequently calls when in the air.* IDENTIFYING HINTS: *The gray mantle (upper surface of the wing), black wing tips, and yellowish legs. Also, in good light, the ring on the bill.* STATUS IN INDIANA: *Does not breed in Indiana. Most common gull found away from Lake Michigan. Occasionally seen in good numbers in wintertime.* RANGE: *Breeds from northern Canada to islands in the Great Lakes area. Winters throughout the United States south to the Gulf of Mexico.*

with us for the longest length of time. It is a crow-sized bird with white body, head, and tail and gray back and wings. The wings have black tips, and the legs are yellowish. As its name indicates, the bill has a black ring near the tip. Unfortunately, it takes up to three years for the ring-billed to obtain its adult plumage, and immature gulls can be difficult to identify.

The ring-billed gulls nest north of Indiana on some of the islands in the Great Lakes and St. Lawrence River and in some of the freshwater marshes of Canada and the northwestern states. When they find a suitable area, they sometimes nest in large numbers in a relatively small space. On one of the small islands off the coast of western New York in Lake Ontario, an estimated forty-five thousand ring-billed gulls nested continually for many years.

The ring-billed gull has been blessed with many attributes that allow it to compete successfully in the world. Its webbed feet enable it to swim and feed on surface-feeding fish, yet it is perfectly at home walking along the shoreline in search of dead fish and other bits of animal matter. At times, the ring-billeds will congregate in large numbers in dumps where they will compete noisily for choice particles of refuse. In the early spring, they vary their diet, as well as perform a valuable service, by eating grubs and other harmful insects.

In Salt Lake City there is a monument that was erected by the citizens of that city in gratitude to a near-relative of the ring-billed gull, the California gull. For three consecutive years, an invasion of black crickets had devastated their fields and wiped out their crops. An enormous flock of these gulls arrived in Salt Lake City in 1848 and ate millions of these crickets, thereby saving the crops upon which the Mormon settlers were almost totally dependent.

The ring-billed's light body and strong, graceful wings allow it to fly great distances with, seemingly, little effort. There are few among us who haven't watched enthralled, at some time in our lives, as a gull made perfect use of the wind and air thermals. And who can watch gulls in flight without a nagging twinge of envy. Oh, for the ability to fly, uninhibited, like a gull!

Wood Duck

[AIX SPONSA]

It is generally agreed that the most beautiful duck in the United States and perhaps in the world is the wood duck. Fortunately, Hoosiers have many opportunities to see this exquisite creature. The wood duck is a relatively numerous duck throughout the state. The only months during which it is difficult to find the wood duck in Indiana are November, December, January, and February.

During March, the wood duck moves up from the South and starts to establish breeding territory in Indiana. There are only a few species of ducks that use a cavity in a tree for nesting, and the wood duck is the only duck common to Indiana that nests in a tree rather than on the ground.

It always had been a puzzle how young wood ducks could survive in getting from the nesting site (at times, twenty to thirty feet above the ground); but recent careful study has shown that the hen wood duck gives a particular call, when she feels her young are ready to leave the nest, and the lightweight young respond by jumping from the lip of the nest, surviving this great fall with surprisingly few fatalities.

Although the wood duck is sometimes seen on lakes and gravel pits, it most often is found along wooded streams and pools located in wet woods. How different the wood duck appears in these surroundings, rather than on display in a zoo or as a mounted specimen in a museum!

The coloring of the male seems to be a combination of most of the colors of the rainbow in a perfect blend. From a distance, the male appears as a small, crested duck with a white striped crown, dark chest and body, and a red and white bill. The female is crested and has a prominent white eye ring. In flight, good marks to look for are the bill, held pointing downward, and the dark, square-shaped tail.

There was a time when the "woodie" was teetering on the brink of extinction, for it was much sought after, not only for food but also for

SIZE: *L. 14–17" (35–43 cm). W. 28" (71 cm).* COLORING: *Commonly considered to be the most colorful of all American ducks. Male, chestnut chest, back patterned in iridescent greens, purples, and blues, with white chin patch. Female, grayish with white eye-ring. Only duck with long, flattish crest.* HABITAT: *Rivers, ponds, and swamps in wooded areas.* NESTING: *Nests made either in natural tree cavity or nesting box, sometimes as high as 50' from the ground; up to 15 eggs.* UNUSUAL MANNERISMS: *One of the few ducks that is a tree nester.* IDENTIFYING HINTS: *Voice, a distinctive rising whistle, usually given when flushed. Long, square, dark tail is good field mark in flight.* STATUS IN INDIANA: *Year-round resident except in winters when there is no unfrozen water. Common nester. Has made good comeback since the elimination of its spring hunting season.* RANGE: *Breeds from southern Canada to Florida. Winters primarily in southern United States.*

its beautiful feathers which made excellent trout flies. This popularity, plus the fact that America was fast losing its swamps and woods, almost spelled disaster for our most beautiful duck. Fortunately, a twenty-year ban on the hunting of the wood duck was strictly enforced, and the woodie is now present in good numbers.

A late March weekend is a good time to see wood ducks. Find a nice stream flowing through a wooded area or a pond nestled in the woods, and you will not only have a good chance of seeing this highly colorful duck, but you will also receive the bonus of discovering the first wildflowers that have started to bloom.

Eastern Meadowlark

[STURNELLA MAGNA]

The eastern meadowlark is a common resident of Indiana. During the months of December, January, and February, most of our meadowlarks move a few hundred miles south to avoid the harshest period of our winters; but, each year, a few of the more adventurous meadowlarks can be found here, searching for weed seeds in a snow-covered field.

Many birds have rather misleading names; for example, the red-bellied woodpecker does not, for all practical purposes, have a red belly. The Cape May warbler is not normally found in Cape May, New Jersey. The long-billed marsh wren does not have a very long bill.

But, the meadowlark is aptly named. It is almost always found in a meadow or field. In fact, there are times, in the spring and fall, when it seems that every uncultivated field has its share of meadowlarks.

When first seen, the meadowlark appears as a medium-sized brown bird. When flushed, the two white tail feathers are very evident. The white outer tail feathers and unique flight of this bird are good identifying field marks, even when the bird is some distance away. When seen at close range, the lemon-yellow throat and breast, with a black "V" across the upper breast, positively identifies the meadowlark.

Size: *L. 9–11″ (23–28 cm).* Coloring: *Brown-streaked back, yellow front, V-shaped black bib, white edging on side of tail.* Habitat: *Open farm fields, pastures, meadows.* Nesting: *Nest on ground in dome-shaped structure. Roof built of grasses, with an opening on the side; 3–5 eggs.* Unusual Mannerisms: *Males usually identify territory by singing from spring to summer. The song says to some people, "Ah, spring of the year!"* Identifying Hints: *Can be identified by flight— several rapid wing beats followed by a short period of sailing. White outer tail feathers also a help when bird is in flight.* Status in Indiana: *Common nesting bird throughout Indiana. Present from March to November. A few winter here each year.* Range: *Breeds from southern Ontario, south to the Gulf states. Winters primarily in the southern states.*

The meadowlark builds its nest on the ground. The nest is made of grasses and is covered by a dome-shaped roof with a side opening. Two broods a year are normal in Indiana.

One of the most engaging characteristics of the meadowlark is its song. There are times, in April, when it is almost impossible to drive out into the country without hearing a meadowlark sing. The normal song of the eastern meadowlark has many variations. In the early spring, it seems to be happily proclaiming that spring has arrived and repeats its musical "spring of the year" song over and over again.

A close relative of our eastern meadowlark is the western meadowlark, found chiefly west of the Mississippi River. To my eyes, the two species are identical an appearance, but their songs are quite different. Many people consider the song of the western meadowlark to be one of the most musical of all bird songs.

The western meadowlark, in recent years, has expanded its range and is now established in our neighboring state of Illinois. There is a good possibility that this trend will continue and that, in future years, both the eastern and the western meadowlark will be breeding birds in Indiana.

Fortunately, in contrast to turn of the century days, there is very little, if any, hunting of the meadowlark today. For one thing, it is strictly against federal law. Also, farmers have long appreciated the value of meadowlarks and take a very dim view of anyone who uses their land to hunt this bird.

Pintail

[A N A S   A C U T A]

March can be a cruel month. Too often, it prematurely announces spring, only then to unleash a snow or ice storm. In spite of the vicissitudes of March, a great number of different species of waterfowl come to Indiana during this month. One of the first of the ducks to arrive is the pintail. As soon as the ice disappears from the reservoirs and ponds,

SIZE: *L. 21–30″ (53–76 cm). W. 35″ (89 cm).* COLORING: *Male, brown head, white breast, white extending into the side of the head. Grayish back. Female primarily brown.* HABITAT: *Marshes, prairie ponds, lakes.* NESTING: *Nest on the ground, hidden in the grasses, lined with down; frequently at some distance from water; 6–8 eggs.* UNUSUAL MANNERISM: *Extremely wary.* IDENTIFYING HINTS: *Long neck, very long, pointed tail. In flight, outer white border of middle area of the wing.* STATUS IN INDIANA: *Common spring and fall migrant. Very uncommon winterer. Does not nest in Indiana.* RANGE: *Breeds from Alaska to northernmost parts of the United States. Winters as far south as Central America.*

the pintails arrive, some from as far away as Mexico and Central America. However, the pintails won't stay in Indiana very long, as most of them move north to Canada and Alaska to nest.

How different the pintails appear in spring from the way they look on their wintering grounds! The males stand out strikingly among the other early migrants, the mallards and the blacks. They always seem to be on the alert, swimming lightly on the surface of the water, head held high, ready to take to the air at any hint of danger. Once airborne, the pintail is a swift flyer and has even been clocked at more than fifty miles per hour. Some hunters claim that the pintail can achieve a speed of up to ninety miles per hour. This powerful flight is necessary for the pintails, since some of them leave their breeding grounds in Alaska to winter off the shores of the Hawaiian Islands—a tremendous task requiring a two-thousand-mile flight over the Pacific Ocean.

The male pintail has a brown head, a long, white neck, and—as its name implies—a long, thin, pointed tail. It is the only duck regularly found in Indiana with such a tail. The female is an all-brown duck that is difficult to distinguish from some of the other surface-feeding female ducks.

In flight the male shows the pointed tail, a white belly, and a single white stripe on the edge of the wing from the middle of the wing to the body. The female also has this white stripe on the wing.

The pintail, one of the first ducks to nest, often builds its nest a considerable distance from the water. Frequently, by June, when other ducks are still incubating eggs, the pintail will have completed its nesting chores. It is among the first of the migrating ducks to return to Indiana in the fall; and, while it is not normally as common here in the fall as it is in the spring, it can be seen in good numbers in September and October.

While there is much to be said for the warm sunshine found in Florida during the winter, March in the South lacks the excitement of March in Indiana. The pintails that I have seen in Florida seem much more bland than the vibrant, wild, energetic birds that come to Indiana when the ice first melts in our lakes and ponds.

Size: *L. 8–9½″ (20–24 cm).* Coloring: *Rusty-brown back. Heavy streaks on upper breast end abruptly against the white belly.* Habitat: *Wet, short-grassed area, golf courses, airports.* Nesting: *Nest is a slight depression in the ground; 4 eggs.* Unusual Mannerisms: *One of the last common migrating shorebirds to give up the secret of where it nests. Extremely long migratory journey.* Identifying Hints: *Well-defined bib is best field mark. Also, yellow legs.* Status in Indiana: *Common spring and fall migrant. Does not nest in Indiana.* Range: *Breeds from Arctic coast of Alaska to Hudson Bay. Winters primarily in southern South America.*

Pectoral Sandpiper

[CALIDRIS MELANOTOS]

Even persons only casually interested in birds are aware of the huge numbers of birds that migrate in the spring. In March, the return of swallows to Capistrano is proclaimed by the jubilant pealing of church bells; also in March, the arrival of the buzzards (turkey vultures) sets off a week-long festival in Hinckley, Ohio. Everyone enjoys seeing the first migrant Canada geese flying overhead, the first robin in a backyard, or the first purple martin returning to a martin house.

Yet, many birds pass through Indiana in the spring unrecognized and unheralded. One such bird is the pectoral sandpiper. Maybe Hoosiers should join together to form a Pectoral Sandpiper Festival Committee to cheer this medium-sized shorebird on as it passes through Indiana on its way to the extreme northern tip of the North American continent. What a journey it has, each year, migrating all the way from its wintering grounds in Peru, Chile, and Argentina to the Arctic coast of Alaska! Even more astounding to me than the long, biannual trip for this small bird is the fact that the young birds that hatch in the summer in the Arctic will fly to South America almost completely unaided by the parent birds. What instincts are involved? How do they find their way? Where do these birds, less than two months old, find the energy for this arduous journey?

The pectoral sandpiper is a surprisingly common shorebird in Indiana and is sometimes seen here in flocks of as many as fifty to one hundred birds. It is most frequently seen here in the spring (April) and, again, during its fall migration (September). In contrast to most shorebirds who use either the Atlantic or Pacific coasts as their main migration route, the pectorals' major spring migration path is through the Mississippi River Valley.

The pectoral is a brown-backed bird with yellow legs. The best field mark is the sharp division between the brown breast and the white belly, appearing almost as if the bird were wearing a brown bib over its white foreparts. The pectoral is more likely to be found in grassy mud flats or short-grassed, wet meadows than feeding along the water's edge, as so many of the shorebirds do. I've also found good-sized flocks of pectorals feeding on insects in freshly plowed fields.

If members of the Pectoral Sandpiper Festival Committee should submit a proposal that they hold their celebration over the Memorial Day weekend, it should be brought to the committee's attention that there is a competing activity in Indiana on this particular weekend . . . something about racing cars trying to travel 500 miles. It seems to me that the pectoral sandpipers' race of more than 12,000 miles far overshadows this other event; so perhaps the planners of the automobile race should concede that Hoosiers might well salute the pectoral sandpipers, rather than racing cars, on the last weekend in May!

Turkey Vulture

[C A T H A R T E S   A U R A]

Two members of the vulture family are found in Indiana. By far, the most common is the turkey vulture. Its close relative, the black vulture, is found only in the most southern part of the state.

The dictionary decribes a vulture as any greedy or ruthless person who preys on others. I don't know how the vulture acquired this reputation. It is not greedy, nor is it ruthless, nor does it prey on other birds. Its counterpart in human life would be our sanitation department —a very necessary and hard-working group of people who perform a most important service. So it is with vultures. They are scavengers in the animal world. They perform a task that nature deemed them best equipped to fulfill.

Turkey vultures move into the state early in the year, in March. I recall counting a migrating flock of vultures the second week in March in Versailles State Park. They started coming in to roost at 4:30 in the afternoon, and by dusk my count had reached over 700 birds. This was the largest group that I had ever seen. There is a town in Ohio—

SIZE: *L. 25–32" (63–81 cm). W. 72" (1.8 m)*. COLORING: *Overall blackish-brown bird with featherless, red head*. HABITAT: *Remote, deciduous forests. Soars everywhere*. NESTING: *Eggs laid on the ground; 1–3 eggs*. UNUSUAL MANNERISMS: *Scavenger, often gathers in good-sized flocks, 25–30, in the evening*. IDENTIFYING HINTS: *In flight, small head, long tail, wings held in shallow "V."* STATUS IN INDIANA: *Fairly common spring and fall migrant, summer resident and nesting bird. Does not winter here*. RANGE: *Breeds from southern Canada to South America. Winters from southern half of the United States south*.

Hinckley—where a week-long festival is staged, celebrating the spring arrival of the turkey vulture!

Vultures build a very rudimentary nest in an inaccessible area, usually on or near the ground. There they lay two eggs, which are incubated for a month. The young are fed by regurgitation on the part of the parent birds. The young bird thrusts its bill into the parent's gullet to receive its nourishment. They mature rapidly, and by the time they are ready to fly, they have almost reached adult size. With rare exceptions, they are absent from the state during the months of November, December, January, and February, wintering in the southern states.

On the ground, vultures remind me of huge awkward, black chickens; but, in the air, they are a thing of beauty. Their great wings, spanning six feet or more, seem to be able to utilize every existing air current. They are able to glide for long distances with minimal movement of their wings. In flight, the best field marks to look for are the large size, headless appearance, two-toned back underparts, and the broad "V"-like pattern formed by their wings.

Look for turkey vultures soaring over the highways and hills anywhere in Indiana; and, remember, they are helping to keep our environment clean—and it doesn't cost one cent of taxpayers' money to reap the benefits of their labors!

APRIL

Spring has arrived and is evident in everything around us: the trees have started to leaf out, the grass has turned green, trillium, crocuses, and daffodils are all in bloom. People seem happier. "Good morning" greetings from associates seem more sincere. Winter is over, and good times lie ahead.

Each week of April brings new groups of birds. First, the fox, the savannah, the vesper, and the field sparrows arrive on the scene—soon to be followed by the white-throat, the white-crowned, and the chipping sparrows. The brown thrasher and the phoebe can be expected to arrive by the middle of the month. Anytime after the fifteenth of April look for the first swallow, usually the tree, then the rough-winged and barn, with the bank and cliff swallows bringing up the rearguard.

Although Indiana is not an especially good state for hawk flights, there is a definite influx of hawks about the third week of April, when the buteos (the red-tailed, the red-shouldered, and the broad-winged hawks) can be seen soaring in their normal manner, moving in a northernly direction. The accipiters, the sharp-shinned and the Cooper's hawks, make an all-too-brief visit and move on within a few days. They and the marsh hawk have not done well in Indiana during the past ten years, and must now be considered uncommon birds here. It is hoped that their status will improve, for the out-of-doors seems a little less exciting without them. Toward the end of the month, the first trickle of warblers will cautiously penetrate our borders—a little like testing bathwater with the tips of one's toes—deciding whether conditions are right to move in en masse. Almost without exception, the first warbler will be the myrtle or, as it is now officially called, the "yellow-rumped warbler."

By the last week in April it is possible to see one hundred different species of birds in a day of birding. Some of the birds that have been with us are now gone and won't return for five or six months. Most of the ducks, the yellow-bellied sapsucker, the winter wren, the hermit thrush, the golden-crowned kinglet, the winter finches, the junco, and the tree sparrow will have moved north to their breeding grounds. We will see them again when there is a feel of chill in the air, when the leaves are turning, and when the last of the tomatoes has been picked. There is a twinge of sadness felt in seeing these birds disappear, but comfort in knowing that they will come back after having fulfilled nature's cycle. It's rather like the feeling a mother gets in sending off her child to kindergarten or a father gets when his son moves out of the household, ready to try out his own wings.

American Bittern

[BOTAURUS LENTIGINOSUS]

Although the bald eagle, the osprey, the pelican, and a few other spectacular birds have received a great amount of attention because of their declining populations, other birds, less obviously, have also had drastic reductions in their numbers.

One bird that I especially miss seeing and hearing is the American bittern. It was a special joy to hear the eerie pumping sound of this heron on an early spring morning. On many occasions I've found this large, brown marsh bird while the ponds were still frozen and a heavy snow lay on the dried cattails; but April is usually the month when the American bitterns pass through Indiana. There was a time when any sizable cattail marsh in the northern states had bitterns either during

SIZE: *L. 23–34" (58–85 cm). W. over 36" (90 cm).* COLORING: *Brown bird with white streaking.* HABITAT: *Cattail marshes and bogs.* NESTING: *On the ground, on a mound among cattails; 4–5 buffy brown eggs.* UNUSUAL MANNERISMS: *Frequently holds head parallel to the tall reeds in which it hides.* IDENTIFYING HINTS: *In flight, the blackish, outer parts of the wings. Call is diagnostic.* STATUS IN INDIANA: *Uncommon nesting bird, primarily in northern part of Indiana.* RANGE: *Nests from Canada to southern states. Winters normally south of Indiana.*

their migration or during their nesting season. Unfortunately, that day has passed.

The two major factors contributing to the decline of the bittern, in my opinion, are the indiscriminate use of various insecticides and, perhaps even more contributory, the decline of the large cattail marshes. I'm sure a few bitterns still nest in the northern part of Indiana where there remain good stands of cattails, but I don't know of any recent nesting records in the central part of Indiana. It is hoped that the decline of this bird is temporary, for there are few birds as fascinating as the bittern.

The voice alone of the American bittern gives it uniqueness. It is an unbird-like sound, difficult to describe in words. Some writers have likened the sound to a guttural, emphatic rendering of the words, "plum pudd'n." To others, the sound is reminiscent of a wooden stake being driven into the soft earth. This sound has great carrying power and, once heard, is not likely to be forgotten.

There are few birds or animals so adept at camouflaging their presence as the American bittern. When not feeding, the bittern typically strikes a pose in which it holds its head and bill parallel to the reeds, remaining absolutely motionless. In this pose the bittern blends perfectly with the marsh vegetation, and it often relies upon this protective coloration, rather than flight, when potential danger approaches. While this ability to blend into its surroundings is important to the bittern, I can attest, from personal experience with an injured bittern, that its bill can be used most efficiently, not only to obtain food, but also to discourage anyone from venturing too close.

The American bittern is a large, stocky, brown bird. The breast is a lighter brown than the back and is streaked with white. In flight it shows black wing tips.

Finding an American bittern in spring may require an element of luck, together with patience and considerable effort, but, then, don't most of the worthwhile things of life call for special effort?

Brown Thrasher

[TOXOSTOMA RUFUM]

Mid-April should be a good time to see the year's first brown thrasher.

Just how the brown thrasher acquired its name is somewhat obscure. True, brown is its predominant color, but why "thrasher"? The most widely accepted theory is that the brown thrasher uses his bill to thrash about among the leaves. A good comparison would be the way one would use a pitchfork in spreading hay with sidewise strokes. The thrasher uses his bill in this manner to send the leaves flying, thus enabling him to find whatever insects and seeds are concealed beneath the pile.

Farmland and brown thrasher seem almost synonymous, for it is down country lanes among the hedgerows that one is likely to see a brown thrasher. Look for a larger than robin-sized bird that is cinnamon-colored above and heavily streaked below. If you are able to get a good look, you will see that he has two white wing-bars, a yellow eye, and a somewhat curved bill.

The brown thrasher is a common nesting bird throughout the state of Indiana and is with us from April through October. Although it will winter here occasionally, it usually winters in the southern part of the United States. In Indiana, the thrasher nests in hedgerows, small trees, or shrubs. As a rule, it will raise two broods per season.

Of all the smaller birds, the brown thrasher is probably the most aggressive defender of its nesting site. It will vigorously attack any cat, dog, or even human that disturbs its nest. Before and after its nesting activities, the brown thrasher seems to be a rather tame and friendly bird that will come to a feeding station or bird bath with little hesitation.

Perhaps the thrasher's most engaging attribute is his marvelous voice. His spring song is a loud, striking, oft-repeated series of short phrases. Henry David Thoreau felt that the thrasher was giving advice to a farmer planting corn: "Drop it, drop it—cover it up, cover it up—pull it up, pull it up."

SIZE: L. 10½–12" (26–30 cm). COLORING: Rufous-red above, white breast, heavily streaked, wing-bars and slightly curved bill. HABITAT: Woodland borders, thickets, hedgerows, gardens. NESTING: Coarsely built nest of twigs, leaves and grass, sometimes on the ground, most often in shrubbery or thorny bushes; 4–5 eggs. UNUSUAL MANNERISMS: Mimics other birds, uses beak to scatter dead leaves. IDENTIFYING HINTS: Long, rufous-red tail, heavy breast streaking. STATUS IN INDIANA: Common spring and fall migrant and summer nesting bird. Uncommon winterer. RANGE: Breeds from southern Canada to the Gulf Coast. Winters primarily in southern United States.

The thrasher is also a good mimicker of other birds, but I don't feel his imitations are nearly as convincing as those of the mockingbird. Although the brown thrasher is normally a bird of the ground or shrubbery, when he is singing his spring song, he frequently will move to a higher elevation, almost as though he wants to be sure everyone will be able to hear his fine song.

Red-shouldered Hawk

[BUTEO LINEATUS]

How welcomed, by the birds, are the first warm days of the year! Cardinals are starting to sing a different tune, crows are beginning to disperse from their winter roosting areas, and the red-shouldered hawks (the most vocal of our nesting hawks) are doing their best to liven up the quiet woods. There are times when the woods will reverberate with the strident call, "kee-yeer, kee-yeer," of the red-shouldered hawk. The first warm winds present an opportunity to the red-shouldered to begin his courtship flights. The male will soar high above the female, then drop suddenly, with wings folded under, until he is beneath her. Abruptly, he will then end his dive and once again ascend above the object of his affection.

Indiana's most common nesting hawks are the red-shouldered, red-tailed, and kestrel. Because of the red-shouldered's tendency to stay close to the woods, it is not seen as often as the red-tailed and kestrel. The red-tailed hawk is often seen soaring in open country, and the kestrel is frequently seen perched on telephone lines near the highways. The red-shouldered hawk exhibits a great loyalty to its favorite woods, nesting there for many years. A pair that I have been watching for about ten years has successfully raised two to four young each year in a small wooded area in Eagle Creek Park. For the past several years, they have nested in a tree located near a road that has a constant stream of cars and people passing by. This situation would never be tolerated

by the red-tailed hawk, which is much more secretive about its nesting site.

The adult red-shouldered hawk is a very colorful bird, showing a cinnamon-streaked breast, a brown back, and a deep chestnut coloring at the bend of the wings. In flight the black and white bands on the tail and the white area toward the tips of its wings are a great help in identifying this bird. Young birds lack the cinnamon-colored breasts but still show the black and white banding on the tail when in flight.

Somehow, this hawk acquired the misnomer of "hen hawk." This is unfortunate, because the red-shouldered hawk has little interest in poultry, and is, in fact, one of the most beneficial birds of prey. Its diet consists of rodents of all types, squirrels, snakes, and frogs; and, in summer, grasshoppers make up a substantial portion of its diet.

Birds of prey, along with all birds, have a difficult time during extremely bitter winters because of the scarcity of food; but, still, the fittest survive, and by late February the red-shouldered hawk is already investigating suitable nesting sites in order to propagate the species.

SIZE: *L. 16–24" (40–61 cm). W. 40" (1 m).* COLORING: *Brown backed, rusty-barred breast, reddish shoulders, black-and-white banding on the tail.* HABITAT: *Deciduous woodlands, often near water.* NESTING: *Nest a large mass of leaves and twigs, generally placed near to tree trunk, 20–50' above the ground; 2–3 eggs.* UNUSUAL MANNERISMS: *A good portion of this bird's diet is made up of snakes and frogs. Is not nearly as secretive about its nesting site as is red-tailed hawk.* IDENTIFYING HINTS: *Black-and-white banding on the tail. Loud call with great carrying power, "kee-yeer"—often perfectly imitated by blue jays.* STATUS IN INDIANA: *Uncommon year-round resident and breeding bird.* RANGE: *Winters in small numbers in northern states.*

SIZE: *L. 12–14″ (30–35 cm).* COLORING: *Raggedy crest, blue-gray above, white below, with dagger-shaped bill. Female has blue band around the upper breast and a chestnut band on lower breast. Male has blue-gray band but lacks the chestnut band.* HABITAT: *Rivers, lakes, gravel pits.* NESTING: *Burrow in bank that has been excavated by the kingfisher, not far from water; 6–7 eggs.* UNUSUAL MANNERISMS: *Is frequently seen hovering, with rapidly beating wings, over water where there are fish. When on its territory often follows the same path, stopping at the same tree on a daily basis.* IDENTIFYING HINTS: *Best mark is to learn the voice: a loud, harsh "rattle" that the kingfisher gives almost continuously.* STATUS IN INDIANA: *Fairly common breeding bird throughout Indiana. Occasionally winters near open water.* RANGE: *Breeds from Alaska south, throughout the United States. Winters as far south as Panama and the West Indies.*

Belted Kingfisher

[MEGACERYLE ALCYON]

The belted kingfisher is the only member of the kingfisher family found in Indiana. Fortunately, it is found throughout the state and is with us each month of the year. During the most severe part of the winter, it must sometimes retreat from the northernmost part of the state to the southern part to find open water, but during the rest of the year just about all the streams, lakes, and reservoirs have a resident pair of belted kingfishers.

Small fish make up more than ninety percent of the kingfisher's diet, and the kingfisher is a very skilled fisherman. It is usually seen perched on a snag or on a dead limb of a tree overlooking a lake or stream. From this vantage point, the kingfisher will scan the water waiting for fish to reveal their presence. When a likely looking victim is spotted, the kingfisher will dash from its perch and, with powerful wings, will quickly arrive at the spot where a fish has been located. Frequently, the kingfisher will hover over the fish and take careful aim before diving down in an attempt to catch the fish. If necessary, the kingfisher will totally submerge itself while pursuing its prey.

The kingfisher is a large bird, about a foot long, and when seen perched, its head and bill seem to be disproportionately large for the rest of its body. But, when flying, the head and bill size seem to add, rather than subtract, to its symmetry. The head, wings, and back are blue. The throat and belly, white. The male has a blue neckband, and the female is identical except that she has a chestnut-colored band across her chest and down her sides. Two additional helpful field marks are the prominent crest (which always reminds me of some teenager's hair that refuses to stay combed) and its ability to hover in one spot. If you see a bird hovering over water in Indiana, it is almost sure to be the belted kingfisher.

The kingfisher nests throughout the state of Indiana. He burrows a hole in a bluff or bank of a river or stream or in the sides of a sand and gravel pit. This tunnel will sometimes extend as much as ten feet into the earth. If the burrow is not destroyed, it will be used more than one year. By July the six or seven young are out of the nest, and the parent birds are busy instructing the young in the art of fishing. They must learn quickly and well, for by the end of that month the family group will break up, and the young are on their own.

The kingfisher doesn't have a song, but rather a loud, penetrating rattle. It is a sound that is held in high esteem by those familiar with the outdoors. The "rattle of the kingfisher" is often referred to in literature. This rattle has qualities about it that imply a love of wilderness and an appreciation of freedom—a sense of confidence that things will turn out well.

Song Sparrow

[MELOSPIZA MELODIA]

Sparrows are looked upon as birds of little beauty and regarded, by many, as nuisance birds. Yet, the bird that is responsible for the poor reputation of the sparrows—the English sparrow or house sparrow—is not even a member of the sparrow family. It is not a native bird in America. Eight pairs brought to New York from France in 1850 have since increased by the millions and have, indeed, become a nuisance. It is unfortunate that the house sparrow has maligned the sparrow name, for those who are acquainted with the song sparrow consider it to be among the most admired of American birds.

The song sparrow is one of Indiana's most beneficial birds. Its diet consists almost entirely of weed seeds and harmful insects. The song sparrow is found in good numbers in every county of the state and is with us every month of the year.

As its name implies, the song sparrow is a persistent singer. Even in the dead of winter when many birds are silent, the song sparrow continues to brighten up the surroundings with its pretty melody. I'm sure that everyone has heard this happy song at some time in his life. It

SIZE: *L. 5–7" (13–17 cm)*. COLORING: *Brown back, white breast with heavy streaking, large, central spot on the breast.* HABITAT: *Parks, farms, cities, suburban gardens, brushy roadsides.* NESTING: *Nest found on the ground, well hidden in tufts of grass or in low ornamental shrubs. Well-made cup of grass and leaves, often lined with hair; 3–5 eggs.* UNUSUAL MANNERISMS: *Persistent singer, gives many variations of song.* IDENTIFYING HINTS: *Heavily streaked breast with central dark spot is best identification help.* STATUS IN INDIANA: *Common year-round resident and nesting bird.* RANGE: *Breeds from Alaska south to mid-America. Winters from Great Lakes area south to the Gulf of Mexico.*

starts with three or four introductory notes and ends in a musical trill, but it gives all sorts of variations upon this theme. Also, in different parts of the country there are other subtle modifications of its typical song.

The song sparrow is brown backed, as are all of our Indiana sparrows, and has a heavily streaked breast. Perhaps the best identifying mark of this bird is the dark spot in the center of the breast.

It most often nests in the grass or under a brush pile, but sometimes it will select a thicket, shrub, or tangle by the edge of a woods or in a suburban backyard. There it will lay three to five eggs and, usually, will raise two families each year. In my own yard song sparrows have nested within six feet of the porch every year. Usually the nest hasn't been evident until the young birds could be heard crying for food.

Stereotyping is always inaccurate and unfair—and so it is with the sparrows. The song sparrow's model behavior and beneficial feeding habits make this sparrow a most welcome member of our fauna.

American Coot

[FULICA AMERICANA]

The first days of spring often bring the American coot to Indiana. I rather like the colloquial names that the coot has acquired, like "mud hen" for its chicken-like appearance and for the fact that it is frequently seen foraging on the muddy shorelines of lakes and ponds. Or "spatter," given because of the coot's manner of spattering water with its feet and wings as it hurries along on top of the water before it becomes airborne.

SIZE: *L. 13–16" (33–40 cm). W. 25" (63 cm).* COLORING: *Slate-gray body with white bill.* HABITAT: *Open ponds and marshes. Frequent visitor at artificial lakes, as found at apartment complexes.* NESTING: *Usually on the water, attached to cattails and reeds; 8–12 eggs.* UNUSUAL MANNERISMS: *Frequently seen on shorelines, rather than on water. Seems to run on the water prior to getting airborne.* IDENTIFYING

HINT: *The only duck-like bird with a white bill.* STATUS IN INDIANA: *Rare nester. Rare winter resident where there is open water. Common spring and fall migrant.* RANGE: *Breeds from western center of Canada south to the Great Lakes area and sporadically in areas south of the Great Lakes. Winters as far north as there is open water, south to South America.*

The American coot is one of the most common waterfowl in Indiana, both in the spring and again in the fall. It is only during the months of December, January, and February that the coot leaves Indiana and winters in the southern parts of the United States. In winter, it is especially numerous in the waters off the west coast of Florida where thousands of coot gather.

Although most often seen feeding and associating with ducks, the coot is more closely related to marsh birds than water birds and shares many of the characteristics of the marsh bird family. The coot, like other members of the marsh bird tribe, gets along very well on land. I've often seen small groups of coots walking along a gravel road, sometimes a considerable distance from water.

The American coot, which looks like a duck with a small head, is dark gray, almost black, and has disproportionately large feet that are lobed rather than webbed. Its most prominent feature is its large, china-white bill. When swimming, it pumps its head back and forth—a mannerism not shared by many of the ducks with which it is usually seen.

The coot builds its nest in shallow water around the edges of ponds and lakes, usually where there is an abundance of cattails. The nest, which may float on top of the water, is firmly attached to the surrounding reeds and vegetation. About eight to twelve eggs are laid each year. The newly hatched chicks are quite comical looking—little black balls of down with almost-bald heads. Within a day or two of hatching, these little mites, only about the size of a silver dollar, are able to swim, dive, and feed themselves.

Two things about the coot have always puzzled me. John James Audubon, in his journals written about 150 years ago, mentioned that the coot does not dive to search for food. This certainly is not true today, for the coot is an accomplished diver and has no hesitancy about diving for its food. Audubon, who birded in areas where the coot was a common bird, most definitely was a careful and keen observer. It's possible that the coot has changed its feeding habits since Audubon's time.

The other puzzle is how the phrase, "you old coot," came into usage. I'm never sure if the phrase is one of endearment or one insinuating a negative characteristic.

Hermit Thrush

[C A T H A R U S   G U T T A T U S]

There is no group of birds more highly thought of than the thrush family. The robin and the bluebird, both members of the thrush family, are recognized by everyone. Yet other thrushes, equally deserving of admiration, pass through Indiana in both spring and fall quickly and quietly, and largely unnoticed.

This is true, unfortunately, of the hermit thrush, for as its name indicates, it is a shy, retiring bird that enjoys solitude. It is usually seen among openings in evergreen plantings where it sits motionless, depending upon its coloring to keep it inconspicuous. Then, when an intruder gets too near, it quickly flies close to the ground to another area where it hopes to go unseen. Consequently, most birders have to be content with brief glimpses of the hermit thrush. This was not the case one early April morning when a small group of us was privileged to see one of these birds as close as six feet and was able to study carefully the thrush's field marks. My guess is that this individual bird had just completed a night-long journey and was too tired and hungry to behave in its normal manner.

The hermit thrush is more hardy than most of the other thrushes and is generally the first to arrive in the spring and the last to leave in the fall. Occasionally, the hermit will winter here when it can find a suitable food supply. A few years ago I found one in February at Eagle Creek Park when the temperature registered 22 degrees below zero. That bird seemed to have a rather unhappy look about it; I imagine it regretted its decision to spend the winter in Indiana.

April and October are the two months when the hermit thrush is most likely to be seen here, for it doesn't nest in Indiana. Its primary nesting area extends from the northern border of the United States north to the mixed evergreen forests of Northern Canada.

Smaller than a robin, the hermit thrush is a brown-backed bird having a rusty tail and white breast with brown spots. A help in

SIZE: *L. 6½–7½" (16–19 cm).* COLORING: *Grayish-brown back, rufous tail, light breast, spotted mostly in upper breast.* HABITAT: *Coniferous or mixed forests, thickets, ornamental shrubbery.* NESTING: *Compact cup of moss, leaves, and rootlets on ground in low bush; 3–4 eggs.* UNUSUAL MANNERISMS: *Normally shy and retiring. Considered to be among the finest vocalists. Song seldom heard in Indiana.* IDENTIFYING HINTS: *Has habit of raising and slowly lowering tail.* STATUS IN INDIANA: *Fairly common spring and fall migrant. Rare winter resident. Does not nest in Indiana.* RANGE: *Breeds from Alaska to northernmost United States. Winters primarily in southern states.*

identifying this bird when seen among the shadows of the evergreens or in any poor light is its habit of raising its tail and then slowly dropping it. The hermit is the only thrush that does this.

During its brief stay here, the hermit thrush does not sing. This is most unfortunate, for the hermit ranks as one of the most gifted vocalists in the bird world. I've heard it in northern Michigan and in northern New York and can attest to the beauty of its flute-like, complicated melody. There is no denying that the hermit thrush is an accomplished singer, but part of its charm is the setting from which the song is given: a lush, moist evergreen forest, most often early in the morning or late, as the sun is setting.

I can describe it no better than to quote John Burroughs' feelings expressed after hearing a hermit thrush, singing at twilight, in the Adirondack Mountains, "I experienced that serene exultation of sentiment of which music, literature and religion are but the faint types and symbols."

Yellow-rumped Warbler

[DENDROICA CORONATA]

It is small wonder that the wood warblers are so difficult to learn. Their very names add to the problem of trying to become familiar with members of the warbler family. For example, there is a yellow warbler, a yellow-throated warbler, and a yellowthroat—all very different looking birds, but birds with very similar names. If this isn't complex enough, the myrtle warbler's name has been officially changed to "yellow-rumped warbler." So now we have yellow warbler, yellow-throated warbler, yellowthroat, and yellow-rumped warbler.

The yellow-rumped warbler, or myrtle, is the most common warbler in Indiana and in all of the states east of the Mississippi River. It is the only warbler that occasionally will winter in Indiana. It is the first one to arrive in the spring and the last one to leave in the fall. The only

SIZE: *L. 5–6″ (13–15 cm).* COLORING: *Male, grayish-blue above, with four spots of yellow—on crown, each shoulder, and rump. Two white wing-bars. Females and immatures, greatly varied but all have yellow rump.* HABITAT: *Mixed and coniferous forests.* NESTING: *Typically in evergreens about 20′ off the ground. Nest cup of coniferous twigs is lined with fine grasses and feathers; 4–5 eggs.* UNUSUAL MANNERISMS: *The hardiest of the warblers and probably the most numerous in the United States.* IDENTIFYING HINTS: *Call note, a sharp "check," which distinguishes this warbler from all other warblers at any season.* STATUS IN INDIANA: *Very common spring and fall migrant; uncommon winterer. Does not nest in Indiana.* RANGE: *Breeds from Alaska south to the northern border of the United States. Winters primarily south of the Great Lakes area to Costa Rica and the West Indies.*

months that it is not found here are June, July, and August, for it does not nest here. It does nest as far north as there are trees, all the way up to northern Alaska and the northern Yukon. A few will nest in the northern part of our most northern states—Michigan, Minnesota, Wisconsin, and the mountains of New York.

In the spring, the male is a most attractive bird—bluish-grey back, wing and tail with white streaking. The belly and throat are white with a dark patch on the breast and sides. Four yellow patches are conspicuous, with one on each side, one on the top of the head, and one on the rump. The female is similarly colored, but the bluish-grey color is replaced by brown.

When these birds return in the fall with their young, the males will have lost their spring coloring. You will see many different varieties of plumage among the males, females, and birds born during the summer, but the yellow rump will always be evident.

The song, to my ears, is not very distinctive. But the rather hard "check" that is frequently given is a help in sorting out the myrtles from the other warblers as they flit through the trees.

The yellow-rumps, like all warblers, move in waves. The males are the first to arrive, followed in the next wave by the females. As a rule, not many myrtles remain in Indiana after the middle of May.

The chances are very good that sometime around the first week of May you will have the yellow-rumped warbler near your home. It's our most common warbler, and I urge you to become acquainted with it.

White-eyed Vireo

[VIREO GRISEUS]

The height of the spring migration lasts from the middle of April until the last week of May. Every few days, as the weather changes, new groups of birds will suddenly appear in our yards, around the farms, and in our parks. Many of these birds will be with us for just a brief

time and will then continue to move north until they reach their breeding grounds. For others, the journey is over; they will stay in Indiana and raise their young.

This is true of a bird that arrives, normally, the last few days of April, the white-eyed vireo. Indiana is the northern extremity of this bird's breeding range, and it is much more common in the southern part of the state than in the northern part.

The white-eyed vireos will be with us all summer; then, by the middle of October most of them will be on their way south to spend the winter in our southernmost states. Their favorite nesting sites in Indiana are amidst brier thickets and, especially, in tangles found along the edges of streams. The nest is most often found a few feet off the ground in low shrubs or in the lower branches of small shade trees. Four eggs would comprise an average clutch.

If you can learn to recognize the call of the white-eyed vireo, you will find many more of them than if you depend on sight alone. Putting words to birdsongs is a helpful way to remember them. To me, the white-eyed vireo seems to say, "Chick'-a-per-weeoo-rickity-chick." The harsh "chicks" at both ends of the song are a distinguishing characteristic. The white-eyed also has some scolding notes and is quite expert in mimicking other birds. Chances are you will hear ten white-eyed vireos for every one you see.

SIZE: *L. 4½–5½" (11–14 cm)*. COLORING: *Olive-green above, white below, with yellow wash to the sides. Yellow spectacles. White wing-bars.* HABITAT: *Dense thickets, brushy hillsides, often along stream banks.* NESTING: *Cone-shaped nest, neatly woven, usually in thick undergrowth; 3–5 eggs.* UNUSUAL MANNERISMS: *One of the few vireos which spends its time low in trees or shrubbery, rather than high in treetops.* IDENTIFYING HINTS: *Gives a variety of scolding notes, beginning and ending with a harsh note "chick'-a-per-weeoo-chick'."* STATUS IN INDIANA: *Fairly common spring and fall migrant and summer resident, less common in northern Indiana.* RANGE: *Breeds south of Great Lakes area to Florida and the Gulf Coast. Winters in the southern states.*

Vireos, in general, appear to be rather drab, slowly moving versions of warblers; however, the white-eyed is a little more colorful than most of the vireos. It has an olive-colored back with two white wing-bars (a good identifying mark), a white throat, and light yellow sides. As its names implies, it has a white eye iris and yellow spectacles. Look for it in low shrubbery and underbrush, rather than in the treetops where most of the vireos are typically found.

It is always a pleasure to welcome back the spring birds. They add a new zest to the landscape. I'm tempted to ask the various insurance companies, restaurants, and motels that line our main streets to print on their marquees some spring day:

"WELCOME BACK, WHITE-EYED VIREOS!"

MAY

MAY IS THE CLIMAX of the year for the birder. It is the month that all birders look forward to all year long. This is the month that brings the greatest number of species, not only to Indiana but to most of the northern states. In Indiana, the peak of the migration is generally between the seventh of the month and the twelfth, depending upon the weather. In some other northern states it is between the tenth and the fifteenth. In western New York (where I have spent a great deal of time), the peak is between the twentieth and the twenty-fifth of May.

This is the month when even non-birders acknowledge that something is different. There's a fresh realization that life shouldn't always be made up of doing the mundane things: that now is the time to plant a garden, to paint the house, to buy a new car. (Or even a time to be more understanding of someone with different views. . . .)

To the birder, May is the month to be out in the field, for he knows that time is fleeting and that each day lost is lost forever. If the solitary vireo is not seen during the first week in May, chances are that it is missed for the entire year, and who knows what the next year will bring? Some of the warblers are with us for only a few days, and it will be twelve months before there is another opportunity to see them.

After the middle of the month, the late migrants move. The late waves of warblers—the mourning, the Canada, the bay-breasted, Wilson's, and the blackpoll—will be followed by the flycatchers—the willow, the alder, and the wood pewee.

May is not the right time to begin to identify the birds of Indiana. One county in Indiana had as high a count as more than 160 birds in one day, and the state count numbered more than 250 different species for this same day. But it is an appropriate time to acknowledge that Indiana has its share, at least, of the birds that are indigenous to the eastern United States and also that learning to identify all the birds of Indiana is indeed a formidable task.

SIZE: L. 7–8½″ (18–21 cm). COLORING: Male, all-over blue-black, with lustrous purple on head and wings. Females, young, and first-year males are duller backed, with light-gray belly area. HABITAT: Open area, often near residential settlements or farmlands. NESTING: Most often in colonies, either in abandoned woodpecker holes or in man-made, apartment-type nesting houses; 4–5 white eggs. UNUSUAL MANNERISMS: Males generally arrive two to three weeks before females to select territory. IDENTIFYING HINTS: Largest of the swallows. The only black-bellied swallow. STATUS IN INDIANA: Fairly common nesting bird, present from middle of April to October. Does not winter in Indiana. RANGE: Breeds from central Canada south to Gulf of Mexico. Winters in South America.

Purple Martin

[PROGNE SUBIS]

One of the birds that has always been subject to wide population fluctuations is the purple martin. It seems to me that I have not seen as many martins in recent years as I have in the past. Some martin houses that used to have thriving colonies of martins now have an oversupply of English sparrows. Of course, there are exceptions. A friend of mine, who lives in the city, has a healthy colony of lively martins annually. I hope my observations aren't accurate and the martins are indeed prospering, for they are among the most admired and beneficial of all American birds.

Credit for erecting the first martin houses in the United States goes to the American Indians. They not only enjoyed the presence of martins in their settlements but also recognized many of the benefits that a colony of martins brings. Indians appreciated the enormous amount of insects that martins eat every day, besides recognizing that they were a help in driving off hawks and other predators which raided the Indians' poultry flocks.

Purple martins cannot survive if a cold spell persists for very long, for their entire diet consists of insects. They are very active birds and require large amounts of food.

Martins winter primarily in Brazil, arriving in Indiana usually by the middle of April. With rare exceptions, they raise one brood a season, and by the middle of September have left Indiana. In fact, by mid-August, martins are already gathering in huge flocks in some of the deciduous trees that border the White River not far from the center of Indianapolis. Soon after Labor Day weekend, they will be well on their way to South America.

The purple martin is our largest swallow. The male, at a distance, seems to be all black, but when viewed in good light, the bluish-purple colors become apparent. The females and young males are dark backed but have dingy, gray breasts.

Not all persons who put up martin houses are successful in attracting martins. In fact, there are more unsuccessful martin houses than successful ones. It is unusual for martins to occupy a martin apartment the first year it is erected.

Adherence to a few rules should increase the possibility of attracting martins. The compartments should be about 8" x 8" with a two-inch diameter entrance hole. Fifteen to twenty feet above the ground is considered, generally, to be the best height. A hinged, or telescopic, pole is a great help in cleaning out the nest and in plugging and unplugging the nesting holes. The number of compartments is not important; any number from four to one hundred will suffice. The number depends only on how ambitious one is. One of the main problems is to keep the very persistent English sparrows from taking over the compartments. This takes constant vigilance, especially when the martins first arrive.

This all sounds like a lot of work, I know, but those who have successful martin houses find it well worth the effort and claim that their yards are almost insect- and mosquito-free during the summer.

It would be interesting to conduct an experiment of erecting martin houses in known mosquito-breeding areas to see just how effective the martins are in keeping down the mosquito population. Martins are reputed to eat their weight, every day, in insects. The idea of martins busily flying overhead, gulping mosquitoes, is much more appealing to me than that of a helicopter spraying insecticides on our environment.

Green Heron

[BUTORIDES STRIATUS]

When asked what the most exciting event held in Indiana during the month of May is, most non-residents of the state would answer that it is the 500-Mile Race at Speedway, Indiana. Yet is it surprising how many Hoosiers are involved at this time of the spring in activities not related to the world-famous race. Most Hoosiers spend the Memorial

Size: *L. 15–22" (38–56 cm). W. 25" (62.5 cm).* Coloring: *Grayish-green backed, chestnut neck, greenish-yellow legs (orange or yellow in breeding season).* Habitat: *Around the edges of lakes, ponds, marshes, and streams.* Nesting: *Rather flimsy nest, usually placed in bush or thicket near water; 3–6 eggs.* Unusual Mannerisms: *Most often calls just prior to taking flight.* Identifying Hints: *Indiana's most common heron. Frequently mistaken for a crow, which it resembles in flight.* Status in Indiana: *Found in Indiana from May to October. Fairly common nesting bird.* Range: *Breeds from southern Canada south to Florida. Winters from South Carolina south to the Gulf Coast.*

Day weekend gardening, boating, fishing, doing yard work, participating in family get-togethers, or just enjoying the out-of-doors during the warming weather.

If a person's activities are water-related, he is likely to spot Indiana's most common member of the heron family, the green heron. In contrast to the rest of the herons, the green heron seems to have maintained a relatively stable population level in Indiana. Why the green heron has fared better than the night herons—the great blue or the bitterns—needs more investigation. One possible factor could be that the green heron winters, primarily, outside the United States, in Mexico and Central America, while the other Indiana herons winter in the middle part of the United States and are subjected to winter storms with prolonged low temperatures, snow, ice, and a consequent inability to find sufficient food.

In Indiana the green heron can be expected to arrive anytime after the first of May. It will nest throughout the state and will leave during the month of September. It usually nests in shrubs or trees not far from water. Occasionally, green herons will group together and nest in small colonies. The few nests that I have inspected were such flimsy affairs, it appeared as if a good, strong wind would destroy them. Four or five eggs would be normal, and occasionally the green heron will raise two broods in a summer.

Like too many birds, the green heron's name is not very appropriate, since the green coloring is only evident under certain light conditions, as is the case with the dark chestnut coloring of the neck. Often, especially when in flight, it appears to be an all-dark bird and can be mistaken for a crow, which it approximates in size.

The food of the green heron in Indiana varies, depending upon where it is feeding. Most often its menu includes small minnows, crickets, water insects, grasshoppers, crayfish, frogs, and small snakes. Some green herons are quite tame and will allow close approach. Fishermen are often joined by a green heron as they sit quietly trying to entice a fish onto their line. If the fishing isn't good, they have at least the consolation of being amused by the antics of the green heron. Being a companion to a fisherman is a suitable activity for the green heron on May days; but if I could offer a sensible suggestion to the intelligent green heron for the Memorial Day weekend at "Indy," it would be this:

"Do not make the mistake of looking for grasshoppers in the infield of the 500-Mile Motor Speedway. True, you may see some unusual characters there, but I don't think you'll find many grasshoppers!"

Sora

[PORZANA CAROLINA]

Rails are a family of birds seldom seen in Indiana. It's not that rails are so rare here, but rather that they are so secretive. The Virginia rail, sora, and king rail all nest in Indiana. The yellow rail and the black rail probably nest here also; but because of their retiring ways, no recent breeding records have been reported.

Occasionally, rails are found in most unusual places. Rails are primarily night migrants, and, at times, when there is a low ceiling, they may become confused by the city lights and get "lost" in civilization, rather than find their preferred habitat, cattail marshes.

The most common of the Indiana rails is the sora. Although it has been known to nest in wet meadows, its preferred nesting site is a bog or a cattail marsh where there is standing water and adequate cover.

The few sora nests that I have seen have been very well concealed, blending perfectly with the surroundings. The soras, like the other rails, lay a large clutch of eggs—up to a dozen or more. It's quite a challenge for the parent birds to incubate such a large number, for, if the eggs get cold, they won't hatch. Many of the eggs and young birds fall victim to hungry weasels, raccoons, possums, and herons.

The sora is a gray, robin-sized bird with a black throat and face. The young birds lack the black face patch. In both the adult and immature plumage, the most distinguishing field mark is the short, yellow bill.

Because of their secretive nature, it is unusual to get a good look at a sora. Most often, the bird is seen only briefly as it feebly flies a short distance after having been flushed. The saying, "skinny as a rail," refers to the rail's ability to move about in the cattails with such agility that its presence is seldom detected.

Size: *L. 8–10" (20–25 cm).* Coloring: *Gray breast, brownish back, with black patch on face and throat. Short, yellow bill. Young birds lack black throat patch.* Habitat: *Marshes, wet meadows, cattails.* Nesting: *Nest made of cattail blades, placed just above the water; 10–12 eggs.* Unusual Mannerisms: *Secretive. Prefers to run, rather than fly, when flushed.* Identifying Hints: *Short, yellow bill best field mark.* Status in Indiana: *Fairly common spring and fall migrant. Rare nester.* Range: *Breeds from central Canada to Great Lakes area. Winters in southern United States.*

It's hard to imagine that this bird, which seems much more at home on the ground than in the air, migrates hundreds of miles each fall and spring. Not long ago, I tried to see if our state conservation department would help in getting rails off the game bird list, but little interest was shown.

It seems logical to me that more Hoosiers would enjoy seeing rails than shooting them. That it is legal for an individual to shoot up to twenty-five of these small birds in a day just doesn't seem right. Most Hoosiers go a lifetime without having the opportunity of seeing a rail, and as our marshes slowly disappear, the next generation will have even less chance to see any of these engaging birds.

Wood Thrush

[HYLOCICHLA MUSTELINA]

One of the best loved birds anywhere is the wood thrush. This bird seems to do especially well in Indiana. Although its preferred habitat is a good-sized woods, in recent years there has been a trend toward its acceptance of small wooded areas as nesting sites. It was once considered to be a shy, retiring bird, and seeing one required great patience and usually a long hike into a deep woods. Nowadays, many people have wood thrushes patronizing their backyard bird baths, and it is even possible to find a wood thrush nesting in some of the wooded areas within the city limits. Fringe areas around golf courses seem also to be favored by this appealing bird.

The wood thrush nests throughout the state of Indiana and is present during the months of May, June, July, August, and September. During the last part of September and the first part of October, the wood thrush leaves Indiana and spends the winter months, for the most part, outside the United States in Mexico and Central America.

The wood thrush is a brown-backed bird, slightly small than a robin. The head is rusty, and the breast is white, heavily covered with black

SIZE: *L. 7½–8½″ (19–21 cm)*. COLORING: *Rusty head, brown back, white upper breast with large dark spots.* HABITAT: *Moist deciduous woods, parks.* NESTING: *Typically 8–12′ above the ground, compact cup of grasses, moss reinforced with mud (similar to robin's); 3–4 pale blue eggs.* UNUSUAL MANNERISMS: *Only thrush, other than robin and bluebird, likely to nest near human habitation.* IDENTIFYING HINTS: *Rusty head, heavy breast spotting, no wing-bars. Flute-like voice outstanding.* STATUS IN INDIANA: *Common spring and fall migrant and summer nesting bird. Does not winter.* RANGE: *Breeds from Great Lakes area south to northern portions of Gulf states. Winters in Mexico and Central America.*

spots. The rusty head, together with the spotted breast and sides, distinguish this bird from the other thrushes.

Although the main diet of the wood thrush is insects, it has a great fondness for fruit and is often found feeding along with other fruit-loving birds in chokecherry and mulberry trees and in berry-producing shrubs.

By far, the outstanding feature of the wood thrush is its song. There has always been a debate as to which of the thrushes has the most beautiful song. Generally, it has come down to the hermit thrush and the wood thrush. Unfortunately, the hermit thrush does not nest in Indiana, so at least in Indiana the laurels must go to the wood thrush. Its song is a series of resounding, flute-like phrases, difficult to describe but unmistakable and unforgettable, once heard. The wood thrush is especially vocal early in the morning, at dusk, and after a rain. When two or three of these birds are singing at the same time, they give the woods a cathedral-like atmosphere.

Black-and-White Warbler

[MNIOTILTA VARIA]

One of the most attractive members of the warbler family is the black-and-white warbler. Bird artists and nature photographers all seem to have a difficult time capturing the beauty of this diminutive bird. I have never seen a reproduction that does justice to the black-and-white warbler. Its modest name hardly hints at what a treat this warbler is to the eyes.

Normally, this bird is an early warbler in Indiana, arriving here soon after the first of April. As a migrant, it leaves Indiana by the third week of May.

Although I don't know of any nesting records for the black-and-white warbler in Marion County, it may nest here if conditions are favorable. It has been recorded as nesting in scattered areas of the state, the Indiana Dunes State Park for one. It prefers to nest on hillsides in deciduous woods. The nest is generally on or near the ground.

Size: *L. 4½–5½″ (11–14 cm)*. Coloring: *Sharply defined black-and-white striping on head, back, and breast.* Habitat: *Deciduous woodlands, especially those with hillsides and ravines.* Nesting: *On the ground, at base of tree or stump; 4–5 eggs.* Unusual Mannerisms: *Often seen creeping around tree trunks, nuthatch-like.* Identifying Hints: *Black-and-white crown stripes.* Status in Indiana: *Common spring and fall migrant, rare nester.* Range: *Breeds from central Canada south to southern United States, east of the Rockies. Winters from the Gulf Coast to South America.*

In other states where I have been an active birder, I have found the black-and-white to be a persistent singer in the nesting area. Each year, it seems, I have to relearn the song of the black-and-white, and other birders have told me they have the same problem. The most likely reason for this difficulty is that, in addition to its typical song, this warbler has variations of its normal song.

It is usually a help in learning bird songs if you can put words to the sounds; and, in the case of the black-and-white, the words "we see" repeated four or five times with the accent on the "see" would be an aid in distinguishing the black-and-white from the rest of the warblers. Also helpful is the fact that the black-and-white's song is among the highest pitched of all warblers' songs.

As its name implies, this warbler is all black and white in its appearance, with a black throat and eye patch, and with the back, wings, breast, and head black-and-white striped. The female is similar to the male, but the blacks and whites are not as intense as in the male.

This bird doesn't act like a warbler; it behaves more like a nuthatch or creeper. While the other warblers are busy flitting about in the tops of trees, the black-and-white is more likely to be seen deliberately moving about on the trunk or limb of a tree, seeking out minute-sized insects. While the other warblers are working in the tops of the trees, the black-and-white spends most of his time in the bottom half of the trees.

It always seems to be a special pleasure to see this bird. While many of the warblers are difficult to see because of their quick, nervous actions, the black-and-white poses no identification problem, and its slower movements afford excellent opportunities to study this bird. Unlike many of the other warblers, the black-and-white has the same plumage in the fall as in the spring.

The majority of black-and-whites winter in Central America, although a few will winter in south Texas and Florida. The frigid temperatures that we sometimes experience in spring slow down the warbler migration, but when the winds come out of the south, a huge influx of birds may occur. Many of the new arrivals migrate at night.

You may wish to try an interesting experiment some warm evening. Pick a night when there is little or no wind, find an area away from traffic noise, and then listen carefully for the flight notes of the thrushes and warblers as they continue on their long journey.

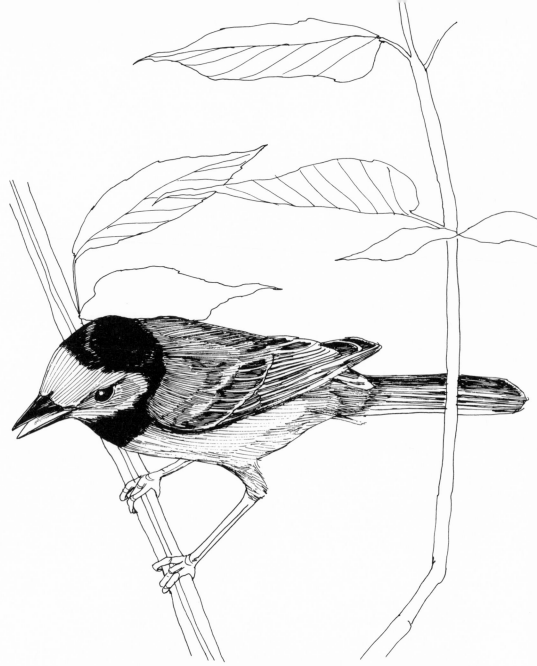

Size: L. 5–5½″ (*13–14 cm*). Coloring: *Male, olive-green back, yellow breast, with black hood encircling the throat and top of head. Yellow face. Female similar but lacks hood.* Habitat: *Moist deciduous woodlands, wooded swamps.* Nesting: *Nest 1–6′ above ground in small tree or bushes. Neat, compact nest, lined with soft grasses and hair; 3–4 eggs.* Unusual Mannerisms: *Most often seen close to the ground.* Identifying Hints: *White tail spots in both male and female evident in all seasons. Male's black hood vivid.* Status in Indiana: *Uncommon spring and fall migrant. Uncommon nesting bird. Does not winter here.* Range: *Breeds south of the Great Lakes to the Gulf Coast. Winters in Central America.*

Hooded Warbler

[WILSONIA CITRINA]

During the first two weeks of May, as many as thirty-five different species of warblers can be found in Indiana. Only about half of them will nest here; the rest of these "jewels of the bird world" will nest with our neighbors to the north. When conditions and timing (sometime between the fifth and the twelfth of May) are just right, it's possible to see half a dozen different species of warblers in one tree.

It's a special treat to be able to show someone, his first time, one of the more colorful warblers and to watch his expression as he savors the extraordinary beauty of one of these birds. Words are inadequate, as are photographs and paintings—warblers have to be seen in real life to be fully appreciated. A good illustration of the truth of this statement is the hooded warbler. True, as the various field guides state, the hooded warbler has a yellow breast and face, with a black crown and bib. What books and paintings can't portray is the vividness of the yellow and the intensity of the black on the crown and bib. The bird must be seen in its typical setting—in the woods, with the bright morning sun at one's back—to bring out the true colors.

Indiana is fairly close to the northern extremity of the breeding range of the hooded warbler, and it is definitely less common in the northern third of the state than in the southern third. Like most of the warblers, the hooded is very selective in the type of habitat that it will use for a nesting area. It requires a deciduous woods of some size, a small ravine where there are trees that haven't reached full growth, and, preferably, a wet area or creek running through the woods. One area that is perfect for the hooded warbler is the Hoosier National Forest, south of Bloomington and near the Monroe Reservoir. When the hooded finds an area like this, it will nest there in some numbers, and every few yards you can find a male loudly announcing that he has staked out his territory. The nest is neat and compact, with the interior lined with soft grasses and various plant fibers. Seldom is it found more than four or five feet above the ground.

Its song, one of the loudest and lowest-pitched of the warblers' songs, can be described by the words, "weeta-weeta-tee-o." The "tee-o" at the end helps to distinguish this song from some of the other similar-sounding warbler songs. The hooded is a persistent singer and, when on territory, will sing constantly, even during the hot summer months when many birds become silent.

This beautiful bird, which will be with us in relatively few numbers from May until October, can sometimes be found during its migration in some very unlikely places, far removed from its normal habitat. For instance, I have found hooded warblers perched and singing in a small, low shade tree almost in the center of the city. By about the middle of October, the hooded warblers will be comfortably settled in the lush foliage of Central America.

Start off some May morning by finding a hooded warbler. There is no way then that the day can be anything but a more pleasant day than the day before.

Scarlet Tanager

[PIRANGA OLIVACEA]

Summer Tanager

[PIRANGA RUBRA]

The male scarlet tanager in breeding plumage, once seen, is a sight not easily forgotten. "Scarlet" really doesn't do it justice. It seems to be a burning, velvet-like red bird with jet black wings, and when seen among the leaves of its favorite tree, the oak, gives an almost startling view. The female hardly seems to be of the same species, with rather dull yellow plumage and none of the brilliance of the male. The scarlet tanager nests rather commonly in Indiana. Its preferred habitat is a deciduous woods.

If one has the opportunity to watch a tanager, he will find that it feeds rather deliberately. It seems to examine each leaf in an unhurried way until it finds a morsel, usually a caterpillar, to its liking.

The tanager song has been described as sounding like a robin with a cold. It always seems to me to have a swing-like quality. The scarlet tanager is a persistent singer and will carol throughout the summer. May, June, July, August, and September are the months that it is normally with us; then it begins its long trip to South America.

The other tanager that comes to Indiana is the summer tanager. It is more common in southern Indiana, and central Indiana is about its most northern nesting range. Since 1972, it has nested in Eagle Creek Park in Indianapolis every year but one. I have never had a record of the summer tanager in upstate New York or in northern Ohio.

The summer tanager is an all-red bird with no crest. It is slightly smaller than a cardinal, the only bird with which it could be confused. The female is an all-yellow bird; again, in sharp contrast to the beautifully crimson male. Its feeding habits are much like the scarlet tanager's, very deliberate. It spend much of its time in the concealing foliage of woodland trees, and if one is not familiar with its rather loud song, it may easily be overlooked. Like the scarlet, the summer tanager leaves us in early fall and travels to Central and South America to spend the cold months.

It seems that the tanagers have a lifestyle that would be the envy of most homo sapiens: whiling away summers in beautiful, bountiful Indiana, where the temperature doesn't go below 32 degrees and where food is plentiful for sustaining themselves and their offspring; and then, at the first sign of approaching adverse weather, taking leave without packing a bag for a grand tour of the southern states and Central America, to their final destination, South America, ready for six months of rest and relaxation in the lush foliage of the tropics.

SCARLET TANAGER

SIZE: *L. 6½–7½" (17–19 cm).* COLORING: *Male, brilliant scarlet, with black wings and tail. Female, dull green above, yellowish below, with blackish wings.* HABITAT: *Both deciduous and coniferous woodlands, parks, and orchards.* NESTING: *Shallow nest, usually placed high and well out on limb of tree; 3–4 eggs.* UNUSUAL MANNERISMS: *Rather deliberate in its movements.* IDENTIFYING HINTS: *Call note a low "chip-bang." No wing-bars.* STATUS IN INDIANA: *Fairly common spring and fall migrant and nesting bird. More common in northern half of state.* RANGE: *Breeds from southern Canada to northern parts of Gulf Coast. Winters in South America.*

SUMMER TANAGER

SIZE: *L. 7–8" (17–20 cm).* COLORING: *Male, solid rose-red all over; female, olive above, yellow below.* HABITAT: *Open deciduous and coniferous woods, orchards, roadsides.* NESTING: *Flimsy, flat nest placed on horizontal limb above the ground and well out from the trunk; 3–4 eggs.* UNUSUAL MANNERISMS: *Often tends to hide in dense foliage.* IDENTIFYING HINTS: *No crest, no wing-bars.* STATUS IN INDIANA: *Uncommon spring and fall migrant. Uncommon nesting bird; more prevalent in southern half of state.* RANGE: *Breeds from south of the Great Lakes to the Gulf Coast and Florida. Winters in Central and South America.*

Blackpoll Warbler

[DENDROICA STRIATA]

There is always a twinge of sadness for me when I start hearing and seeing the blackpoll warbler; for when the blackpoll is present in the spring, it's a sure sign that the height of the warbler migration is past.

SIZE: L. 5–5½″ (13–14 cm). COLORING: *Male, gray-striped back, solid black cap, white cheek patch. Female and young birds, olive-green above, dingy yellow below, two white wing-bars.* HABITAT: *Breeds low in coniferous forests.* NESTING: *In small conifers, small twigs and weeds, lined with rootlets, hair, and feathers; 4–5 eggs.* UNUSUAL MANNERISMS: *In migration frequently moves to the top of tall trees.* IDENTIFYING HINTS: *Song, very high, all on one pitch, increasing and then decreasing in volume. Solid black cap.* STATUS IN INDIANA: *Common spring and fall migrant, does not nest or winter here.* RANGE: *Breeds from Alaska south to the northernmost border of the United States. Winters in South America.*

While it is true that we will still have some warblers with us for several more weeks, they will become fewer in number as the month of May progresses. Less than a third of the warblers that are seen in Indiana stay on to nest here.

The blackpoll warbler is a surprisingly common warbler in Indiana, but relatively few people recognize just how common it is. For one thing, it is a treetop warbler and is with us for only a short time. It is not an obvious warbler; although when carefully observed, it is a handsome bird.

The male has a black crown, a white face patch, and a white throat. The female is not as clearly marked and can easily be confused with a number of other birds. In fact, in the fall, differentiating the blackpoll from the bay-breasted warbler and the pine warbler is a very difficult task. A great help in identifying the blackpoll in the spring is to learn its song.

The song is a short one and is among the highest pitched of all bird songs. It is on one pitch and can best be described as being crescendo and diminuendo—all on the same tone. It is a unique song and one well worth learning. I've heard as many as ten different blackpoll warblers singing while driving down one street (Meridian) from 62nd Street to 38th.

Unfortunately, the song is so high pitched that many people cannot hear the blackpoll at all. A friend of mine—one with whom I birded for many years—lost the ability to hear the blackpoll after he reached the age of sixty.

The migrating mystique of the warblers continues to baffle ornithologists; it is hard to imagine, for example, how the little five-inch blackpoll travels the great distance from Brazil to Alaska and then makes the same 5,000-mile journey again in the fall. To make this incredible feat even more astounding, most of the trip is made at night.

Spring is the time to see the blackpoll; for when it returns to Indiana in September, it will be silent and will be wearing an entirely different plumage. Look for the blackpoll in the tops of trees. Because it is with us for such a short time, and because of its small size and habit of feeding in the treetops, it goes unnoticed by most people.

Common Nighthawk

[CHORDEILES MINOR]

Chimney Swift

[CHAETURA PELAGICA]

A city is not the place that you normally associate with birds. However, a large number of birds can be seen in the very center of all our cities. Two birds seem to show a decided preference for urban living. Both the common nighthawk and the chimney swift can be readily seen, every night, in every city in Indiana from June to September.

The nighthawk is not a hawk, but rather a member of the goatsucker family. The name, "goatsucker," came from an old superstition which held that these birds nursed from goats, a fable never substantiated by facts. The nighthawk is a medium-sized bird with prominent white stripes across the wings. It is generally seen at dusk, energetically pursuing flying insects. It seems to have a special fondness for public places that are illuminated by street lights or flood lights. These lights, of course, attract large numbers of moths, flying ants, mosquitoes, and other tempting morsels that make up the main part of the nighthawk's diet.

It is almost impossible to look up at seven o'clock in the evening at any of our shopping places without seeing nighthawks, during the months they are with us. They build no nest, but rather lay their two eggs on a flat rooftop where they are relatively safe from any enemies. They have a rather spectacular fall migration and frequently are seen by the hundreds as they gather for their flight to South America.

The chimney swift is another bird that likes city life. In earlier times, the chimney swift nested in hollow trees, but later it discovered that there are many more chimneys than hollow trees. It builds a nest, primarily of twigs, attached to the inside of the chimney by a salivary secretion that has adhesive qualities. It is essential that the nest is firmly attached, for it must survive heavy summer downpours. After the nesting season, in July, the swifts gather in large flocks and find suitable chimneys in which to roost for the night.

The chimney swift was one of the last birds to give up the secret of where it spends the winter. It wasn't until the late 1930s, when natives of the interior jungles of Peru brought some banded chimney swifts to the marketplace, that their wintering grounds were known.

Take half an hour from television viewing some evening at dusk and watch the amazing aerial display as the swifts, sometimes hundreds of them, circle a chimney and then, suddenly, drop into the chimney to roost for the night.

COMMON NIGHTHAWK

SIZE: *L. 8½–10" (21–25 cm)*. COLORING: *Dark gray, long pointed wings, white patches on the outer wing*. HABITAT: *Most often seen in open areas. In cities can often be found hunting for flying insects near shopping centers or near any bright lights as at baseball fields*. NESTING: *Does not build a nest, but lays 2 eggs on the ground or, more commonly, on graveled rooftops of city buildings*. UNUSUAL MANNERISMS: *Mostly nocturnal, although often seen late in the day. Gather in large numbers during September migratory period*. IDENTIFYING HINTS: *Broad white patch across the wing*. STATUS IN INDIANA: *Common summer resident and nesting bird. In Indiana from May through September*. RANGE: *Breeds from northern Canada to the southern parts of the United States. Winters in South America.*

CHIMNEY SWIFT

SIZE: *L. 5–5½" (13–14 cm)*. COLORING: *All grayish-brown body, with stubby tail*. HABITAT: *Found in all types of open areas*. NESTING: *Primarily in chimneys, although has been known to nest in barns, attics, silos, hollow trees; 4–5 white eggs*. UNUSUAL MANNERISMS: *Appears to beat its wings alternately rather than in unison, as do most birds. One of the most aerial of birds, seldom seen at rest. Considered to be one of the fastest flying birds in the bird world*. IDENTIFYING HINTS: *Dark color, appearing tailless. Crescent shape of the wings*. STATUS IN INDIANA: *Common nesting bird, present from April to middle of October*. RANGE: *Nests from southern Canada to the Gulf of Mexico. Winters in Peru.*

JUNE

JUNE IS THE CRITICAL MONTH for most birds. It is the month when nesting must take place. Behind is the long trip from South America or from the southern borders of our country. Behind are the decisions of selecting a mate and a nesting site. The serious business of raising young is at hand. Because the lifespan of most birds is short (four to six years), the necessity of successfully raising young is paramount.

Each species is guided by instinct to a particular place—a particular tree, field, meadow, or marsh. If the grasses become too high, the Henslow's sparrow and the short-billed marsh wren find it unsuitable. If cattails disappear or become too sparse, the gallinules, rails, and long-billed marsh wrens know that their chance of a successful nesting is limited. Let the trees become too tall or disappear, and the catbird, brown thrasher, white-eyed vireo, or any number of other birds that depend upon small trees and shrubs will have to look elsewhere for a nesting site. Many ducks and birds of prey will tolerate little disturbance near where they will attempt to raise young. The line between suitable and not suitable habitat is sometimes very delicate.

A warbler, the Kirtland's warbler, will nest only in a small area in Michigan where the jack pine tree is found—and also will use only a jack pine area where there has been a fire ten years previously and the trees are now under twenty feet tall, with an ample growth of underbrush around them. This type of extreme selectivity undoubtedly accounts for the rarity of this warbler.

Extreme selectivity is also the reason for the rarity of a Florida bird, the Everglades kite, for it must eat a special kind of snail found only in a swamp in central Florida to survive. If a bird cannot accept a less than perfect habitat, or if it cannot learn to vary its diet, it is doomed to suffer whenever the environment changes. Those birds which have been able to make these changes will prosper. The red-winged blackbird, many years ago, required a cattail marsh in which to build its nest; but, with the decrease of cattail marshes, the red-wing changed its nesting requirements, and it has now been recorded nesting in all sorts of different habitats. The killdeer is no longer dependent upon a deserted shoreline, but will nest on parking lots spread with gravel. The chimney swift has found that there are many more unused chimneys than hollow trees and has adapted to city life very successfully.

June is a lovely month in Indiana. Warm weather has arrived, schools are letting out, gardens are flourishing, and vacations are just around the corner. By the end of June, the question of whether or not birds have had a successful nesting will, for the most part, have been resolved. More than 120 different species regularly nest within the confines of Indiana. I recommend a project that will give you much satisfaction—see how many of our nesting birds you can discover for yourself each year.

Rose-breasted Grosbeak

[PHEUCTICUS LUDOVICIANUS]

All too often our most attractive birds are seen by very few people. The members of the colorful warbler family are so small (four to five inches in length), move so fast, and stay so high in the tops of tall trees that they often go unnoticed, even when they are abundant. Other attractive birds that are larger are not fully appreciated because they are so commonly seen, like the mallard, the robin, and the cardinal. A compromise between these two extremes is the rose-breasted grosbeak. It arrives in Indiana soon after the first of May and will be present for about a month. Rarely will it nest south of Indianapolis, but in the northern part of the state it can be termed a regular but uncommon nesting bird.

Each year when I see my first rose-breasted grosbeak, I'm reminded of the story told of a woman living in southern Texas who called the Audubon Society to report a flock of beautiful birds in her yard that had been "injured and were bleeding from their chests!" What she had seen, of course, were male rose-breasted grosbeaks that had just arrived,

Size: *L. 8" (20 cm).* Coloring: *Male, black back, white wing-bars, white belly, bright rose-colored bib. Female resembles plump sparrow— brown, heavily streaked. Two white wing-bars, white eyebrow.* Habitat: *Deciduous, second-growth woods. Moist woodlands adjacent to open fields.* Nesting: *Loosely made nest, often placed in fork of deciduous tree; 4–5 eggs.* Unusual Mannerisms: *Very beneficial bird,*

exhausted and hungry, from their winter home in Central and South America. If you have never seen this bird, you are doing yourself a disservice if you don't make an effort to add it to the list of birds you have sighted.

The male rose-breasted grosbeak is an absolutely gorgeous bird. It is robin-sized and has a black back, white wing-bars, and a snow-white breast splashed with a triangle of red on the upper part of the breast. The female looks nothing like the male. She always reminds me of a sparrow with an excess weight problem! The best identifying mark on the female is the white stripe over the eye.

One of the difficulties in identifying some birds is that so many of them have rather weak, insignificant songs, but this is not so with the rose-breasted grosbeak. Not only does it have a long, lovely song (robin-like in quality), but it has a propensity to announce its song with an unbird-like sharp "check" that can be simulated by hitting two stones together. It can be likened to a conductor's hitting the podium with his baton to signal that the orchestra music is about to begin and everyone should pay attention.

If ever a bird had all the positive qualities, it is the rose-breasted grosbeak. It has exquisite coloring, a melodious song, a pleasing personality; and with both parents sharing the responsibilities of raising the young grosbeaks, it is a model family member. To top it all, the grosbeaks' feeding habits are entirely beneficial to man's interests. Half of its food is made up of such harmful insects as tent caterpillars, gypsy moths, leaf beetle larvae, and the like. The other half is primarily made up of weed seeds and wild fruit.

As you have probably gathered by now, the rose-breasted grosbeak is one of my favorite birds; and if you become acquainted with it, I'm sure you will like it also.

as well as one of the most beautiful North American birds. IDENTIFYING HINTS: *Announces its song, in both spring and fall, by giving single, sharp, unmusical "clink." Song is robin-like in quality, but more musical and longer.* STATUS IN INDIANA: *Resides in Indiana from last week in April to second week in October. More common as a nesting bird in northern portions of the State.* RANGE: *Breeds from southern Canada to central United States. Winters from Mexico to South America.*

Size: L. 4½–5" (11–13 cm). Coloring: *Male bright yellow with rusty streaks on the breast. Female lacks rusty breast streaking.* Habitat: *Hedgerows, roadside thickets, edges of swamps, marshes.* Nesting: *Nest found 3–8' off the ground, a compact cup made of milkweed fibers, plant down, lined with hair and fine grasses; 4–5 eggs.* Unusual Mannerisms: *This bird frequently victimized by cowbirds' parasitic habits.* Identifying Hints: *Song, "sweet, sweet, sweet-e-ly, sweet."* Status in Indiana: *Fairly common spring and fall migrant and nesting bird.* Range: *Breeds from Alaska to northern South America. Winters from Mexico south to Brazil.*

Yellow Warbler

[DENDROICA PETECHIA]

The yellow warbler seems to thrive in Indiana. One June I heard singing males at the Dunes State Park, Bluffton, Yellowwood State Forest, McCormick's Creek State Park, Nebo Ridge, Monroe Reservoir, Geist Reservoir, and Eagle Creek Park in Indianapolis. In just a two-hour survey at Eagle Creek, five different singing males were heard.

It's a good thing that the yellow warbler is so widely distributed throughout Indiana, for it is frequently victimized by the cowbird. The cowbird is the only bird in Indiana that does not build its own nest but lays its eggs in other birds' nests instead. When this happens, it is usually the cowbird that survives, for the young cowbirds are very aggressive, and they mature quickly.

I remember watching a yellow warbler feeding a young cowbird. The cowbird was about twice the size of the warbler, yet the warbler dutifully responded to each vociferous hunger plea of the cowbird by frantically searching for insects to satisfy the cowbird's seemingly insatiable appetite.

The yellow warbler has no difficulty in recognizing the latent danger in having a cowbird egg in the nest, for it often will either desert the nest or build a nest over the cowbird egg. There have been yellow warbler nests found containing as many as six floors, each added as the warbler tried repeatedly to avoid hatching a cowbird egg; but it seems that, once the egg has hatched, the warbler's maternal feeding instinct is so dominant that it will continue to feed the young cowbird until it can fend for itself.

The yellow warbler is the only small bird in Indiana that appears to be all yellow, although close scrutiny of the male will reveal faint chestnut streaks on the breast. Another mark to look for are the yellow tail spots. It is the only warbler that has them. Although the song varies, the song most often given in Indiana is a cheerful, rhythmic refrain: "sweet, sweet, sweet-e-ly sweet!"

133

Its favored nesting sites are found in the shrubs and small trees that border a river, stream, or pond. Young willow trees are especially popular with this bird. The nest is more often below eye level than above. In Indiana the yellow warbler is present during the months of May, June, July, and August. By the end of July the family groups have broken up, and the yellow warbler has started on its long trek to southern Mexico and South America.

The yellow warbler is a bird with virtually no faults. Its beautiful yellow color, lively song, and appealing mannerisms brighten up any landscape. It seems to endure the hardship of being victimized by the cowbird without complaint and never allows this adversity to alter its pleasing personality. Maybe the yellow warbler should consider authoring a self-help book, "How Best to Handle Hardships"—sure to be a best seller!

Common Yellowthroat

[GEOTHLYPIS TRICHAS]

The beginning of June marks the end of the spring migration in Indiana. Almost without exception, the birds that are present on June first will stay to nest. Over a hundred species of birds will find Indiana a suitable place to raise their young.

One very attractive bird that nests in Indiana on a regular basis is the yellowthroat. The yellowthroat is a member of the warbler family and is referred to, in the early bird books, as the "Maryland yellowthroat." In other bird guides it is called the "northern yellowthroat."

SIZE: *L. 4½–5½"* (*11–14 cm*). COLORING: *Male, olive-brown above, yellow below, with black face mask. Female and immatures lack the face mask and are dingier in color below.* HABITAT: *Moist thickets, hedgerows, dense low cover.* NESTING: *Bulky nest placed on or near the ground. Lined with rootlets, hair, and fine grass; 3–5 white eggs.* UNUSUAL MANNERISMS: *Wren-like in behavior. Almost always seen*

close to the ground. IDENTIFYING HINTS: *Black mask of male unmistak-able. Clearly given song, "witchity, witchity, witchity, witch."* STATUS IN INDIANA: *Fairly common spring and fall migrating and nesting bird. Does not winter in Indiana.* RANGE: *Breeds from southern Alaska south to Florida and the Gulf Coast. Winters from the Carolinas to the Gulf, Florida, and Mexico.*

Officially, it is now called the "common yellowthroat." This bird, like so many of our birds, is heard more often than it is seen. Anyone who has spent any amount of time near a lake or reservoir in Indiana could hardly avoid hearing the rather loud, distinctive song, "Whichity, whichity, which," of the yellowthroat. The song is almost always given while the yellowthroat perches in a low shrub, tangle, or cattails. It is a persistent singer and sings from the time it arrives in May until about the middle of July. Then, for the next two months of its stay here, it is mostly silent.

In contrast to so many warblers, this bird seems to have a reluctance to leave the low vegetation, and it is seldom seen high in a tree. The yellowthroat builds a surprisingly large nest for so small a bird. The nest is usually located on the ground or just off the ground in low bushes or weed stalks. Four eggs are normally laid, and most often, two broods are raised each season.

The male common yellowthroat is very distinctively marked and can hardly be confused with any other bird. It has an olive-green back, a lemon-yellow throat, and a black mask that gives this bird one of its nicknames, "the bandit bird." The females and young birds are much less vividly marked; they are olive backed with a less bright yellow throat than the adult males, and they lack the black mask.

Like a number of other birds that have been able to prosper in spite of a changing environment, the yellowthroat is not as selective as it once was in the type of habitat that it requires. I recall that as a teenager I had to go to a marshy area to see the yellowthroat; but now this insect eater can be found in areas entirely devoid of water, such as uncultivated pastures, hedgerows, meadows (where there is sufficient cover) and even in dense shrubbery in suburban backyards.

June is the critical month for most Indiana birds. They must successfully raise young birds during this month or face the prospect of leaving the breeding grounds without replenishing the birds that will normally be lost through death or accident. The yellowthroat's ability to change its habitat and the fact that it usually will attempt to raise a second brood are the two most important reasons for the success of this bird.

Wasn't it stated in *Poor Richard's Almanac* that "diversification and determination are the key ingredients for success"?

Northern Oriole

[ICTERUS GALBULA]

Orchard Oriole

[ICTERUS SPURIUS]

The oriole family is well represented in Indiana by the northern oriole (formerly called the "Baltimore" oriole) and the orchard oriole. Both species winter primarily in Central America and are common nesting birds in Indiana, arriving in May and departing in September.

It has been said that if the bluebird is a harbinger of spring, the oriole is the essence of spring. The orioles' arrival in Indiana seems to coincide with the blossoming of our fruit trees. Few sights in nature rival the sight of a male northern (Baltimore) oriole in a newly flowered apple tree. The vibrant orange body in contrast to the black head and chest, together with its enthusiastic song, makes its presence known to even the casual observer.

One of the most intriguing attributes of both orioles is their ability to weave a hanging basket-like nest. What instinct is involved in this elaborate, time-consuming nest-building activity is unknown. It is known that the oriole will return to the same tree for many years, and rather than repair the nest used the previous year, it will make the considerable effort required to construct a new nest.

Both the northern and the orchard orioles perform a great service by eating large numbers of harmful insects. They especially like cater-pillars and have been credited with destroying entire infestations of orchard tent caterpillars. The orchard oriole is not nearly as well known as its more colorful relative, the northern oriole. Its prefered habitat is, as its name implies, orchards in rural areas near human dwellings, but it can also be found in shade trees along village streets or country roadsides. It is almost never found in heavily wooded regions or forests.

137

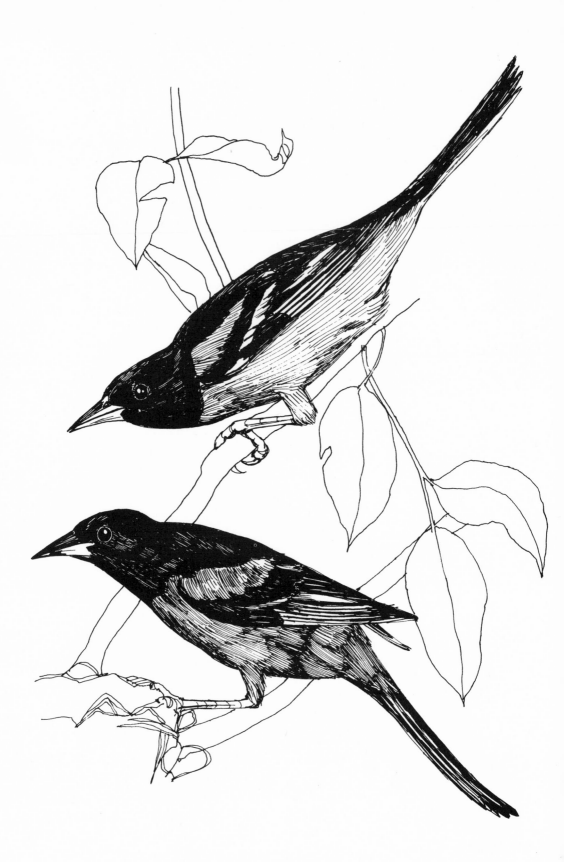

NORTHERN ORIOLE

SIZE: *L. 7–8½" (18–21 cm). COLORING: Male, black head, black wings with white wing stripes, fiery orange breast, rump and shoulder patch. Female, olive-brown back and wings, two white wing-bars, subdued orange underparts. HABITAT: Dedicuous woodlands, shade trees. NESTING: Well-woven, pendent nest made of plant fibers, hair, and, frequently, yarn, 25–30" above the ground. Formerly nested in elms, now primarily in maples and willow trees; 4–6 eggs. UNUSUAL MANNERISMS: Unique and well-crafted nest difficult to find until leaves of trees have fallen. During migration large numbers are found moving en masse. IDENTIFYING HINTS: Combination of brilliant orange body and jet-black head, together with flute-like whistles. STATUS IN INDIANA: Common summer resident and breeding bird, present from May to October. RANGE: Breeds from middle of Canada to the southern states. Winters in southern Mexico and Central America.*

ORCHARD ORIOLE

SIZE: *L. 6–7¼" (16–18 cm). COLORING: Male, black head, black wings and tail, white wing-bar. Deep chestnut body and rump. Female, olive-green head, back, and breast. Dark wings with wing-bars. HABITAT: Orchards, country roadsides, shade trees and suburban yards. NESTING: Pouch-shaped nest, 10–20' above ground, deeply hollowed; 4–5 eggs. UNUSUAL MANNERISMS: Often nest fairly near other orioles, suggesting a loose colony. IDENTIFYING HINTS: When male is seen in poor light, it gives the illusion of being an all dark bird. Voice, robin-like in quality, is quite dissimilar to northern oriole's voice. STATUS IN INDIANA: Uncommon nesting bird, more common in southern than in northern half of Indiana. RANGE: Breeds south of Great Lakes to Gulf of Mexico. Winters from southern Mexico to northern Colombia.*

The orchard oriole has the same sequence of colors as the northern, except the fiery orange is replaced by a deep chestnut on the breast and rump. In poor light the male orchard can appear to be completely black. It is a persistent singer, and its song, to my ears, is much more musical than the northern's. The orchard, also, is a bird most beneficial to man. Various studies have shown that over ninety percent of its food is made up of animal matter or insects, and the bulk of these insects are caterpillars, grasshoppers, and beetles.

It would be difficult to put a monetary value on orioles. Consider that the young are fed perhaps one hundred times a day for about a three-week period, with each nest producing four young birds who will stay and feed in the area for the summer. Multiply this consumption of harmful insects times the number of orioles—then consider the cost of artificially controlling these insects, and you can readily see that our orioles represent a plus figure on the right-hand side of the ledger.

Yellow-billed Cuckoo

[COCCYZUS AMERICANUS]

Black-billed Cuckoo

[COCCYZUS ERYTHROPTHALMUS]

Indiana is host to two members of the cuckoo family, the yellow-billed cuckoo and the black-billed cuckoo. In general, the black-billed is more common in the northernmost part of Indiana and the yellow-billed in the southern part of the state. Both cuckoos are found in the central area, but I would say the yellow-billed outnumber the black-billed five to one.

Identification of the two birds requires close scrutiny. Both are long tailed, brown backed, and have white underparts. The yellow-billed has chestnut-colored wings and rather prominent white tail spots. When viewed from a short distance, the color of their bills and eyes are reliable field marks. The yellow-billed has, of course, a yellow lower bill and yellow eyelids. The black-billed has a dark lower bill and a red eye ring.

Habitat would be another aid in identifying the two; the yellow-billed likes the fringe area of a woods, while the black-billed is more likely to be seen in the woods. Voice is still another guide to identification. The yellow-billed has a rather long series of notes that sound like the word, "cow," with accentuation on the beginning and a retarded, drawn-out ending. The black-billed's most common song is a series of notes that sound like "cow" grouped in two's and three's without the slowed-down ending.

Cuckoos are found just about everywhere in the world. The European cuckoos are parasitic; that is, they do not build their own nests or rear their own young. Rather, they lay their eggs in other birds' nests, usually to the detriment of the host birds. In America, the cuckoos do build their own nests but will occasionally lay their eggs in other birds' nests. There have been records of yellow-billed cuckoos laying eggs in black-billeds' nests and vice versa. So the nest-building instincts do not seem to be as strong in the cuckoos as in other birds.

Both of our cuckoos have a fondness for hairy caterpillars. Many times an outbreak of caterpillars is followed by an invasion of cuckoos. Studies have been made that indicate that when caterpillars are unusually plentiful, the brood size of the cuckoos increases.

I don't know where the phrase, "crazy as a cuckoo," originated, but I hardly think it's warranted. I have never heard of a cuckoo's blood pressure going up because of a statement made by a politician or of a cuckoo's becoming depressed because of a downturn in our economic climate, nor have I heard of a cuckoo's being unduly concerned because of an offspring's failure to get straight "A's" in school. Maybe "wise as a cuckoo" would be more appropriate.

YELLOW-BILLED CUCKOO

SIZE: *L. 11–12" (28–30 cm)*. COLORING: *Dull brown above, white below, rufous in the wings. Prominent white spots in the tail.* HABITAT: *Thickets, stream banks, overgrown pastures with small trees. Seldom found in heavy woods.* NESTING: *Frail, flimsy nest, usually in large shrub or small tree; 2–4 eggs.* UNUSUAL MANNERISMS: *Rather secretive in behavior. This bird is heard much more often than seen.* IDENTIFYING HINTS: *Rufous in wings and white wing spots obvious in flight. (Yellow lower bill is an aid in identification only at close range.) Call is rapid series of "cow, cow, cow," with a retarded ending.* STATUS IN INDIANA: *Present in Indiana from May to October. More common as a nesting bird in the southern half of state.* RANGE: *Breeds from southern Canada throughout the United States. Winters in South America.*

BLACK-BILLED CUCKOO

SIZE: *L. 11–12" (28–30 cm)*. COLORING: *Brown back, white belly, indistinct white tail spots.* HABITAT: *Similar to yellow-billed, but has tendency toward thicker undergrowth.* NESTING: *Frail, flimsy nest, usually in large shrub or small tree, seldom above 6' off the ground; 2–4 eggs.* UNUSUAL MANNERISMS: *Rather secretive in behavior. This bird is heard much more often than seen. Very beneficial bird because of its habit of feeding on tent caterpillars and other insects.* IDENTIFYING HINTS: *Black bill, red eye, and lack of rufous in wings in flight. Call is series of two to five "cow, cow, cow," all on the same pitch.* STATUS IN INDIANA: *Present in Indiana from May to October. More common as a nesting bird in the northern half of state.* RANGE: *Breeds from southern Canada to mid-United States. Winters in South America.*

SIZE: *L. 5½" (14 cm).* COLORING: *Male, deep orange head and body, blue-gray wings, no wing-bars. Female similar, but duller.* HABITAT: *Wet woods, deciduous woods near water, wooded swamps.* NESTING: *Nest in a tree cavity, old woodpecker holes. Has accepted bird houses. Stuffs cavity with moss; 4–6 eggs.* UNUSUAL MANNERISMS: *One of the few warblers to use tree cavity for nest.* IDENTIFYING HINTS: *Song, a loud "sweet, sweet, sweet, sweet, sweet, sweet." Vivid orange coloring of male unmistakable.* STATUS IN INDIANA: *Uncommon spring and fall migrant, uncommon nesting bird. More common in southern half of Indiana.* RANGE: *Breeds from area south of Great Lakes to northern Florida and Texas. Winters from southern Mexico to northern South America.*

Prothonotary Warbler

[P R O T O N O T A R I A   C I T R E A]

If a beauty pageant were conducted for birds, certain warblers would undoubtedly end up in the final ten. When all the judges' ballots were tallied, I'm sure the prothonotary warbler would place in the top five of the most beautiful birds in America. The dictionary defines "prothonotary" as a chief clerk of any of the courts of law. This is certainly an inappropriate name for this gorgeous creature. Flame bird, sun bird, golden bird, and swamp bird would all be more fitting.

The prothonotary can hardly be confused with any other bird. The male has a golden or orangish head, breast, and body. The wings and back are an off-blue. The female is a duplicate of the male, but her colors are somewhat duller.

Part of the appeal of this bird is the idyllic habitat in which it is normally found. The prothonotary is a bird of wet areas and is seldom found away from water. The most likely place to see a prothonothary is along the banks of a river or in a wooded area where the base of the trees are submerged in standing water.

The prothonotary can be termed an uncommon nesting bird in Indiana. Where conditions are right, it will be found nesting in the state; but unfortunately, there are relatively few areas that are suitable. It may nest in areas surrounding some of the major reservoirs and in the flooded flats found along riverbanks. This bird is the only warbler in the eastern United States that nests in cavities, rather than in the open. A hole made in a tree by a downy or hairy woodpecker is most frequently used by the prothonotary, although it will also use a man-made wren or bluebird house to raise its family. The male arrives a week or so before the female and selects a possible nesting site; then when the female arrives, she approves or disapproves his selection.

The song of the prothonotary, once heard, is easily remembered. It is a surprisingly loud song for so small a bird and can be heard from a long distance. It seems to say, "sweet, sweet, sweet," all on one tone.

The prothonotary is the bird that gained notoriety a number of years ago during the famous Alger Hiss perjury trial (in 1948). Whittaker Chambers, when questioned about what hobbies Mr. Hiss pursued, testified that he was an amateur ornithologist and had once seen a prothonotary warbler. When Mr. Hiss was questioned, he admitted he had seen a prothonotary, and the jury felt that this added to Mr. Chamber's credibility.

It's unfortunate that so few people have an opportunity to see this beautiful warbler. It is a rather tame bird and is most often seen on the ground or not very high up in a tree or shrub. Most warblers are elusive and stay in the tops of the trees, but this is not the case with the prothonotary. If you are able to spend some time in an area that would be suitable prothonotary habitat, by all means, make the effort to find this beautiful bird. The sight of a prothonotary will stay in your memory the rest of your life.

Great Crested Flycatcher

[MYIARCHUS CRINITUS]

Living up to a name or tradition can be a difficult task. If your last name happens to be Aristotle, Roosevelt, Churchill, or De Gaulle, you may feel a special compulsion to be a leader. If you come from a long line of physicians, certified public accountants, barristers, or scientists, you may be directed to certain fields. If you were given the name of "great crested Flycatcher," how would you handle that? Would you abdicate the responsibility that your name implies, or would you make a special effort to rise above the proletariat?

The great crested flycatcher makes a reasonable compromise. He knows that he lacks the hardiness of the phoebe and the aggressiveness of the kingbird, but he also knows that the rest of the flycatcher family is not a threat to his dominance of the woods. He recognizes that he is larger and more colorful than most of the flycatchers, and he uses these advantages, along with his strong vocal efforts, to lord over the flycatchers' scene.

SIZE: *L. 8–9″ (20–23 cm).* COLORING: *Brown above, yellow below, rufous wings and tail. Crested.* HABITAT: *Orchards, open forests, fringe edges of woods.* NESTING: *Nests in tree cavities (only eastern flycatcher that does so). Will accept man-made birdhouses; 5–6 eggs.* UNUSUAL MANNERISMS: *Frequently uses snakeskin in nest lining.* IDENTIFYING HINTS: *Large-headed. Feeds in flycatcher manner. Call, a loud, whistled "ka weet."* STATUS IN INDIANA: *Present in Indiana from May to October; a fairly common nesting bird throughout the state.* RANGE: *Breeds as far north as southern Canada. Winters chiefly from southern Mexico to Colombia.*

The great crested flycatcher, which spends the winter months in Mexico, Central America, or South America, is found in Indiana from the middle of April until the middle of October. A surprisingly common nesting bird throughout the state, it normally nests in tree cavities, frequently in holes that have been excavated by one of the larger wood-peckers. There has been a definite trend during the past twenty years or so for the great crested flycatcher to use man-made houses. Bluebird houses and purple martin houses seem to be used with some degree of regularity.

A peculiarity of the great crested flycatcher's nesting habits is its use of a snakeskin or a substitute material, like plastic, that resembles a snakeskin. The two most widely accepted theories as to the purpose of the snakeskin are, one, that the snakeskin discourages snakes or preda-tory animals from entering the nest and eating the eggs or the young birds and, two, that the snakeskin is used because it is light and airy and helps bring a measure of ventilation to the close confines of the nesting cavity.

The great crested flycatcher is quite a noisy bird and makes a variety of different sounds. That most often heard is a loud, ringing "ka weet" that has great carrying power.

This large member of the flycatcher family has a yellow belly, two white wing-bars, and a chestnut tail. It is often seen perched on a dead branch from which it will dart out to catch a flying insect, and then return to the same branch.

Living up to a name like "great crested flycatcher" can be quite a burden, but this flycatcher carries the responsibility well.

Ruby-throated Hummingbird

[ARCHILOCHUS COLUBRIS]

The ruby-throated hummingbird is aptly named, for the male has a deep, glowing red throat that, in certain light, does have a color like the ruby gem. In the female, the red throat is replaced by white, but both birds have the green back and long, nettle-like bill. It is the only hummingbird found in Indiana and can hardly be confused with any other bird east of the Mississippi River. West of the Mississippi, identification is not so simple, with more than a dozen different species of "hummers" found in some of the southwestern states.

After wooing and mating, the male ruby-throat evidently feels that his domestic responsibilities have been fulfilled. The females does most of the nest building and rearing of the young. One early Sunday morning, a group of us watched a female on and around her nest for an hour or so, and no male was to be seen. As a rule, the hummingbird lays two white, pea-sized eggs, incubates them for about two weeks, then spends two weeks feeding the young.

Many students of bird behavior have made significant contributions to science by close scrutiny of the habits of the hummingbird. It was thought for many years that the hummingbird preferred red-colored flowers, but various studies, conducted under controlled conditions, prove rather conclusively that it is flowers colored in contrast to their background that attract the hummer.

It also was assumed that nectar or honey made up the main diet of the hummingbird, but examinations of the stomachs have revealed that their main foods are insects and spiders. The small sizes of the insects can be realized by the fact that one stomach was found to contain more than fifty such insects. It is concluded that the hummingbird has acquired a taste for sweets while gathering insects which were attracted to the nectar-laden flowers.

Many photographers have accepted the challenge of getting pictures of the hummingbird in flight. Crawford Greenewalt, while a chief

SIZE: *L. 3½–4″ (9–10 cm).* COLORING: *Metallic green back, iridescent red throat, whitish underparts. Female lacks red throat.* HABITAT: *Mixed woodlands, orchards, suburban gardens, parks.* NESTING: *Walnut-sized nest, positioned in small fork of tree, a finely woven structure of plant down held together with spider silk. Outer surface decorated with lichens; 2 white pea-sized eggs.* UNUSUAL MANNERISMS: *Has the ability to hover in flight and even fly backwards (the only bird with this*

executive officer of the DuPont Company, took an extended leave of absence to visit the jungles of South America, where he procured some outstanding pictures of hummers that had never been photographed before. These were published, and the edition is available in many libraries and in some book shops.

The hummingbird is the only bird in this hemisphere that can fly backwards, and this unusual maneuver can be verified by those who have seen it feeding on the flower of the trumpet vine. Again, it was scientific photographers who, using very sophisticated equipment, captured the mechanics of this phenomenon.

One secret of the ruby-throated hummingbirds that is yet to be unraveled is how they manage to maintain a reservoir of energy that enables them to fly, non-stop, across the Gulf of Mexico. Just consider— the beats of their wings have been timed at seventy per second, and their speed of forward flight at fifty miles per hour. The distance from southern Florida to Central America is approximately five hundred miles. How can this three-inch bird, which weighs less than one ounce, beat its wings more than two million times without any intake of energy? (Energy czar—take note!)

ability). Will come to man-made feeders for sugar-water. Frequently are seen in garden areas that contain jewel weed, trumpet vines, coral bells, or other flowers, especially tubular shaped ones. IDENTIFYING HINTS: *Insect-like buzz is often first clue of presence of "hummer" in an area. Indiana's only hummingbird.* STATUS IN INDIANA: *Summer resident, here from May to October. Fairly common nesting bird.* RANGE: *Breeds in southern Canada and throughout eastern half of the United States. Winters chiefly from Mexico to Panama.*

KILLDEER

SIZE: *L. 9–11" (23–28 cm).* COLORING: *Brown above, white below, two black bands on the upper breast. Rufous tail.* HABITAT: *Open country, golf courses, plowed fields, gravel-topped parking areas.* NESTING: *Nest placed in an open area, a modest depression in the ground, sparsely lined with grass; 4–5 eggs.* UNUSUAL MANNERISMS: *When protecting the nest area, adults frequently resort to giving the appearance of being wounded, hobbling along with a wing dragging, then making a rapid "recovery" and flying away normally.* IDENTIFYING HINTS: *Two black bands on the breast and rufous tail most evident in flight. Calls its name.* STATUS IN INDIANA: *Our most common nesting shorebird—nests commonly throughout Indiana. Winters here in small numbers near open water.* RANGE: *Breeds from northern Canada south to the United States and Mexico. Winters from the southern edge of the Great Lakes to our most southern states.*

SPOTTED SANDPIPER

SIZE: *L. 7–8" (17–20 cm).* COLORING: *Brown-backed. In the spring white breast has black spots which are lacking after the breeding season.* HABITAT: *Along the edges of ponds, lakes, streams.* NESTING: *Nest is grass-lined depression in ground, often placed a considerable distance from water; 4 eggs.* UNUSUAL MANNERISMS: *Constantly bobs its tail up and down.* IDENTIFYING HINTS: *In the spring the heavily spotted breast; in the fall the white shoulder mark. In flight the wings are held below the horizon and give very rapid, shallow wing beats.* STATUS IN INDIANA: *Our second most common nesting shorebird. Found in Indiana from May to October. Does not winter here.* RANGE: *Breeds from northern Canada to the southern United States. Winters from southern United States to South America.*

Killdeer

[CHARADRIUS VOCIFERUS]

Spotted Sandpiper

[ACTITUS MACULARIA]

The two most common nesting shorebirds found in Indiana are the killdeer and the spotted sandpiper. Virtually every pond, lake, and gravel pit has one or the other, or in some instances both of these birds nesting in close proximity. The killdeer, a member of the plover family, is with us every month of the year, although it becomes scarce during December, January, and February. Its brown back, white breast, and two black neckbands, together with its rusty rump, assure easy identification of this colorful shorebird.

One of the best known characteristics of this bird is the "broken wing" act performed by the female when trying to draw any intruder away from the nest. The nest of the killdeer is extremely rudimentary. Much of the time, it is composed of a slight indentation in a driveway or gravel parking lot. Camouflaged coloring of the eggs is the ingredient that is essential for a successful nesting of killdeers, and because of this success, it is probably the most familiar of all American shorebirds.

The spotted sandpiper also has characteristics that make it unique. It is our only shorebird that has a spotted breast. It has a mannerism of teetering while it feeds—rocking back and forth. It flies with its wings held under the center of its body. In late August it loses its spots, and then the best field mark is the white shoulder mark. Unlike the killdeer, the spotted sandpiper does not winter in Indiana—or even in the United States—but rather moves south to Central and South America. Both the spotted sandpiper and the killdeer are extremely beneficial birds and feed on a multitude of aquatic insects.

Shorebirds have always been of special interest to man. I think one reason is that we tend to associate shorebirds with the fresh smell of the surf and sand, and perhaps when we witness shorebirds, we are reminded of a pleasant vacation spent on the beach, away from our normal day-to-day stresses.

Red-eyed Vireo

[VIREO OLIVACEUS]

Most birds greatly reduce their singing after the breeding season. Some birds cease singing altogether once the young leave the nest. This is not the case with the red-eyed vireo. Its song is one of the most common songs heard during the summer. Even on a hot summer's afternoon when the woods are silent, the red-eyed vireo continues to serenade anyone who will pause to listen.

The song is a series of two and three-noted phrases somewhat robin-like in quality. By using a little imagination, the red-eyed seems to say, "See me? Here I am—up in a tree! See me?" This song is repeated over and over.

This vireo is by far the most common of the vireos in Indiana. If a survey could be taken of the red-eyed vireo in the state during the months of June and July, I'm sure the count would be surprising. Just about every wooded area in the entire state has a few pairs of red-eyed vireos. They are very beneficial birds because they are so common and because more than eighty percent of their diet consists of harmful insects. They are especially fond of caterpillars. The red-eyed is a resident in the state during May, June, July, August, and September. By the middle of October most of these charming birds will be on their way to South America where they will spend the winter.

The red-eyed vireo is not a spectacularly colored bird—olive-green above, with white underparts. It does not have white wing-bars, as do many of the other vireos. The best identifying mark of the red-eyed is the white line over the eye. As this bird is generally seen from below,

while it is feeding in the treetops, it sometimes takes a little patience to get a good look at the face pattern. It usually builds its nest in the fork of one of the smaller branches of a deciduous tree, about five to ten feet above the ground. Four eggs are normally laid, and one nesting a year is most common.

It seems to me to be a valid criticism of our times and values that such a common, beneficial creature goes largely unheard of and unrecognized. The red-eyed vireo spends all of its time doing good—eating insects, raising young, singing—and yet if the average person were given two photographs to identify, one of Charles Manson, and the other of the red-eyed vireo, everyone would recognize Manson, while probably only one out of a thousand would recognize the red-eyed vireo.

SIZE: L. 5½–6½" (14–16 cm). COLORING: Olive-green above, white below, no wing-bars, white stripe over eye. HABITAT: Deciduous woods, occasionally mixed woods, shade trees in residential areas. NESTING: Deep-cupped, pendent nest, attached to slender, forked branch; 3–4 eggs. UNUSUAL MANNERISMS: Very unobtrusive, often overlooked because of shy manners. Lack of bright coloring. IDENTIFYING HINTS: Very persistent singer. White eye stripe. STATUS IN INDIANA: Very common spring and fall migrant and summer nesting bird. RANGE: Breeds from northern Canada to the Gulf Coast states. Winters in South America.

JULY

In July, hot weather is with us, and temperatures soar into the eighties and nineties. Most of the birds stop singing during the day. The necessity to sing is now past, and only those birds that seem to find special pleasure in singing persist in filling the air with their music.

There are many theories as to why birds sing, but it is known that bird song is involved with mate selection, with the establishment of territory, and with the males' proclamations that they are the dominant males in an area. There are a number of species that continue to sing long after there is any practical reason to sing. The red-eyed vireo is the most persistent singer of our nesting birds and is in full song even during the heat of the day. The mockingbird is another bird that continues to sing after young are out of the nest. In fact, the "mocker" often sings all night long. The wood pewee and the indigo bunting, also, are obvious summer singers, but most of Indiana's nesting birds either slow down their vocal efforts or stop singing altogether during July.

With the exceptions of the goldfinch and the cedar waxwing, most nesting activity has stopped. This is the time of the year when birds have a little leisure. The nesting season is over, and migration, for the most part, has not yet begun. It's time for relaxing and enjoying life— a time to move away from the nesting area and play, eat, and put on weight. There is an instinct in birds that tells them that leisure is a fleeting luxury, that if they are to return to Indiana the next year, their physical condition must be as close to perfection as possible. The young birds must learn quickly that they are living in a very exacting world and that the least imperfection will render them incapable of surviving in the world. They must learn their lessons well and fast, for soon it will be time for them to leave Indiana and start a long trip south, a trip that will prove the undoing of over half of the young hatched here.

Red-headed Woodpecker

[MELANERPES ERYTHROCEPHALUS]

A Fourth of July weekend would be a most appropriate time to learn to know the red-headed woodpecker. Early bird literature refers to the red-headed woodpecker as the "flag bird" or the "patriotic bird." Its colors are red, white, and—with a little stretch of the imagination—blue.

In early July, the red-headed is very much in evidence, for it is then that young birds are in the nest and must be continually fed. A habit that tends to make this beautiful woodpecker easily seen is its tendency to sit at the top of a dead tree, by the road, in search of flying insects. The red-headed woodpecker can hardly be confused with any other bird; it is our only woodpecker with an all-red head and neck. This, together with its flashing dark and white wing patches, makes identification of the adult bird unmistakable.

In Indiana the red-headed woodpecker is found throughout the state. It tends to be migratory, but a few will winter in areas where suitable food and cover are found. In the fall and winter, the red-headed woodpecker is frequently seen storing beechnuts and acorns in available cavities in anticipation of a decline in supply of its favorite foods.

Much has been written about the negative habits of the red-headed woodpecker. It has been accused of having a fondness for cherries and other cultivated fruits. It is not very tolerant of other species of birds when they fly in close proximity to its nesting place, and it is very jealous of its food supply. Another bad habit attributed to the red-head is that of destroying other birds' eggs and killing young birds. While the negative characteristics may be somewhat valid, the red-head has many redeeming attributes. It eats huge numbers of harmful ants, moths, and beetles, especially "June bugs."

Perhaps its greatest asset is its exuberant response to life. Few birds seem so gay and so fearless of man. They often will allow very close approach and, at times, seem to be playing "hide-and-go-seek" as they

159

SIZE: L. 9–10″ (23–25 cm). COLORING: *Entire head and neck area are bright red. Black back and tail, large white wing patches. Immature bird lacks red head.* HABITAT: *Golf courses, open forests, rural roadsides, and farms.* NESTING: *Nests in cavity in trees, utility poles, or fence posts; 5 white eggs.* UNUSUAL MANNERISMS: *Often flies low across roads. Frequently feeds in flycatcher manner.* IDENTIFYING HINTS: *Prominent white wing patches evident in flight.* STATUS IN INDIANA: *Fairly common spring and fall migrant and nesting bird. Uncommon winter resident; more common in southern part of Indiana.* RANGE: *Breeds from southern Canada to the Gulf states and Florida. Winters primarily in the southern parts of its range.*

move from fence stake to fence stake. This fearlessness often is the red-heads' undoing, as they are frequently killed by cars when flying slowly across the roadways.

A number of years ago, there was concern that the red-head would have a much more restricted range than it now has. It seems to me to be holding its own, and maybe slightly increasing in population.

Now that we have passed the two hundredth anniversary of our country's birthday, let's hope that both our great nation and our flagbird, the red-headed woodpecker, continue to prosper.

Eastern Kingbird

[TYRANNUS TYRANNUS]

Aggression is a trait that is admired by many people—a trait even considered essential in many fields. Many times aggression can make up for natural inability in certain fields. In athletics, properly directed aggression can often make up for physical shortcomings or for a lack of outstanding coordination. In promoting a service or product, aggression can often be harnessed and used as an effective tool.

Among birds, aggression is a frequently encountered mannerism. Hawks and owls depend upon a high degree of aggression for survival. But why a member of the flycatcher family, the eastern kingbird, should be so aggressive is a puzzle to me.

The kingbird is not physically equipped to be an aggressive creature; it does not have sharp talons or a sharply-honed beak. As a member of the flycatcher family, the bulk of its diet is made up of flying insects. Yet the kingbird is among the most aggressive of birds. It is most often seen chasing a larger bird—a crow, blackbird, or hawk—away from an area that the kingbird has proclaimed as its special territory.

Like most of the members of the flycatcher family, the kingbird is absent from Indiana when insects are not present. The kingbird is here for the months of May, June, July, August, and September. During

Size: *L. 8–9″ (20–23 cm)*. Coloring: *Black-backed, white front, black tail with definite white tip.* Habitat: *Open woods, orchards, fencerows, edge of golf courses.* Nesting: *Bulky nest made of weed stalks and grasses and lined with fine grass. Built 10–20′ above the ground, often near water; 3–5 eggs.* Unusual Mannerisms: *Flycatcher habit of returning to the same exposed perch after darting out to catch a flying insect. White tip on dark tail.* Identifying Hints: *Aggressive behavior, intolerant of any blackbirds or birds of prey near nesting area.* Status in Indiana: *Common nesting bird throughout the state, present from May to October. Does not winter here.* Range: *Breeds from central and southern Canada to southern United States. Winters from Peru to Bolivia.*

these five months, it will raise its family of four young and then move south to South America.

The kingbird is most often seen in orchards and open, wooded areas and is seldom seen in deeper woods. Another likely place to see this bird is along stream and river banks, especially if there are dead stumps or dead tree limbs bordering the water. Golf courses also are favored by the kingbird.

Look for a robin-sized bird, black on the back, with white underparts. The black tail has a white band at the tip which is a good field mark when the bird is flying.

Although the kingbird has little tolerance for potential enemies, it doesn't seem to mind, in the least, nesting in the same tree with other other birds with which it is compatible. But if a hawk or crow should come into the kingbird's view, watch out for a battle royal!

In many years of birding, I have never seen any of the large birds victorious in a battle with a kingbird. Its agility in the air, together with its pugnacity and utter fearlessness, give the kingbird all it needs to drive off any bird that it wishes, no matter what the size difference may be.

After the issue has been settled, the kingbird returns to the exposed limb or stump that it occupied prior to the encounter and resumes feeding on flying insects. It almost seems to be saying, "Now you know why I'm called the *kingbird*."

Red-tailed Hawk

[BUTEO JAMAICENSIS]

The red-tailed hawk is our most evident bird of prey. It is the large hawk that we see circling in the sky on warm, summer days. It always causes me to wonder what it would be like if men could fly as easily as it does. It certainly would relieve some of the congestion on our super highways! I like to think that the Wright brothers were inspired by the

flight of the red-tail—that perhaps it was the red-tail that germinated the thought that it might be possible for a "heavier than air" craft to fly.

Red-tailed hawks are one of a group of hawks called "buteos," or large hawks with broad wings and fan-like tails. Other members of this group seen in Indiana are the red-shouldered, rough-legged, and broad-winged hawks. The distinguishing field marks of the adult red-tailed are the red tail and white breast, separated by a dark belly band.

A closer look at the red-tailed hawk would reveal that it is a permanent resident throughout Indiana, nesting in the larger stands of deciduous woods. The red-tail, which generally mates for life, may stay in the same wooded area for many years. Frequently it picks the tallest tree in the woods in which to build its rather large nest.

An interesting feature of the nest building is that when the pair has selected a suitable nesting site, and after the nest has been constructed, the male habitually brings a branch of an evergreen tree to the nest—rather like a young man presenting his ladylove with a ring! Nesting takes place early, in March, and both the male and the female help in rearing the young. By May, the two young are ready to take their places in the world.

SIZE: *L. 18–25" (46–63 cm). W. 48" (1.2 m).* COLORING: *Brown-backed, adult has rufous tail.* HABITAT: *Deciduous woods and adjacent open country.* NESTING: *Nest is well-constructed platform of sticks, usually placed high in a tall tree; 2–3 eggs.* UNUSUAL MANNERISMS: *Extremely secretive about nesting. Pairs are reputed to nest for life.* IDENTIFYING HINTS: *When perched, shows dark belly band, contrasting with whitish breast. Is the most common soaring hawk in Indiana.* STATUS IN INDIANA: *Year-round resident, nests throughout the state.* RANGE: *Nests from Alaska and northern Canada south to Central America. Winters from the Great Lakes area south.*

The red-tailed hawk has been mistakenly called a "chicken hawk." It used to be considered an admirable feat to shoot red-tails and other hawks and put them on display, strung out along a fence row. Thankfully, that era is now past. Careful analysis of the food habits of the red-tailed hawk has revealed that more than three-fourths of its diet consists of rabbits, squirrels, and rodents. Any farmers who have resident red-tailed hawks on their farmlands should feel especially blessed and should do everything possible to see that these great hawks are not disturbed.

All the buteos have extremely keen eyesight. This attribute allows them to spot their prey from great distances. Many times I've seen a red-tail, seemingly dozing on the limb of a dead tree, suddenly spring from the limb and fly a considerable distance to investigate a movement in the field that only the hawk's eye could detect.

Many bird lovers look with disfavor upon the feeding habits of the hawks; but if I may do some plea bargaining on behalf of these birds, they do not hunt indiscriminately. They tend to capture the prey least able to escape, the bird or animal that has some imperfection, the bird that is just a trifle less alert, maneuverable, or swift.

The surviving birds are the ones that are best equipped to compete in a tough world. Darwin called it "the survival of the fittest." It is an exacting system, but one that has worked well.

Yellow-breasted Chat

[I CTERIA VIRENS]

The strangest warbler in Indiana or, for that matter, in the United States is the yellow-breasted chat. It's an unusual warbler because it doesn't look, act, or sound like a member of the warbler family. Early scientists wrestled with the problem of how to classify this bird and came to the conclusion that it had more physical characteristics of a warbler than of any other type of bird.

Size: *L. 6½–7½″ (16–19 cm).* Coloring: *Yellow breast, olive-green back.* Habitat: *Thickets, tangles, brier patches.* Nesting: *Off the ground in small saplings; 4–5 eggs.* Unusual Mannerisms: *Best known by unwarbler-like songs—a series of croaks, whistles, honks, and squeaks.* Identifying Hints: *Largest of the warblers; white spectacles.* Status in Indiana: *Common nesting bird here from May to September. More common in the southern than the north part of Indiana.* Range: *Breeds from southern Canada to Florida. Winters in Mexico and Central America.*

In upstate New York the chat is a rare bird; and each year, when I lived there, a group of us used to make a special trip in June to view the only nesting chat within fifty miles of Rochester. Hoosiers don't have this problem, for the chat is a relatively common nesting bird throughout the state, with the exception of the northernmost parts. In central Indiana it is one of the most common nesting warblers. For example, in the Eagle Creek Park area there are as many as twelve pairs nesting yearly, and in one small area just west of the Indianapolis Museum of Art there are usually three pairs nesting.

Chats can be seen in Indiana from the middle of May until the middle of September. They winter south of the United States, primarily in Central America. During migration, they are secretive, quiet birds, often moving through an area without being reported; but on their breeding grounds, it is a different matter. The chat sounds like no other warbler. It has such a variety of whistles, wheezes, honks, squeaks, and screeches that trying to put words to the chat's vocalizations is a thankless task. One early writer, when asked to put into words what the chat was saying, claimed, tongue in cheek, that it repeated the following: "Your gun won't work—your ramrod is broken—you haven't got a gun—you are a bald-headed cripple—there is a horrible suicide in the bushes and a big snake and a nasty skunk—your house is on fire—your baby is crying—you have missed the road to the poor farm—you have gone to seed and should move west and grow up in the country—you are taking too much of his valuable time and must excuse him for a moment!" Often, while going through all this, the chat is hopping about from branch to branch in a large tangle or shrub, and he even continues his tyrannical utterances while he is in mid-air!

Look for the yellow-breasted chat in deserted pastures or unculti-vated fields that have an abundance of unkempt tangles, brier thickets, or multiflora hedges. The yellow-breasted chat is our largest warbler, half again the size of most of the warblers, and is much more deliberate and slower-moving than the other warblers. The yellow-breasted chat is olive green above, with a lemon-yellow throat and breast and a clear, white belly. A prominent mark of the chat is the white eye spectacles that accentuate its dark eyes.

Although no one has the option to choose from which family he will come, I'm sure the chat is pleased that he has been included in the warbler family.

Cliff Swallow

[PETROCHELIDON PYRRHONOTA]

Bird nests come in all sorts of sizes, shapes, and forms. They range in size from the half-ton structures of the American bald eagle to the silver dollar-sized cradles of the hummingbird. Some birds, the orioles, for instance, are masters at weaving a complicated hanging basket-type nest; while others, like the turkey vulture, build little or no nest at all.

One of the most expertly crafted nests is that of the cliff swallow. Its nest embodies the disciplines of engineering, sculpturing, and brick-laying. Both the male and the female participate in building the nest. They must first find a sufficient supply of soil that has just the right consistency of dry earth and mud so that when it is combined with the birds' saliva, it will adhere to the structure to which the nest will be attached. Sometimes as many as one thousand dabs of mud are needed to form the globe-shaped nest.

It was once true that the cliff swallow nested mostly on the sides of steep bluffs or cliffs; now barns (preferably unpainted ones) and bridge abutments are also used by this colorful member of the swallow family. When conditions are favorable, they will nest in large colonies.

Although I happened upon two active cliff swallow nests under a bridge near my home one recent summer, it must be admitted that this is not a very common bird in Indiana. It is much less likely to be seen here as a nesting bird than as a migrant during the months of May and in September.

Early ornithologists either ignored it or didn't recognize it. From the turn of the century until about 1930, it was considered to be a fairly common bird in the East. From that time until now it seems to have had a constant struggle to maintain a stable population. Its main problem seems to be an inability to compete with the house sparrow, which often manages to evict the cliff swallow from its nests.

The cliff swallow is not difficult to identify. It is blue backed, like the barn swallow, but lacks the deeply forked tail of the barn swallow.

SIZE: *5–6″ (13–15 cm)*. COLORING: *Upper parts blue-black, underparts white, with chestnut neck area. Pale brown rump area.* HABITAT: *Farmlands, cliffs, open country, near buildings.* NESTING: *Gourd-like, mud nest under bridges, against cliffs, or beneath the outside eaves of barns; 4–6 white eggs.* UNUSUAL MANNERISMS: *Sometimes nest in large colonies.* IDENTIFYING HINTS: *Light rump area, square-shaped tail.* STATUS IN INDIANA: *Uncommon migrant, spring and fall. Uncommon nesting bird. Does not winter here.* RANGE: *Breeds from southern Alaska south to Tennessee, northern Alabama, and northern Georgia. Winters in South America.*

The best field mark of the cliff swallow is a light rump, which is absent in all of our other swallows. This light rump enables one to identify the cliff swallow even at a considerable distance.

Midwesterners are often accused of being too conservative and blasé about their viewpoints. When the cliff swallows return each year to the Capistrano Mission in southern California, they are greeted with wild acclaim: crowds cheer; bells peal; and the wire services, newspapers, and television commentators all make much ado about the swallows. When the cliff swallows return to Indiana, they are greeted by unconcealed yawns. Maybe some sort of compromise between the two extremes would be in order.

Mockingbird

[Mimus polyglottos]

If there is a better mimic than the mockingbird, I've never heard it. My son, Scott, and I kept track, for half an hour, of the various birds that a mockingbird nesting on our property imitated. The list finally totaled nineteen, including such diverse species as red-shouldered hawk, bluebird, killdeer, red-eyed and white-eyed vireo, bobwhite, robin, blue jay, chickadee, rough-winged swallow, and barn swallow. These calls were given, one after the other, with no hesitation between songs. The mockingbird truly should be awarded the accolade, "Caruso of the birds!"

In Indiana, it is a persistent singer from early spring until late fall, and it really pulls out all the stops on a clear, moonlit summer night. If you hear a bird singing a variety of songs at night in Indiana, it is almost certain to be a mockingbird.

When one thinks about mockingbirds, visions of mint juleps, magnolias, and stately plantations come to mind. Actually the "mocker" has been extending its range northward for many years and is now established as a breeding bird in all of the northern states east of the Mississippi. I recall a number of years ago keeping track of a mockingbird in upstate New York that was trying to survive the severe winter

SIZE: *L. 9–11" (23–28 cm).* COLORING: *Gray above, white below, large white patches on the wing and tail.* HABITAT: *City parks, suburban backyards, farmlands, open country with thickets.* NESTING: *Nests in a tree or shrub 3–10' above the ground. Loosely constructed nest; 3–5 blue-green eggs.* UNUSUAL MANNERISMS: *One of the few nocturnal singers. This bird has amazing ability to imitate other bird songs.* IDENTIFYING HINTS: *White patches on wings and tail when in flight. In winter can frequently be found perched on chimney tops.* STATUS IN INDIANA: *Common nesting bird and year-round resident. Less common in northern portions of state.* RANGE: *Breeds south of Great Lakes area to Gulf of Mexico. Winters throughout its breeding range, but more common in the southern portion of its range.*

common to that area. This bird seemed to sense that the chimney was a source of heat, and in late afternoon would fly to the top of the chimney to spend the night. The bird did survive—and subsequently bred in the nearby area. It was, I believe, the first time that a mocker completed the entire life cycle in that county.

Identification of the mocker is not difficult. It is a good-sized, gray bird with white wing patches that are easily seen when the bird flies. It frequently lays its four eggs in a nest located in a small tree or shrub not far from human habitation.

The mockingbird rates with the bald eagle and the bluebird as a favorite bird of many Americans. No less than five states have designated the mocker as their state bird.

In spite of these credentials, it has been criticized by some gardeners and orchardists because of its feeding habits. It likes fruit and berries. Personally, I feel that if I could sing like Caruso, and if I could bring as much joy to the world as the mockingbird has, I would be entitled to eat whatever I pleased!

House Wren

[TROGLODYTES AEDON]

Folklore has it that if you have a house wren nesting on your property, you will have good fortune for the coming year. I hope this is true, for each summer I usually have two families of house wrens nesting on my property.

Once a friend and I watched a pair of house wrens feeding young, and we timed the number of times that the parents fed the babies. They started at approximately six o'clock in the morning and concluded at about eight in the evening. They fed the young approximately every four minutes; so, during a fourteen-hour period, the young were fed a total of 210 times. The range of insects brought to feed the young included slugs, moths, flying ants, caterpillars, and beetles—just about any insect that was found in the area. It struck me just how beneficial house wrens are in our environment.

Consider that after the young are out of the nest, each of the fledglings will continue to search out insects. Realizing that each of these pairs of wrens will raise an average of ten young (two broods of five each) per year, we can appreciate the great quantities of insects they are consuming annually.

Not too many years ago, there was concern that the house wren population was decreasing rapidly, and the house wren was put on the "amber" list. That is, it was not considered to be an endangered species, but one needful of concern and one perhaps susceptible to a further decrease in numbers. Indiana seems to be a fertile area for this bird, and it seems to me that the lot of the house wren here is improved.

The male wrens arrive in Indiana in May, about a week before the females, and immediately search for possible nesting sites. When the females or "jenny wrens" arrive, they make the final selection. For some reason wrens appear to be more prone than most birds to nest near human habitation.

Wrens are very aggressive. They will seldom allow other birds to build near their nests and have even been known to puncture holes in the eggs of other birds who attempted to locate their nests nearby.

The house wren is a very small, grayish-brown bird with a tail usually held erect. Its bubbling song is rendered all day long. If you put up a man-made wren house or hang a gourd, and if the bird that occupies this house does not have a white eye stripe, you can be sure that you have a house wren.

The indefatigable house wrens, who are very conscientious about feeding and taking care of their young, manage to keep up a continually cheerful exterior. I wonder how many human parents would be pleasant after feeding their offspring 210 times in one day!

SIZE: *L. 4½–5¼" (11–13 cm).* COLORING: *Dusky brown above and below. No wing-bars or eye stripe.* HABITAT: *Residential areas, suburban gardens, farmlands, woodpiles.* NESTING: *Nests in natural cavity in tree stump, old woodpecker holes, bird houses, almost any cavity. Uses twigs and sticks; 6–7 eggs.* UNUSUAL MANNERISMS: *Often builds a number of dummy nests to confuse potential enemies and to protect territory.* IDENTIFYING HINTS: *Like many of the wrens, tail often held erect. Lack of wing stripes and eye line. Song is persistent, bubbling, and exuberant.* STATUS IN INDIANA: *Common spring and fall migrant and nesting bird. Does not winter in Indiana.* RANGE: *Breeds from southern Canada to the middle states. Winters in Gulf states, Florida, and Mexico.*

SIZE: *5–6″ (13–16 cm)*. COLORING: *Male, all-over deep blue, appears black in poor light. Female, dull brown, with no distinguishing field marks.* HABITAT: *Uncultivated fields, edges of woods, hedgerows, thickets.* NESTING: *Low trees, tangles, seldom above 10 feet. Well-woven cup of dried grasses, twigs. Usually 3–4 white, or occasionally pale blue, eggs.* UNUSUAL MANNERISMS: *Persistent singer. Allows rather close approach.* IDENTIFYING HINTS: *The only all blue bird. Song, lively, cheerful, repetitive. Call note a distinctive, harsh "chip."* STATUS IN INDIANA: *Very common nesting bird. Resides in Indiana from May to September.* RANGE: *Nests throughout eastern United States. Winters in south Mexico and Central America.*

Indigo Bunting

[PASSERINA CYANEA]

One-word adjectives are often used to describe birds. Eagles are referred to as being majestic; rails as being mysterious; scarlet tanagers as being beautiful; and chickadees as being energetic. At the risk of being dubbed a sentimentalist, I suggest a one-word adjective which describes the indigo bunting—sweet. This bird has a lovely song that, once learned, always stands out among all other bird songs heard during the summer months.

The indigo bunting has a warm, pleasant personality, always seeming to be happy, not sad or introspective. It seems to delight in its adornment, for it exudes the confidence of a being that knows that it is beautiful. It also has the confidence of knowing it can make the journey from Central America north to the eastern United States each year and survive in spite of adversity.

The male indigo bunting can hardly be mistaken for any other bird —it is an all blue, sparrow-sized bird. If it is true, as a poet has written, that the bluebird carries the blue of the sky on its back, then the entire indigo bunting must have been dipped in the blue of the oceans. When seen in poor light and from a distance, it sometimes seems to be a small, dark bird. But seen at close range in good light, the deep velvet-blue sets this bird apart from all other birds.

The female looks nothing like the male and hardly seems to be a member of the same species. She is a plain, brown, sparrow-like bird with no distinguishing field marks other than utter plainness.

One day while out on a walk I saw a male indigo bunting and a male goldfinch perched on the same weed stalk. The blend of brilliant blue, yellow, and black, in such close proximity, would cause anyone, as it did me, to pause and marvel at the color combinations that are always visible in the out-of-doors.

177

Common Flicker

[COLAPTES AURATUS]

Indiana is well favored by the woodpecker family. All of the woodpeckers found east of the Mississippi River, with the exception of the
three-toed woodpecker and the red-cockaded woodpecker, can be seen
in every county of the state. Perhaps the most visible woodpecker in
Indiana is the common flicker. Since the turn of the century, the flicker
found east of the Mississippi has been called the yellow-shafted flicker
and the one found west of the Mississippi the red-shafted flicker. A few
years ago, it was decided that, while there were some obvious visual differences between the two flickers, they were not separate species. Now,
both the western form and the eastern form are called common flickers.

In Indiana, flickers are with us all year, but they are much more
common in the summer than in the winter. Ornithologists feel that most
of the flickers that winter here are birds that have nested north of us.
In the spring and fall the migration of flickers is very much in evidence.
I can recall watching hundreds of migrating flickers along the shores of
both Lake Ontario and Lake Erie, and the flicker migration, in early
spring, at Point Pelee, near Detroit, is well worth driving several hundred miles to see. Inland, the arrival of flickers in the spring is not as
spectacular, but it is an event much appreciated by those who enjoy
watching the migration of birds.

The flicker, our second largest woodpecker, is larger in size than a
robin. In flight the undulating pattern, typical of all woodpeckers, is
very obvious. The yellow wing linings and powder puff-like, white
rump enable one to identify the flicker in flight, even at a considerable
distance. When seen close at hand, the beautiful blending of browns and
yellows is a treat to the eye. The male and female are very much alike,
except the male has a black moustache which the female lacks.

The courtship display of the flicker is a complicated and elaborate
process. The male goes through all sorts of wing and tail spreading, head
bobbing, and drumming on hollow trees or even tin roofs and gutters.

SIZE: *L. 12–14″ (30–35 cm)*. COLORING: *Golden-brown backed, with black bars and spots. Black bib on front. Prominent white rump and yellow wing linings show in flight. Adult male has black moustache marking.* HABITAT: *Open country with trees, orchards, farm woodlots.* NESTING: *In tree cavity or will accept man-made birdhouse; 6–7 white eggs.* UNUSUAL MANNERISMS: *The woodpecker most often seen on the ground, searching for ants. More vocal than most woodpeckers. Frequently repeats its name, "flicka, flicka, flicka."* IDENTIFYING HINTS: *Deep, undulating flight. White rump.* STATUS IN INDIANA: *Common nesting bird and year-round resident. Less common during winter months.* RANGE: *Breeds east of the Rockies, from the limit of trees in Canada south to Florida. Winters as far north as the states bordering the Great Lakes.*

In the spring both the male and female engage in enthusiastic aerobatics that seem to be part of the courtship. First, the male will pursue the female, flying vigorously around trees and through the woods. Then the female will take up the chase, and the pursuer becomes the pursued. During all this romantic foreplay, the selection of a suitable nesting site is determined.

Why some birds have a complicated ritual prior to nesting, and others make little or no display, I don't know. Maybe for the same reason that some couples have long engagements and large church weddings, while others feel a brief visit to a justice of the peace is sufficient.

Whip-poor-will

[CAPRIMULGUS VOCIFEROUS]

Nocturnal creatures have always held a special fascination for man. The fact that these creatures function most efficiently when man is normally at rest adds to the attraction. Indiana is one of the few states that has these two members of the goatsucker family nesting within its borders, the whip-poor-will and the chuck-will's widow. The chuck-will's widow is a rare bird in Indiana, although it is reputed to nest in the knobs area of southern Indiana, between New Albany and Evans-ville. The whip-poor-will nests in favorable habitats throughout the central and northern parts of Indiana. Both of these birds are very vocal and do not hesitate to proclaim loudly their presence in the area.

The differences between the two species are that the more southern bird, the chuck-will's widow, is a larger bird and gives a four-syllable song and has a brown neck stripe. The whip-poor-will has a three-noted song and has a white neck stripe. Both birds arrive in Indiana in the middle of April and depart in the middle of September. Both lay their two eggs on the ground and depend upon their natural camouflage for protection.

Many years ago I recall hearing my first whip-poor-will. After an

SIZE: *L. 9–10″ (23–25 cm)*. COLORING: *Overall brown with gray streaking. Male shows white outer tail patches.* HABITAT: *Dry, open deciduous woods, often near water.* NESTING: *Two white eggs placed in leaves on the ground.* UNUSUAL MANNERISMS: *Nocturnal. Nighttime song given persistently.* IDENTIFYING HINTS: *Song, "whip-poor-will."* STATUS IN INDIANA: *Uncommon spring and fall migrant; uncommon nester; does not winter in Indiana.* RANGE: *Breeds from southern Canada to southern United States. Winters from Gulf Coast south to Central America.*

afternoon of playing sandlot baseball, I lingered to walk through a wooded area that had a small stream passing through it. While walking along the edge of this stream, as dusk was descending, I heard what to my ears was a wondrous song. None of my fellow would-be major leaguers could help in identifying this enthusiastic nocturnal vocalist. I recall going to the local library and satisfying myself that what I had heard was a whip-poor-will. Although my memory of that spot stays fresh, the area where I first heard the whip-poor-will has gone through many changes. During World War II it was a "victory garden"; later a housing development for returning veterans was located there, and now it is the site of a senior citizens' project. Descendants of my first whip-poor-will, when passing over this area, must be puzzled to know why such a lush, wet, green, and inviting woods has been changed into a blacktopped, mundane area. While a man would call this efficient use of our environment, the whip-poor-will might question our priorities.

A friend of mine once told me of counting the number of times the whip-poor-will repeated his call during the course of an evening in Brown County. With little hesitation, this bird repeated singing his name 323 times. John Burroughs, famous nature writer, tells in one of his books of counting the whip-poor-will's song repeated more than one thousand times! Unfortunately, the whip-poor-will is seldom seen or heard in the cities; but if you happen to be in the areas of Brown County, Monroe County, or McCormick's Creek at dusk, take a little time to listen to the wonderful song of the whip-poor-will.

Blue-gray Gnatcatcher

[POLIOPTILA CAERULEA]

Many people are reluctant to venture out-of-doors when the temperatures rise to the eighties and nineties, but those who do are always rewarded with a sight or sound that makes the effort worthwhile. Wild

SIZE: *L. 4½–5" (11–13 cm)*. COLORING: *Blue-gray above, white below, with white eye-ring.* HABITAT: *Open woodlands and brushy thickets, frequently beside stream or pond. Wooded swamps.* NESTING: *Builds exquisitely constructed nest-cup of plant down and spider webs, covered with lichens—one of the most beautiful of nests, and also one of the best camouflaged.* UNUSUAL MANNERISMS: *Seldom sits still.* IDENTIFYING HINTS: *Look for white eye-ring and listen for song, which may easily be overlooked, insect-like, with a nasal quality.* STATUS IN INDIANA: *In Indiana from the middle of April until the middle of September. Surprisingly common nesting bird throughout most of Indiana; less common in extreme northern part of state.* RANGE: *Breeds from northernmost United States to the Gulf of Mexico. Winters from the Carolinas to Mexico.*

flowers of all shapes, sizes, and colors are now in full bloom. While it is rewarding to watch a beautiful domestic rose mature and bloom, the beauty of the tea rose pales when compared to a field of wild daisies and black-eyed susans basking in the sun.

One bird that doesn't seem to be intimidated by the summer's heat is the blue-gray gnatcatcher, one of our smallest and liveliest birds. The gnatcatcher is seldom seen sitting still and is almost always seen busily moving about the foliage of trees and shrubs, searching for minute insects that make up the majority of its diet.

The blue-gray gnatcatcher is the only gnatcatcher found in Indiana. It nests throughout the state but is more common in the southern part of Indiana. It is one of a number of birds that at one time was considered a bird of the South but during the past thirty years has gradually moved north. It is now firmly established as a nesting species in most of our northern states.

Because of its small size and rather insignificant voice, the blue-gray gnatcatcher often goes unnoticed, even in areas where it is common. It is a pale blue-backed bird with white underparts. Its tail is often held erect, like a wren's. Another mark to look for is the white eye-ring. The months to look for this bird in Indiana are April, May, June, July, and August. During September the gnatcatcher moves south and generally winters in our most southern states.

The nest of this mite of a bird is a thing of beauty. It is usually situated on a horizontal branch not over twenty feet from the ground. The cup-shaped nest is bound together with spider webs and covered externally with lichen. The nest opening is about the size of a silver dollar. It always surprises me that these delicate nests can survive some of our violent storms, but survive they do, and the gnatcatcher seems to be thriving in Indiana.

July is truly a lovely month in the Hoosier state. The famed home-grown sweet corn and tomatoes are starting to be available at the roadside stands, the uncultivated fields are profuse with an exquisite array of wildflowers, and our outstanding state parks are conveniently located for all to enjoy. Air conditioning is fine, and a great convenience, but now is the time to be out-of-doors. Who knows, you may even make a new acquaintance, the blue-gray gnatcatcher!

AUGUST

AN ANTICIPATION OF THE COMING change in season is now evident in the behavior of many birds. At the beginning of the month small groups of mixed blackbirds—red-wings, grackles, cowbirds, and starlings—can be seen moving about just before sunset. Their numbers will increase almost daily, and by the end of the month, they will have gathered into huge flocks.

Swallows, also, have started to prepare for migration. First to gather are the bank swallows, which can often be seen lined up on telephone wires not far from where they have nested. Shortly after the bank swallows have left, the purple martins take their place on the wires, to be followed shortly by the barn swallows. Other swallows—the rough-winged and a few cliff—will follow their lead, and within a month, only the tree swallows can be found lingering briefly here. It boggles the mind to see thousands of swallows in mid-August and realize that within thirty days most of these birds will have departed the country, with some already having accomplished the long journey to South America.

The movement of the swallows and blackbirds is obvious, but there are subtle signs also that a change of seasons is imminent. Some of the shorebirds that have nested to the north of us have already returned to pay a brief visit here. The semipalmated plover, the solitary sandpiper, the lesser yellowlegs, and the short-billed dowitchers have completed their nesting and are on their way south. Herons have a period after the breeding season when they wander away from the nesting sites, and August is the month when one is most likely to see some of the southern herons during their postbreeding wanderings. Yellow warblers and blue-gray gnatcatchers, along with a number of other warblers, are ready to make their move southward.

A bird hike at this time of the year will reveal that springtime is not the only time when wildflowers are abundant. The late summer array of flora can be spectacular. The thistle, black-eyed susan, Indian paintbrush, and Queen Anne's lace are all very much in evidence. Although not belittling the lovely, diminutive spring blossoms, it is true that at no other time of the year than late summer are the myriad colors in nature so manifest. Those who have not experienced being chest-high in a field of black-eyed susan and thistle blooms have missed a facet of life that enriches one.

By the end of the month, there will be a chill in the air. Some evenings, it will be necessary to sleep under a blanket. Many of the birds will have lost their brightly colored appearance. Even such colorful ducks as the wood duck, blue-winged teal, and mallard—which have all begun to bunch up now—will be in "eclipse" plumage and difficult to identify. This is the time when the new birder must guard against discouragement. It is a time to decide that the difficulties involved in identifying fall birds will not bring dismay. Part of the satisfaction in being a birder is that it is not an interest that can be started and concluded in a brief time. Rather, it is an interest that can best be pursued for a lifetime.

Screech Owl

[OTUS ASIO]

Nocturnal creatures have always held a special fascination for man. These creatures that function more efficiently at night and rest during the day possess skills that set them apart from the rest of the animal world. The owls are good examples. The owl has unusually soft, fringed wing feathers that allow it to fly very quietly. It has abnormally large eyes that are set forward in the skull, and the owl's ears are also large and located in its head in such a fashion that it can detect the faintest of sounds. All of these peculiarities enable the owl to hunt skillfully in the dark of night.

The screech owl nests throughout the state of Indiana and is a year-round resident here. It is about the size of a robin. In Indiana, the two color phases—gray and red—of the screech owl are found. Early orni-

Size: *L. 8–10″ (20–25 cm).* Coloring: *Two color phases, red and gray. Red phase, a rich rufous on back, wings and breast area, with yellow eyes. Gray phase, almost solid gray back, wings, and breast area, with yellow eyes.* Habitat: *Suburban areas, deciduous woods, orchards.* Nesting: *Nests in tree cavity, often abandoned woodpecker holes, or man-made houses; 4–5 white eggs.* Unusual Mannerisms: *Very aggressive in defense of nest.* Identifying Hints: *Ear tufts and voice— gives low whinny, a tremulous whistle.* Status in Indiana: *Fairly common nesting bird and year-round resident.* Range: *Breeds from southern Canada to Gulf Coast and Mexico. Winters throughout its breeding range.*

thologists thought they were separate species, but study has shown that this is not not true. The screech owl has ear tufts which separate it from the other small owls found in Indiana. If you spot a robin-sized owl with ear tufts, you are seeing a screech owl.

Many more screech owls are heard than seen, for they are strictly nocturnal, spending the day quietly resting in the cavities of dead trees. Both the red and gray phases of the screech owl blend perfectly into their surroundings during the day, and they can be present in a neighborhood for years without being observed. The best way to locate a screech owl is to learn first to imitate its call—a low, mournful whinny, going down the scale. It is easy to imitate if you can whistle. Try going to the edge of a wooded area and imitating the call. It's surprising how often an owl will return the call.

The screech owl nests in an abandoned woodpecker's hole or natural cavity in a tree. It raises one brood a year, and if it is successful in its nesting activities, it will return for many years to the same nest.

There has been much investigation of what the screech owl eats. Some studies have shown that its diet consists primarily of other birds; other research has shown that the screech owl mainly eats rodents. The general conclusion is that this small owl eats whatever is most convenient for it to catch. If it is nesting where there is a preponderance of rodents, rodents will be the primary source of its food. If birds are the more abundant creatures in the area, birds will be the main source of food for the owl.

As evidenced by the physical adaptations with which it has been blessed, the owl is well equipped to function in the night when most other creatures are sleeping. It makes us aware that, while we are sleeping, the drama of life continues.

Bank Swallow

[RIPARIA RIPARIA]

The month of August signals a change in the behavior of most of Indiana's nesting birds. The urgent compulsion to breed and perpetuate the species is now past for all but two or three species.

August is generally a carefree month for Indiana birds—a time to frolic and to enjoy the beauty and bounty of the countryside, family responsibilities all but forgotten. Perhaps the first bird that recognizes that it soon must leave its breeding grounds and return to its winter home is the bank swallow.

Around the first of August, bank swallows begin to gather into large flocks, and by the end of the month, ninety percent of them will be well on their way to South America. In order to survive, they must avoid being caught in a prolonged cold spell that is followed by a killing frost.

The bank swallow is usually the last swallow to arrive in Indiana (the last week of April or first of May) and the first to leave (the last week in August or first week of September). It is our smallest swallow and the only one that will not nest in man-made bird houses or in buildings or barns near man.

The bank swallows nest in burrows in sandbanks and gravel pits. When a suitable area is found, they will nest in colonies of hundreds and will return each year to the same area. Even when the area changes, the bank swallow will return in hopes that a suitable nesting site will be available.

One area that I have watched for a number of years has changed drastically during the past ten years. First, there were natural sandbanks, and hundreds of bank swallows nested there successfully. Then the area changed to a sand and gravel mining operation, and the swallows set up housekeeping in the mounds of gravel. One year the gravel mounds were disturbed during the time the swallows were feeding young, and very few survived. Yet, the next year they returned and attempted to nest there again. In recent years the area has contained a combination of

189

SIZE: *L. 4¾–5½" (12–14 cm).* COLORING: *Brown back, white breast, crossed by brown band.* HABITAT: *Rivers and streams, shows decided preference for sandbanks.* NESTING: *Burrows into gravel pits, sandbanks, and roadcuts; 4–6 white eggs.* UNUSUAL MANNERISMS: *Most often nest in dense colonies.* IDENTIFYING HINTS: *Smallest of the swallows; dark band across white breast.* STATUS IN INDIANA: *Common spring migrant and nesting bird. Leaves Indiana late summer and early fall.* RANGE: *Breeds from Alaska south to middle states. Winters in South America.*

sandbanks and gravel mounds, and the swallows have been able to nest there successfully.

The bank swallow is a small, brown-backed bird with white underparts. There is a dark band across the neck that can be seen when viewed with binoculars. Like all swallows, the bank swallow is known for its agility in the air.

The bank swallow anticipates that adverse conditions lie ahead—that life won't always be sunshine and roses—that all too soon the harsh realities of winter will dominate the scene. He knows he must forgo the serenity of idyllic todays if he is to experience any tomorrows.

Great Blue Heron

[ARDEA HERODIAS]

The great blue heron is the largest—and most dramatic-looking—member of the heron family. Its status in the state seems to have changed rather drastically in recent years; for instance, in the Indianapolis area the great blue heron population is down drastically. The former high counts of fifty to one hundred at Eagle Creek Park have been reduced now to four or five birds. This reduction in heron population seems to be part of a nationwide trend, but nowhere else is it as obvious as in central Indiana. The reasons for their reductions vary, but usually the diminishing of suitable habitat is the main cause.

Great blue herons are always a delight to observe. Just their size causes one to stop what he is doing and gaze at this huge bird. It stands over four feet tall, and its wingspan can exceed six feet. In flight its slow, labored wingbeats, together with its folded neck and trailing legs, make identification easy.

The great blue heron, which has few rivals as a fisherman, uses either one of two methods of fishing. One is to find a likely spot—usually close to the bank and in shallow water—patiently wait until an unsuspecting victim ventures too near, and then in a flash shoot out his dagger-like bill. Most often, the heron has secured his fish dinner.

SIZE: *L. 39–52″ (99–132 cm). W. 70″ (1.8 m).* COLORING: *More gray than blue, with yellow bill. White area about the head and neck.* HABITAT: *Lakes, rivers, marshes, ponds.* NESTING: *Most often nests in colonies, generally placed high in deciduous tree; 3–5 eggs. Same rookery may be used for many years.* UNUSUAL MANNERISMS: *Will patiently stand, motionless, in one place until a fish suitable for eating swims by.* IDENTIFYING HINTS: *Huge size, second largest wading bird in Indiana. In flight, its folded neck and trailing legs are evident.* STATUS IN INDIANA: *Fairly common summer resident, nesting in Indiana in small colonies. Common spring and fall migrant. Uncommon wintering bird.* RANGE: *Breeds from Alaska to Mexico. Winters from Great Lakes area south to South America.*

The other method is to stalk very slowly, its large feet barely making a ripple, its eyes ever alert for the slightest movement. Then, rapier-like, the bill darts out. If its prey is a good-sized fish, the heron tries to impale the fish on its bill, bring it to shore, and then eat it. If its victim is a small fish, the heron will grasp it between its mandibles and quickly swallow it whole.

The great blue, along with other herons, prefers to nest in colonies, called rookeries. They usually pick an inaccessible, large, wooded area for the nest and there lay their usual four eggs. Exploration of the great blue heron rookeries that I have visited is not recommended for the queasy. Undigested and rotted fish abound in the area, making the rookery an odorous site.

In spite of their poor housekeeping habits, the herons have always inspired artists. The herons' dignified, stately manner and the serene settings that are their normal haunts make them suitable models for discerning eyes.

American Goldfinch

[CARDUELIS TRISTIS]

One of the most widely known birds in Indiana is the American goldfinch. It is found in every county each month of the year. In the summer the male is a small, bright, lemon-yellow bird with black wings and a black forehead. The female is a dull yellow bird with dark wings showing two white wing-bars. In the winter the male adopts a plumage very similar to the summer plumage of the female. Two other helpful field aids in identifying this bird from a distance are the undulating flight (flying in a wave-like pattern), and its cheerful call notes which sound like "kur chick-a-dee," with an accent on the second syllable.

Goldfinches are one of the species of birds that nest late in the season. Most of our songbirds nest in May and June; but the goldfinch nests in

SIZE: *L. 4½–5″ (11–14 cm).* COLORING: *Male, bright yellow with black forehead, wings, and tail. Female and winter birds, dull olive-yellow with darker wings showing white wing-bars. Unstreaked breasts.*
HABITAT: *Open country, brush thickets, tangles near water.*
NESTING: *Compact, neat nest, lined with thistle and cattail down Usually placed in small tree or shrub; 4–5 bluish-white eggs.*
UNUSUAL MANNERISMS: *Late nester. Will readily patronize a thistle feeder at summer's end.* IDENTIFYING HINTS: *Undulating flight, also sings in flight, "kur chick-a-dee." Adult males are unmistakable in bright breeding plumage.* STATUS IN INDIANA: *Common year-round resident and breeding bird. Frequently gathers in large flocks in winter and feeds on weed seeds of various kinds.* RANGE: *Breeds from southern Canada south to Georgia, Alabama, and Arkansas. Winters from Canada to southern Mexico.*

July and August, and it is not unusual to find an active nest in September. The goldfinch seems to wait for the maturing of the thistle plants before it gets serious about raising a family. It uses the thistle seed as food and the thistle down for nesting material. In fact, early ornithologists called this bird the "wild canary" or "thistle bird."

In recent years, people have been putting out special feeders that are made to contain thistle seed. I've seen as many as two dozen goldfinches clustered on one long, tubular feeder at one time. One unfortunate aspect of the popularity of these feeders is that the price of thistle seed has, at times, gone as high as a dollar a pound, and in some instances the demand has exceeded the supply. Who would have thought that the lowly thistle seed would become such a sought-after commodity!

In the winter goldfinches tend to gather in flocks. I've seen literally thousands of these birds feeding on weed seeds in December and January at Eagle Creek Park. They never seem to have any trouble finding food, even in the dead of winter.

If you have the opportunity to be out in the country any weekend, don't miss the chance to get a good look at a goldfinch. I'm sure it will brighten your whole day, and maybe this winter you'll be able to think back to that lovely, warm summer day when you saw a goldfinch perched on a thistle stalk .

Cedar Waxwing

[BOMBYCILLA CEDRORUM]

One of the attributes which makes birds appealing to so many people is their beautiful coloring. The orange of the orioles, the red of the cardinal, the blue of the bluebird are all colors that appeal to everyone. These birds have plumage that is obviously attractive.

There are other birds able to blend less striking colors in such a manner as to make them at least equal in beauty to the spectacularly colored birds. The cedar waxwing is a perfect example of these.

The cedar waxwing is a blend of soft yellows, grays, and browns, except for a black mark through the eye and the small spot of red on the

Size: L. 6½–8″ (16–18 cm). Coloring: *Overall soft brown, black mask, yellow-tipped tail, prominent crest, red wax-like spots near the tip of the wings.* Habitat: *Open woodlands, orchards, residential areas where there are fruit-bearing ornamental shrubs.* Nesting: *Loosely woven nest of weed stems, twigs, and grass; 4–5 eggs.* Unusual Mannerisms: *Often gathers in flocks to feed on fruited trees, hawthorns and multi-flora rose hedges, in particular.* Identifying Hints: *Combination of crest and black mask. High, thin, whistled song.* Status in Indiana: *Common spring and fall migrant, common nesting bird, more so in northern half of Indiana. Uncommon winter resident.* Range: *Breeds from southern Alaska south to Georgia. Winters from the Gulf states south to Panama.*

wing that looks downright artificial and resembles sealing wax (whence the waxwing gets its name). The total effect of this blending gives the waxwing a very neat, sleek, elegant, and regal look.

The waxwings never seem to have a feather out of place (rather like individuals who always seem to know what tie to wear with the right suit, or what handbag to carry with the right dress). The best identifying field marks of the waxwing are the yellow tip of the tail and the crested head.

The cedar waxwing normally is a late nesting bird and frequently is still feeding young in Indiana in late August and even into September, long after most of our nesting birds have finished their housekeeping chores.

It is possible to see waxwings every month of the year in Indiana, although there is a period from November to March when their presence here is dependent upon the availability of berries or wild fruit. Consequently, during those years when the berry-bearing trees and shrubs have a poor crop of fruit, the waxwings are scarce or absent.

Although the major portion of their diet is berries, waxwings do consume insects when they are readily available. During August and September, they frequently can be seen catching flying insects and generally behaving like members of the flycatcher family.

The waxwings don't have a "song" in the sense that we normally think of as bird song. Rather, they give a very high, hissing-like whistle. Given singly, it can go undetected altogether; but waxwings are most often seen in groups and when they are all giving this high whistle, the sound, very pleasant to the ear, will often reveal a flock of waxwings in an area where they might have gone unnoticed if they had remained silent.

Cedar waxwings seem to me to have a very gentle personality. Even around the nest, they do not seem to possess aggressive traits that are so evident in most birds. When feeding in groups, as they often do, in a chokecherry tree or other fruit-bearing tree, they never quarrel over the tidbits, as most birds have a tendency to do. They are content to eat the food in front of them and let their neighbors also eat without interference.

I've never seen them exhibit hostility either toward their own kind or toward other birds with which they sometimes gather. Yet, the waxwings seem to have done well in the world. Their numbers do not seem to have decreased, and they still can be found in areas that history tells us they have occupied for over one hundred years. Maybe they are familiar with the Beatitudes and believe that "the meek shall inherit the earth."

Mallard

[ANAS PLATYRHYNCHOS]

The mallard is not only the most common duck found in Indiana, but it is also the most common duck in the United States—and probably in the world. It is present in Indiana each month of the year and is one of the few ducks that can be considered to be a common nesting species in this state.

Although it most often hides its nest in tall grasses, it has been known to nest in trees or on the top of a building, or even inside a barn or garage. Ten or more chicks are raised each year.

The male, or drake, is a most attractive bird with a brilliant green head separated from the chestnut breast by a white ring around the neck. The female looks like a number of other female surface-feeding ducks: she is all brown. After the breeding season, the males adopt a very similarly dull plumage called the "eclipse" plumage. During this one- or two-month period, the mallards can be very difficult to differentiate in the field from some of the other ducks which are also in their eclipse plumage.

It has been said that the mallard is the most important duck in the world. Wild mallards are the chief waterfowl of most game preserves. Domesticated mallards have supplied man not only with untold tons of table fare, but also with eggs and feathers.

All too often, things of beauty are not given proper recognition because they are close at hand or seen daily. The maple tree, as it changes from winter to spring and then leafs out to its full summer foliage, is usually not properly appreciated by those upon whose land it is growing.

SIZE: *L. 18–27" (46–68 cm). W. 36" (90 cm).* COLORING: *Male, green head with white neck-ring, chestnut breast, and grayish body. Female, brown with white tail, purplish-blue speculum.* HABITAT: *Ponds, lakes, and marshes, almost any size.* NESTING: *Nest usually placed in tall grass, thick, dead reeds, or hidden in a brush pile near the shore; 8–10 greenish eggs.* UNUSUAL MANNERISMS: *Commonly interbreed with domestic ducks and other wild ducks, most notably the black duck.* IDENTIFYING HINTS: *Female quacks like domestic barnyard fowl. In flight, dark head and the white outer wing stripes are helpful.* STATUS IN INDIANA: *Common year-round resident and nesting bird. Winters in good numbers as long as there is unfrozen water. Hybrids between wild mallard and domestic fowl often seen on canals and farmyard ponds.* RANGE: *Breeds from Alaska south to central United States. Winters from the Great Lakes south to the Gulf of Mexico.*

Often, it is the tourist or stranger who will bring to our attention the outstanding architectural features of a building that we have passed daily on our way to work but have taken for granted. Many times it is an outsider who will point out to us an outstanding quality or feature of one of our own children—a feature that we had overlooked. So it is with the mallard.

It is usually a new birder or a youngster who will enthusiastically point out to us that the green head of the mallard is a spectacular shade of green, that the chestnut-colored breast seems to blend perfectly with the rest of the body, and that the mallard is, indeed, a most handsome bird!

Great Egret

[CASMERODIUS ALBUS]

The American egret, now officially named the great egret, is a bird not normally thought of as being indigenous to Indiana; yet each year a few of these large, white, wading birds make a brief visit here. On three or four occasions, I have seen this marvelous bird in the spring, but usually the bird is seen in Indiana in August. The great egret, like all members of the heron family, tends to move north after its breeding season is over. The reasons for this postbreeding wandering are obscure. We do know that a trend showing it is nesting north of its normal breeding grounds has become evident, and this August showing of the egret could be a factor in its range extension. Whatever the reason, it is a delight to see in Indiana, especially for the benefit of those who aren't fortunate enough to be able to make the long trip to Florida where this egret is common. Identification is not difficult; it's a large, three-feet tall, all-white bird except for its black legs and yellow bill.

The great egret and the Audubon Society have become synonymous; in fact, the egret is the official symbol of the National Audubon Society. About the turn of the century it was considered very fashionable for a lady to adorn her chapeau with egret plumes. The egret has these plumes only during the breeding season; consequently, when the birds that

Size: L. 35–41" (89–104 cm). W. 55" (1.4 m). Coloring: *All white, with black legs and feet, yellow bill.* Habitat: *Marshes, salt and fresh water, brushy lake borders, deciduous woods with tall trees.* Nesting: *Nests in trees over water, often in colonies with other herons. Nest made of sticks and twigs; 3–4 pale blue eggs.* Unusual Mannerisms: *Feeds by spearing fish and other aquatic creatures. Frequently stands, apparently motionless.* Identifying Hints: *Large size, black legs and feet, and white plumage separate this bird from any other heron.* Status in Indiana: *Rare spring migrant, uncommon fall migrant, most often seen during its wandering period, from August to September. At one time nested sparsely throughout the state.* Range: *Breeds from mid-central states south to Florida. Occasionally has been known to nest north of its regular range. Winters from South Carolina to Gulf Coast.*

were ready to breed were killed, there were no offspring—and the egret population rapidly declined. At one auction sale of two pounds of egret plumes, it was estimated that 200,000 adult egrets had been killed to produce this many plumes. As the egret declined, the price the millinery trade was willing to pay for the plumes skyrocketed. At one point, an ounce of egret plumes was worth twice the price of an ounce of gold! The battle lines were drawn, and the question of whether a priceless resource would be sacrificed for the material gain of a limited few had to be resolved. By extraordinary efforts the Audubon Society was successful, and its position prevailed. In retrospect, the issues seem clear. Should a beautiful part of nature be sacrificed so that ladies could have long, white feathers for their hats? This story has a happy ending: the great egret is doing well, and a few even get to Indiana each year. The millinery industry is still functioning, and ladies' hats are more attractive without the silly-looking, long, white feathers.

The Audubon Society, which has grown to a membership numbering around one-half million members, continues to be in the forefront of the various conservation and environmental struggles. One of the major efforts of the Audubon Society today is to try to discourage the killing of big cats (leopards, jaguars, tigers, et al.) for their fur. A popular slogan that is thought-provoking is, "Real ladies wear fake furs."

Blue-winged Teal

[ANAS DISCORS]

If a survey could be taken to find out why people like to watch birds, I'm sure some surprising answers would be revealed. For some, it's a fun activity combining good exercise and an excuse to enjoy the out-of-doors. I'm sure a surprisingly large number of birders would confess that they like to feel they are contributing, in a scientific way, not only to our knowledge of birds, but also to our knowledge of the environment. Many times seemingly insignificant observations made in different

SIZE: *L. 14–16" (35–40 cm).* COLORING: *Male, brown back and sides, white crescent in face, blue wing patch, whitish patch forward of tail. Female, overall brown with blue wing patch.* HABITAT: *Marshes, shallow ponds, swamps, lakes.* NESTING: *On ground, frequently beside muskrat house; 10–13 eggs.* UNUSUAL MANNERISMS: *Gathers in large numbers, 50–75 birds, in August and September.* IDENTIFYING HINTS: *Common spring and very common fall migrant. Uncommon nesting bird in northernmost part of Indiana.* STATUS IN INDIANA: *Breeds from northern Canada south to the Great Lakes area and south along the Atlantic Coast. Winters in southern states and as far south as South America.*

parts of the country can indicate a change in the status of a bird or show that the environment of an area has been altered.

The blue-winged teal has always been considered to be a duck very sensitive to cold weather. Usually, it is among the last of the ducks to arrive in the spring and is not often seen here until April is well underway. During the month of August, when most ducks are still busy raising their young, the blue-winged teal starts its southward migration. By mid-August, groups of twenty to twenty-five blue-winged teal can be found on many of our reservoirs and ponds; by the end of October, most of them have left the country. Some years, a number of blue-winged teal will be seen a month or so ahead of the normal arrival time, but careful monitoring over a number of years is needed to determine whether the change is permanent or merely temporary.

The blue-winged teal is a rather small duck which prefers small ponds and the marshy edges of the larger bodies of water. In Indiana it can be termed a common bird, both in spring and early fall. It has been known to nest in the northern part of the state.

In the spring the male blue-winged is a dark-looking bird with a crescent-shaped white patch on the face and a white mark at the base of its tail. The female, like many of the female ducks, is a drab brown. In the fall the male is most often seen in its eclipse (darkened) plumage and looks very much like the female. The best field mark, for both the male and female in the spring and fall, is the large blue wing patches that are very much in evidence when the bird is in flight.

While it is true that amateur ornithologists can and have added to our bank of information about birds and our environment, I've found that most birders will find any excuse to pursue their hobby.

SEPTEMBER

IN THE ORNITHOLOGICAL WORLD, Labor Day weekend marks the end of summer and the beginning of the fall season. Gone are the carefree days of July and August. In September there are more birds in Indiana than in any other month. They are not as evident as they are in May, their colors are more subdued, and—for the most part—they are silent, but the facts are that those birds that passed through Indiana in May have returned and brought with them their offspring. Theoretically, there are three times as many birds in Indiana in September as in May.

Migrating ducks have moved in. Warblers and other land birds are everywhere. On a clear, quiet night the migrating hordes can be heard as they pass overhead—thrushes, warblers, shorebirds, and sparrows. When there is a full moon in early September, many of these night migrants can be seen as they pass before the moon's outline. The September migration of the nighthawk in our state is worth noting.

Indiana does not normally have an outstanding shorebird flight, but it is possible, in the right place on the right day, to see fifteen different species of shorebirds in Indiana. Unfortunately, our shorebird numbers pale when compared to the thousands of shorebirds that congregate in favorable sites along coastal areas of the Great Lakes and down the eastern coast of America. Nevertheless, by careful study, most of the shorebirds that are regularly seen east of the Mississippi River can be seen in Indiana during the month of September.

Identifying ducks and warblers in their fall plumage can be challenging, but there is a satisfaction in knowing that after careful thought and close scrutiny, you have correctly named a difficult bird. Roger Tory Peterson once wrote that it takes ten years for the average person to learn fall warblers. I would say this is a conservative estimate. Each September I find that I have to re-learn the fall warblers. A good case in point is differentiating the blackpoll and bay-breasted warblers in

205

their fall plumage, for they look very different from the way they did when they were with us in May; furthermore, neither bird sings here in the fall. Both birds are olive green above and dingy yellow below. Both have white wing-bars. The most reliable field mark separating these two warblers is the color of their legs—the blackpoll has light legs, and the bay-breasted warbler dark legs. Now this sounds simple enough; but trying to ascertain the leg color of a five-inch long, fast-moving bird in a heavily foliaged tree is not easy. In fact, there may be a latent danger in becoming too academic and hence missing the pleasure of enjoying birds for what they are.

Birds mean different things to different people. To some birding is an intellectual pursuit; to others it is a way to relate to nature. Still others find birding an escape from problems of daily living, but almost every-one finds it a stimulating hobby. Whatever your interest, September is the month to see fall warblers and other birds that are intriguing because it is difficult to put the proper "moniker" on them. Don't be unduly concerned if you can't identify them all—just relax and enjoy them!

Northern Phalarope

[PHALAROPUS LOBATUS]

It is always a red-letter day when a phalarope is seen in Indiana, for many persons who have birded here all their lives have not had the thrill of seeing one of these fascinating birds. It is regrettable that phalaropes are so uncommon in Indiana, because they are one of the most intriguing birds. Occasionally a northern phalarope is seen at Eagle Creek Park or Geist Reservoir in Indianapolis, or a number of these small, ocean-loving sandpipers may be reported from Hammond or other areas.

There are three species of phalaropes in the United States, the Wilson's, the northern, and the red. If you have ever taken an ocean voyage, chances are good that sometime during your trip there were phalaropes feeding on the marine insects stirred up by your ship's wake. The

SIZE: *L. 7–8″ (18–20 cm).* COLORING: *Male, breeding plumage, grayish-brown backed, white bellied. Female, gray backed, white bellied, rufous-red on side of neck. Winter plumage, both sexes, gray backed, white fronted, dark legs and beak.* HABITAT: *Mud flats, beaches, open ocean.* NESTING: *A hollow in the ground; 4 eggs.* UNUSUAL MANNERISMS: *Females more colorful than the males. Males assume housekeeping duties as soon as eggs are laid.* IDENTIFYING HINTS: *In flight, prominent white wing stripes. Long, thin bill, dark mark through eyes. Spinning action during feeding.* STATUS IN INDIANA: *Rare spring and fall migrant. Does not nest or winter in Indiana.* RANGE: *Breeds in extreme northern area of North America. Winters in open oceans in the southern hemisphere.*

phalaropes are very much at home on the oceans. In fact, it is suspected that the northern phalarope winters on the oceans of the southern hemisphere, south of the equator. Just imagine a seven-inch-long bird nesting near the Arctic Circle and then spending the winter, far from land, on the open sea.

The phalaropes have a unique way of feeding that is an aid in identification, even from a considerable distance. They sit on the water and spin like little tops; then they quickly shoot out their sharp bills to pick off any insects that have been brought to the water's surface by the spinning action of the phalaropes' bodies.

Shorebirds are not known for their colorful plumage, but phalaropes are among the more colorful of the shorebirds. In the spring the northern phalarope has a chestnut-colored ring across its throat and upper breast. In August and September, when it is most likely to be seen in Indiana, it appears to be a gray-backed, white-fronted bird that shows prominent white wing stripes when in flight.

An unusual characteristic of the phalarope is that the role of the sexes is reversed. The females are more colorful and are the aggressors in the courtship. After the eggs are laid, the females evidently figure that their family responsibilities are over, and it is the males who incubate the eggs and take the major role in raising the young birds. The males seem to be perfectly content with their "stay at home" position, and the females appear to enjoy their freedom from caring for the young birds.

It seems that in the phalaropes' world not only has the Equal Rights Amendment been passed but has been accepted with relish, and that it has worked out to the mutual satisfaction of both the male and female phalaropes.

House Sparrow

[PASSER DOMESTICUS]

The most frequently seen bird in Indiana—and in the United States—is the house sparrow or, as it used to be called, the English sparrow. It is familiar to most people primarily because it is seldom found away from human habitation and seems to enjoy city life especially. In fact, for many city dwellers the house sparrow is the only bird seen on a regular basis. It would be interesting to trace how many people first became interested in birds and the out-of-doors from watching the antics of a house sparrow.

The house sparrow, a native of England, Europe, and Asia, is not really a sparrow but a weaver finch. It has an unusual history in this country. It is said that in the 1850s and 1860s a number of persons who had emigrated from England to America became lonesome for their beloved homeland and decided that if they could import one of the common birds of England it would help them adjust to their new country. The bird they selected they called the "English sparrow."

This bird found America ideally suited to its lifestyle, and within fifty years it had spread from the east to the west coast. During the 1920s it was estimated that there were more house sparrows in America than any other bird. Because of their aggressiveness and determination, they were able to secure the more favorable nesting sites and had displaced a number of our native birds. It was generally agreed that the house sparrow had become a nuisance, and grumbling could be heard that those who had imported the house sparrow should gather them all up and return them whence they came.

In the 1930s and 1940s there were indications that the population explosion of this species had subsided. This welcome change seemed to coincide with the replacement of the horse with motorized vehicles. (When was the last time you saw a horse-drawn wagon?) What was once a source of food for the sparrows—undigested grain from horse droppings—was replaced by a mechanical device—a device that, instead of serving as a food source, was a safety hazard.

Size: *L. 5–6½" (13–16 cm)*. Coloring: *Male has gray coat, chestnut nape, black throat, and white cheek patches. Female and young are dull brown above, dingy white below. Female has indistinct eye stripe.* Habitat: *Farm buildings, cities, and villages.* Nesting: *Loose and bulky mass of grasses, feathers, paper, string, and other debris placed in natural cavity or any cavity; 5–6 eggs.* Unusual Mannerisms: *Very tame. Aggressive in feeding and nesting habits.* Identifying Hints: *Male, black throat. Female, dull brown with whitish eye stripe.* Status in Indiana: *Abundant year-round resident and breeding bird.* Range: *Breeds from middle Canada south to Mexico. Winters throughout its range.*

The house sparrow has been able to adjust to this development very well and is now found in reasonable numbers in all our cities and towns. It can still be a problem bird because of its aggressive nesting instincts; for instance, one summer I had to remove sixteen house sparrow nests from a purple martin house.

The house sparrow has found its niche in America, and—as has historically been the case in America with other immigrants—the furor that once surrounded this immigrant from across the ocean has died down; and it is now being accepted and allowed to blend into our melting pot.

Carolina Wren

[THRYOTHORUS LUDOVICIANUS]

The Carolina wren is our most loyal wren—loyal in that it is the only member of the wren family present in Indiana every month of the year. This hasn't always been true. The Carolina wren historically has been a bird of the South. During the past twenty years, however, the Carolina wren has gradually moved north and is now firmly established in Indiana as a year-round resident. In severe winters it may have some trouble surviving in Indiana; but, ordinarily, the Carolina wren is the most obvious member of the wren tribe and is one of the most vocal birds to be found during all seasons.

I can remember banding a Carolina wren in upstate New York a number of years ago. It was the first record of the Carolina wren's raising young successfully in that part of New York. Even today, the Carolina wren has difficulty making it through the long winter there, but they are becoming more common.

Although it has a number of scolding notes and modifications of its normal song, the wren's common song seems to say, "Teakettle, teakettle, teakettle." Many birds sing only during the breeding season, but the Carolina wren sings even in the dead of winter, and often the "teakettle, teakettle, teakettle" song is the dominant sound in the woods.

SIZE: *L. 5½–6″ (14–16 cm).* COLORING: *Rich chestnut brown above, buff below, prominent white line above eye.* HABITAT: *Thickets, sub-urban gardens, rocky slopes that have good cover.* NESTING: *May nest in natural cavity, old woodpecker hole, or bird house. Bulky nest with side entrance, lined with feathers, moss, and fine grasses; 5–6 eggs.* UNUSUAL MANNERISMS: *Often nests near human habitation—in porches, garages, flower boxes, barns, outbuildings.* IDENTIFYING HINTS: *White line over eye. Voice—a loud persistent calling of "teakettle, teakettle, teakettle."* STATUS IN INDIANA: *Fairly common year-round resident and breeding bird, but extreme winters often decimate its population.* RANGE: *Breeds south of the Great Lakes to the Gulf states, Florida, and southern Mexico. Winters throughout its range.*

The Carolina wren is the largest wren found east of the Mississippi River. It has a reddish-brown back and light brown body. The white stripe over the eye is evident in both the male and female and is the best means of identifying this wren.

One of the intriguing habits of the Carolina wren is a penchant for building its nest in unusual places. Each year seems to bring new examples of the Carolina wren's odd nesting sites—in old tin cans, clothes hanging on a line, inside garages. There is one old record of a successful nesting in a farm tractor that was being used daily. The most recent "fad" seems to be nesting in hanging flower baskets, so popular today.

It seems strange for a bird that is normally shy to abandon this shyness during the breeding season and raise its young so close to human activity. The Carolina seems to have a talent for selecting a place to nest where there are people who will not harm the wren nor disturb its nest.

Gray Catbird

[DUMETELLA CAROLINENSIS]

Even before fall officially arrives, many of the birds that nest in Indiana have left the state. In spite of having lost most of the swallows and flycatchers by early September, there are more birds present at this time than there were in the spring. The reason for this is that the birds that passed through Indiana in April and May plus the birds that nested here have all returned with their young birds hatched in the summer. Theoretically, then, there are three times as many birds here in September as there were in May—two adults plus an average of four young per pair.

Fall birds are much less obvious than spring birds in coloring, in behavior, and in personality. In the spring, the males were in their bright breeding plumage; but when they return in early fall, they are in a much more subdued plumage. This is especially true of many of the warblers and waterfowl.

In the spring, there are mornings when it seems as though each bird is engaged in a singing contest with its neighbor. Not so in the fall! What little song is heard is but a short, soft rendering of the spring song. In the spring, bird song is a necessity, used both to attract a mate and to establish a territory. In the fall, bird song has no practical purpose, and consequently it is normally given listlessly and rather perfunctorily.

The spring birds seem to me to have more energy than they do in the fall. In the spring, they appear never to stop chasing about the trees and shrubs; while in the autumn they seem to be more concerned with staying out of sight, hiding behind leaves or skulking among the tangles.

One bird that should still be very much in evidence in early fall is the gray catbird. The catbird is a common nesting bird throughout the state. It generally arrives during the month of April and by the middle of October is settled for the winter in the more southern states. Sometimes a catbird will attempt to winter in Indiana, but I'm not aware of any that have been successful in surviving all winter.

The gray catbird is an all slate-gray bird except for its dark cap and a deep chestnut area under the tail. Closely related to two outstanding songsters, the mockingbird and the brown thrasher, it is a fine vocalist in its own right. It is the cat-like "meow," usually given from a thicket, that alerts one to the presence of the catbird.

Even in the spring, when many birds seek out a prominent, exposed place to observe their surroundings, the catbird stays hidden in its world of dense tangles and brier patches—almost as if it were trying to say, "Let others have the limelight and acclaim; I'm content with my niche in the world."

SIZE: *L. 8–9¼" (20–23 cm)*. COLORING: *All slate-gray except dark cap, chestnut undertail.* HABITAT: *Thickets, hedgerows, gardens, underbrush at edge of woods.* NESTING: *Bulky nest of twigs and dried weeds, hidden in brush, 3–10' off the ground; 4–5 eggs.* UNUSUAL MANNERISMS: *Delights in hiding in dense cover when giving its cat-like call.* IDENTIFYING HINTS: *Must have good light to see chestnut undertail. Black cap.* STATUS IN INDIANA: *Common spring and fall migrant in Indiana. Common summer nesting bird; rare winterer.* RANGE: *Breeds from southern Canada to southern United States. Winters primarily in southern states south to Panama.*

American Redstart

[SETOPHAGA RUTICILLA]

Come September, there is a new chill in the morning air and the hours of daylight are noticeably shorter as the transition from summer to fall becomes obvious to everyone. One glance at the countryside reveals that the greens of spring are being replaced by the yellows and browns of fall. The cornfields, that but a few months before were a velvet green, are now brown and brittle. Goldenrod confidently furnishes color to the roadside and fields, unaware that, soon, the first frost will spell its demise.

The yellow and brown sunflower blossoms, that seem to strain to lift their heads to catch the morning sun, always remind me of bright-eyed, neatly garbed school children on their way to their first day of school. Monarch butterflies are in the midst of their fantastic migration all the way south to Mexico and can be seen in mid-September, even in the center of cities.

Warblers have often been referred to as the "butterflies of the bird world" because of their bright colors and the insect-like flitting in which some warblers engage. A warbler that is most butterfly-like is the American redstart, a surprisingly common nesting bird throughout Indiana. During the nesting season, it is found along the fringe areas of woods and in the smaller trees that border lakes and streams. In the

SIZE: *L. 4½–5½" (11–14 cm).* COLORING: *Male, black, orange patches on wing and tail, white belly. Female, olive-brown above, white below, yellow wing and tail patches.* HABITAT: *Young deciduous woods, thickets, roadside trees.* NESTING: *Well-made cup of grass, spider webs, lined with grass and hair, usually in the fork of a tree; 4 eggs. Often victimized by parasitic cowbird.* UNUSUAL MANNERISMS: *Both sexes, opening and closing of fan-like tail.* IDENTIFYING HINTS: *Brilliant coloring of male. In fall young birds and females most often seen. Look for yellow patches on wings and tail.* STATUS IN INDIANA: *Common spring and fall migrant, common nester. Does not winter in Indiana.* RANGE: *Breeds from northern Canada to mid-United States. Winters from Mexico to South America.*

fall, while on its journey to Central and South America, the redstart can be found almost anywhere.

I recall with pleasure pointing out to an acquaintance his first male redstart and watching the expression of awe on his face as he savored the beauty of this exquisite creature. The male American redstart is a jet-black bird with a white belly and bright orange patches in the wings and tail. The female is primarily an olive-brown bird with yellow patches in the wing and tail. In the fall, the young birds all resemble the female; consequently, the duller plumaged birds outnumber the males by about four to one.

Both the males and females share the habit of frequently spreading their fan-like tails and exposing, in the case of the male, the bright orange patches and, in the case of the female, the yellow tail patches.

Most of our redstarts and other warblers will leave for the south in September, and the countryside will be less exciting without them. The twinge of sadness that is felt with the departing of the warblers is mitigated by the knowledge that the woods will be brightened, on some fresh spring morning next year, by the return of the redstart.

Osprey

[PANDION HALIAETUS]

Sometime ago, the eagle, the peregrine falcon, and the osprey were put on the President's endangered species list. It was predicted that these three great birds of prey would be eliminated as nesting birds east of the Mississippi River. Fortunately, the increased control of some of the more harmful insecticides has made the prognosis for these and other birds more favorable. The eagle and peregrine falcon populations in the East are still a matter of grave concern, but there are indications that the osprey, at least, is holding its own. It is now possible to see the osprey each year at such places as Muscatatuck National Wildlife Refuge near Seymour; Monroe Reservoir near Bloomington; and Eagle Creek Park in Indianapolis.

The osprey, frequently called the "fish hawk," is a large, eagle-like bird with a wingspan of five feet or more. The white belly and black wrist marks are the most reliable field marks when the bird is flying. When perched, its large size, together with the white head and a dark patch through the eyes, are the best marks.

The osprey's diet is almost exclusively fish. It prefers surface-feeding fish but will, if necessary, dive underwater to secure finny delight. An osprey I recently watched at Eagle Creek was fishing in its normal manner: slowly flying thirty or forty feet above the water, scanning the area for a likely victim, then hovering over the fish before going into a dive. The osprey is superbly equipped for its role of fish hawk with its keen eyesight, long, sharp talons, and maneuverability in flight. Unlike the bald eagle, the osprey shuns carrion and will take a dead fish only under extraordinary conditions.

I am not aware of any successful nest in the state of Indiana, but I have heard of ospreys returning to nest at some of their former nesting sites in the East. This is encouraging. They build a large nest and, if successful, will use the same nest for many years. There have been records of ospreys using the same nest for more than fifty years. Like many of the large birds of prey, the ospreys mate for life. They generally lay three eggs and incubate the clutch for about a month. The young birds are in the nest for approximately two months; then they are on their own. Although some ospreys leave the United States for more tropical climes, the majority winter in our southern coastal states, principally Florida, Texas, Mississippi, and Louisiana.

The best months to see the osprey in Indiana are September, October, April, and May. Ospreys are always near water; so if you are planning a trip to one of Indiana's larger bodies of water on a weekend, you might keep an eye out for this noble bird. It's a sight worth seeing and remembering.

SIZE: *L. 21–24″ (53–61 cm). W. 54–72″ (1.4–1.8 m).* COLORING: *Blackish above, clear white below, white head with broad black patch through cheeks. In flight shows the combination of white belly and black marks at the end of the wing.* HABITAT: *Lakes, rivers, and sea-coasts.* NESTING: *Nest occasionally found on the ground, but most often in trees, utility poles, or man-made structures 40–50′ from the ground. A bulky mass of sticks and debris; 2–4 eggs.* UNUSUAL MANNERISMS: *Hovers over water until suitable fish is spotted; then dives, sometimes even becoming completely submerged.* IDENTIFYING HINTS: *In flight flies with crook in its wings. This, plus white belly and black mark at bend of wings, best field marks.* STATUS IN INDIANA: *Rare spring and fall migrant. Formerly nested in Indiana. Listed on endangered species list.* RANGE: *Breeds from Alaska to the Gulf of Mexico. Winters from the Gulf Coast to Argentina and Chile.*

Common Snipe

[CAPELLA GALLINAGO]

A number of Indiana cities annually conduct a Christmas bird census. One of the more unusual birds seen on the Indianapolis count in recent years was the common snipe. Not that the snipe is rare in Indiana, for it is not; but it is a surprise to find one still located in central Indiana after a sustained·period of cold weather. The snipe must have unfrozen earth in order to find food. The snipe that was found on the Eagle Creek census was seen feeding along the bank in an area that still had flowing water.

Snipes are most frequently found in Indiana during the months of September and October and then again in April and May. Northern Indiana is included in the nesting range of the snipe, and early ornithological literature cites a number of successful nesting records in and around the Lake County area. I'm not aware of any recent nesting of

the snipe in the central part of the state, nor have I heard or seen there any of the antics that the snipe performs during its breeding season.

I'll confess that, to me, there is something lacking in a spring season that passes without hearing the winnowing of a snipe. It is a sound unlike any other sound. It is a surprisingly loud sound with great carrying power. It gives me an uncomfortable feeling to hear this unearthly sound coming from a small speck, high up in the sky. With a little imagination, one can envisage creatures from another planet trying to communicate with earthlings.

The common snipe is a medium-sized brown bird with white striping on the head and back. Its most prominent feature is its long, thin bill which it uses to probe deeply into the earth, searching for its favorite food, earthworms. The woodcock is similarly colored and also has a long bill, but the two birds prefer different habitats. The snipe is seldom found away from mud flats and shorelines, whereas the woodcock spends almost all of its time in a wooded area. Another aid in identifying the common snipe is learning to recognize the sound it makes when flushed. It seems to be saying, "scape" or "escape," as it flies away in a zigzag pattern.

The snipe is still considered a game bird in Indiana, and it is legal to bag up to eight of these birds per day during the hunting season. Somehow, the shooting of this ten-inch bird seems archaic in this day and age.

SIZE: L. 10½–11½" (26–29 cm). COLORING: *Back, brown with white striping, has brown-and-white striped crown. Long bill.* HABITAT: *Marshes, ponds, wet meadows, and fields.* NESTING: *Nests on the ground in dried clump of grass; 4 eggs.* UNUSUAL MANNERISMS: *Spectacular courtship display, both in voice and by aerial maneuverings.* IDENTI-FYING HINTS: *Very long bill, twice as long as the head. When flushed, inevitably gives nasal rasping note.* STATUS IN INDIANA: *Common spring and fall migrant, uncommon breeding bird in northern Indiana. Rare winter visitor.* RANGE: *Breeds from northern Alaska to Great Lakes area. Winters from Great Lakes area south to Gulf of Mexico.*

SIZE: *L. 8–8½" (20–21 cm)*. COLORING: *Male, zebra backed, red cap, red throat. Dull yellow wash on breast, long white wing stripe. Female lacks red throat.* HABITAT: *Both deciduous and coniferous woods. During migration, suburban yards and gardens.* NESTING: *In tree cavity; 5–6 white eggs.* UNUSUAL MANNERISMS: *Often seen boring holes in regular pattern, encircling tree.* IDENTIFYING HINTS: *Vertical right wing stripe. Cat-like "mewing."* STATUS IN INDIANA: *Common spring and fall migrant. Rare breeding bird in Indiana; uncommon winterer.* RANGE: *Breeds from northern Canada to the Great Lakes area of the United States. Winters primarily in the southern states to the Gulf of Mexico.*

Yellow-bellied Sapsucker

[SPHYRAPICUS VARIUS]

If on a Monday morning you told your next-door neighbor that you had an intoxicated sapsucker up in one of your trees over the weekend, I wonder what his reaction would be. Would he alert the vice squad or contact one of the alarm system companies to increase the security of his domain? Perhaps it would be best if you checked first to see if your neighbor is a birder. If he is, he would be happy to hear that the sapsucker has returned.

The yellow-bellied sapsucker is aptly named, for it does have a yellowish-colored belly, and it does indeed have a fondness for sap. In fact, sap is a staple in the sapsucker's diet. The yellow-bellied sapsucker is the only member of the sapsucker tribe found in Indiana and is a common migrant through Indiana in both the spring and fall. It is reputed to nest only in the northwest section of the state and will rarely winter in Indiana.

It is in the spring that the sapsucker is most evident, for in the fall he is a quiet and unobtrusive visitor. In the spring he is anything but quiet and unobtrusive; at this time of the year, the sapsucker becomes very animated and vocal. The most easily recognized call is a cat-like "meow." The yellow-bellied sapsucker has a variety of other sounds that he makes only in the spring. Even his drumming seems to have a quality distinctive from that of the other woodpeckers.

The most reliable field mark is the long, white, vertical stripe on the wing. This white stripe is always present, even on the brownish, immature birds that come through Indiana in the fall. The male sapsucker has a red forehead and throat. The female also has a red forehead, but the throat is white.

The yellow-bellied sapsucker seems to have favorite trees that he works on each year. A close examination of these trees will reveal a series of punctures around the tree where the sapsucker has worked in previous years. Unfortunately, the sapsucker is capable of damaging trees by continuing to open up these holes, which, at times, leaves the trees susceptible to infections. The damage done in Indiana is insignificant, however, because this bird is with us for only a brief two or three weeks each spring and fall.

One of the early nature writers claimed that the sap from some trees in Indiana contains intoxicants and that the sapsuckers tend to be an intemperate group. I don't know if this is true or not, but I rather doubt that it is. It seems to me that if we had trees in Indiana that contained intoxicating sap, our political leaders surely would have found a way, by now, to impose some sort of tax on it!

White-throated Sparrow

[ZONOTRICHIA ALBICOLLIS]

White-crowned Sparrow

[ZONOTRICHIA LEUCOPHRYS]

In fall, two of the more colorful members of the sparrow family make their semiannual pilgrimage through Indiana. Small numbers of both the white-throated sparrows and the white-crowned sparrows will be seen, starting in September, and their numbers will swell until winter sets in.

A few of both species will attempt to winter with us. Just what percentage of these birds survive is unknown. My guess is that the increase of backyard feeding programs has helped the survival percentage of both these sparrows, as well as of other birds that normally winter farther south. Many years ago, it was almost unheard of to find a wintering white-crowned sparrow in the North, but now they are reported each year, sometimes in good numbers.

The *white-throated sparrow* is about one inch larger than the song sparrow, our most common true sparrow. It has an unstreaked breast and a white throat. The head has black and white stripes. Unfortunately, the majority of the white-throats that we see in the fall and winter are immature and are not as clearly marked as the adult birds. The white-throats normally nest north of Indiana, the major nesting grounds being the evergreen belt of southern Canada.

One of the most appealing characteristics of the white-throated sparrow is its song. Put into words, it seems to be plaintively saying, "Poor Sam, Peabody, Peabody, Peabody"—all given in a minor key. Our neighbors to the north claim that they sing, "Oh see, Canada, Canada, Canada." In any event, it is a haunting melody and one that tends to be remembered, once heard.

The *white-crowned sparrow* is also a handsome bird. As its name implies, it has a black-and-white crown. At times, it almost appears as though it has a new chapeau and is wearing it for some special occasion. The white-crowned, like the white-throated sparrow, has an unstreaked breast. Another good field mark of the white-crowned is the pink bill which is prominent in both the adult and immature plumage. It is one of the northernmost nesting birds and nests almost up to the tundra in northern Canada.

The song of the white-crowned sparrow, while it has a beginning like the white-throated's, has an entirely different ending. To me, the ending phrase has the sound of wilderness in it, bringing to mind the beautiful wild areas where it breeds.

Many of the members of the sparrow family are difficult to identify, but that's not the case with the white-throated or the white-crowned sparrows. Today might be a good time to add these two to the list of birds seen in your own backyard.

WHITE-THROATED SPARROW

SIZE: *L. 6–7" (15–17 cm)*. COLORING: *Clear breast, white throat, black-and-white crown, dark bill, brown back.* HABITAT: *Brushy undergrowth, thickets, edges of forests.* NESTING: *On or near the ground, cup-like nest of grasses and moss; 4–5 pale green eggs.* UNUSUAL MANNERISMS: *Often seen in groups of 20–30.* IDENTIFYING HINTS: *Striped crown, prominent white throat. Distinctive, clear, whistled song.* STATUS IN INDIANA: *Common spring and fall migrant; uncommon winterer. Does not nest in Indiana.* RANGE: *Breeds from central Canada south to northernmost United States. Winters primarily from central states south to Gulf of Mexico.*

WHITE-CROWNED SPARROW

SIZE: *L. 6–7½" (15–19 cm)*. COLORING: *Clear breast, pinkish bill, bold black-and-white striping on the crown, brown backed. Immature birds' head striping is buff and dark brown.* HABITAT: *Grassy area with brush cover; often along edges of streams and lakes.* NESTING: *On or near the ground, bulky cup of grasses, moss, bark strips; 3–5 pale green eggs.* UNUSUAL MANNERISMS: *Habitually shows off handsome crown.* IDENTIFYING HINTS: *Pinkish bill, striped crown, clear breast.* STATUS IN INDIANA: *Rather common spring and fall migrant. Does not nest in Indiana; rare winterer.* RANGE: *Breeds from Alaska to northern Canada, as well as to the western mountains of northern New Mexico and California. Winters south from New Jersey to Oregon.*

Size: *L. 10–13" (25–33 cm)*. Coloring: *In spring, black belly, black-and-white patterned back. In fall, gray above and whitish below, lacking the black belly.* Habitat: *Beaches, coastal marshes, plowed fields.* Nesting: *Nests in hollow in the ground lined with mosses; 3–4 eggs.* Unusual Mannerisms: *Very wary.* Identifying Hints: *Largest of the plover family. In flight shows black patch under the wings and white rump. Plaintive, whistled call, "pee-o-wee."* Status in Indiana: *Uncommon spring and fall migrant. Does not nest in Indiana.* Range: *Breeds in Arctic. Winters along the Atlantic coast from North Carolina south to northern South America.*

Black-bellied Plover

[PLUVIALIS SQUATAROLA]

Shorebirds have always offered a special appeal to the serious birder. They are a group of birds that you won't find in your backyard; they are birds that you have to seek out—that you have to make a special effort to see. They won't come to your feeder.

Identification of shorebirds is difficult, but not impossible. There are about twenty-five different species of shorebirds to be seen in Indiana. It ordinarily takes at least five years before a new birder feels relatively comfortable in identifying the local shorebirds.

I've tried to fathom the reason that birders evolve into devotees of shorebirds. I suspect that part of the appeal of shorebirds is their mysterious ways. Except for the killdeer and spotted sandpiper, they are with us just briefly; then they leave to fulfill their destinies. They are always associated with water. Water and things related to water have always fascinated man. One has only to visit a lake, reservoir, or beach to see evidence of this.

One of the most appealing members of the shorebird fraternity, the black-bellied plover is occasionally seen in Indiana. In fact, these colorful shorebirds are sometimes seen at the Indianapolis sewage treatment plant, for many years the best local place to view shorebirds in late summer. In early fall the plover is often still in its gaudy, spring plumage—gray above, with black belly, chest, and throat.

In flight the black mark under the wing is a good field mark. A little later in the year, the black-bellied plover will lose its dark underparts. In this plumage it can be confused with a couple of other shorebirds, but if the bird can be flushed, a glimpse of the white rump and tail, together with the black mark under the wings, will eliminate the possibility of its being any other bird.

The black-bellied plover nests in the Arctic and passes through Indiana in the spring and again in the months of August and September.

About the turn of the century, it was considered a most prized game bird, and thousands of these beautiful shorebirds were killed each spring and fall during their migration. So many were killed that their population was greatly reduced, and there was grave concern that the black-bellied plover would join the ranks of other birds that man has eliminated. Fortunately, the Migratory Bird Treaties, signed into law in the early 1900s, stopped the senseless slaughter of these and other shorebirds.

The black-bellied plover has made a fine comeback, and once again graces our landscapes with its presence. A trip to the sewage treatment plant may not appeal to many persons, but if a birder wants to see black-bellied plover, this location offers a likely prospect for finding it.

OCTOBER

IF A SURVEY WERE TAKEN to determine the Hoosiers' favorite month, I would venture to guess that October would win, hands down. The trees are in full color, and many of them are already dropping their leaves, forming quilts of gold and crimson on the ground. The skies are a special shade of blue. The first killing frost is in the air. Nights are refreshingly cool. Some of the birds that have been present all summer know that the time to leave Indiana is now at hand. The wood thrushes, indigo buntings, cuckoos, orioles, and the tanagers seem to know that, if they don't hasten, they are doomed. Already, most of their compatriots are no longer to be found in the north. Gone are most of the warblers, swallows, and flycatchers.

Most of the woodpeckers have decided that they can withstand the rigors of the coming season. The song sparrow will stay north, as will the chickadee and the white-breasted nuthatch. The cardinal, mocking-bird, and Carolina wren decided years ago that Indiana is a suitable place to winter. It is strange that these southern birds have survived the cold temperatures here so successfully, although there is evidence that many perish during a long, severely cold winter.

There are still quite a number of birds that haven't quite made up their minds as to whether to move south or to take a chance on the vicissitudes of Indiana weather. The great blue heron, killdeer, king-fisher, towhee, brown thrasher, and the meadowlark still vacillate in their decision. A good percentage of these birds will eventually decide to stay for the winter. If the winter proves to be mild, a fair portion of these hardy birds will survive; if the winter weather is extreme, they will not.

Sharp-shinned Hawk

[ACCIPITER STRIATUS]

Some birds always seem to generate excitement whenever they are near. The mere presence of a sharp-shinned hawk will liven up an entire woods. The first indication of a sharp-shinned in the area is usually an alarm or distress call from the other birds; for they always seem to be on the lookout for the sharp-shinned hawk. Well they may be, because its main diet is other birds! When the "sharpie" is serious about pursuing another bird, it is the epitome of unleashed fury. It will often attack a bird larger than itself.

The sharpie is well equipped for its role in nature with its razor-sharp talons, sharply hooked beak, and a long, streamlined tail that allows it to maneuver precisely, even in heavily wooded areas. It has a single-minded dedication to purpose that gives it an advantage over its intended victim. I recall once watching a starling eating suet at my feeding station, when a sharp-shinned dashed in and killed the starling before it could even attempt to get away. The whole drama took place

SIZE: *L. 10–14" (25–35 cm). W. 21" (0.5 m).* COLORING: *Adults, bluish back, cinnamon fronted. Immatures, brown backed with heavily streaked breasts.* HABITAT: *Prefers substantial stands of coniferous woods.* NESTING: *Well-made nest, usually placed in an evergreen tree; 4–5 eggs.* UNUSUAL MANNERISMS: *Extremely aggressive and persistent in pursuing its prey, mostly small birds and rodents. In migration seen annually in large numbers at various hawk-watching places in the United States.* IDENTIFYING HINTS: *Accipiter flight (several quick wingbeats, followed by a sail).* STATUS IN INDIANA: *Uncommon migrant in spring and fall; also, uncommon as winter resident. Decreasing as nesting bird, but may occasionally nest in Indiana.* RANGE: *Breeds from Alaska to northern Mexico and east to South Carolina. Winters in the southern part of its range.*

in a few seconds, not ten feet from where I was standing. Normally, the sharp-shinned is leery of getting too close to man, but when hungry, will disregard any other factors to satisfy its hunger.

The sharp-shinned hawk, one of the smaller birds of prey, is not much bigger than a kestrel or a grackle. The adult is blue backed and has a chestnut-colored, streaked breast. Immature birds are brown backed, with light-colored breasts streaked with brown. As with all of the hawks, the females are larger than the males. A help in identifying the sharp-shinned is its manner of flying, giving three or four quick wing beats, then a short sail. This flight pattern will establish that you are seeing an accipiter. Accipiters are short-winged, long-tailed, woodland hawks. There are three species of hawks of the accipiter type in Indiana—the goshawk, the Cooper's hawk, and the sharp-shinned. The sharp-shinned is the most common and the smallest of the accipiters; so if you see a hawk-like bird flying as described, the odds are good that you are seeing a sharp-shinned.

The sharp-shinned is most often seen in Indiana during the months of March, April, and May, and then again in September and October. It will occasionally winter here. Early literature lists the sharp-shinned as a fairly common nesting bird within the state, but this is certainly not true today. The sharp-shinned, like its larger relative, the Cooper's hawk, has greatly decreased as a nesting bird east of the Mississippi River.

Unfortunately, Indiana does not have the conditions necessary to produce great hawk flights. Hawk watching has become a popular pastime for many. In fact, thousands of birders anxiously await, each year, the right conditions for a good hawk flight. The dramatic spring and fall flights of the sharp-shinned are well worth a special trip made to such places as Duluth, Minnesota; Cape May, New Jersey; Hawk Mountain, Pennsylvania; upstate New York; or Point Pelee, Canada. All have great annual flights of sharpies and other birds of prey. Witnessing one of these great spectaculars is an impressive experience.

Tufted Titmouse

[PARUS BICOLOR]

October is an ideal time to start a winter's program of bird feeding in Indiana. A mesh bag filled with suet and a dispenser of some sort for sunflower seeds are really all that is needed for a basic program. One of the birds that you are almost sure to attract is the tufted titmouse.

Although the tufted titmouse is a year-round resident of Indiana, it is during the colder months that it is most in evidence. Indiana is close to the northern limits of the tufted titmouse's breeding range. It is one of a group of southern birds that has been gradually expanding its range northward. It is now firmly established in Indiana as a year-round resident and will readily come to a backyard winter's feeding station.

I guess I especially enjoy the tufted titmouse because in my hometown in upstate New York this perky little bird was seldom seen. I clearly recall the first time I heard an unfamiliar "peter, peter, peter!" call one spring morning. After a long search I found I had tracked down a tufted titmouse.

During the breeding season, this bird becomes shy and secretive and is much less likely to be seen around suburban yards. Its favorite nesting site is in a natural tree cavity. The titmouse is not capable of drilling into a tree to make its own cavity, so it is dependent upon finding a natural hole or one that has been excavated by one of the woodpeckers. It is surprising how many animals and birds depend upon cavities in dead trees both for nesting sites during the summer and for shelter during the winter.

The female tufted titmouse is identical to the male—gray-backed and white-breasted, with a wash of chestnut down each side. As its name implies, it has a prominent crest, but it can hardly be confused with our other crested birds, the blue jay, cardinal, cedar waxwing, or kingfisher.

The titmouse, like so many of our wintering birds, is very fond of sunflower seeds. Wouldn't this fall be a good time to get started on a bird feeding program? I'm sure one of your first customers will be a tufted titmouse.

SIZE: *L. 6–6½" (15–16 cm)*. COLORING: *Gray above, white below, pale rust-colored sides, gray crest.* HABITAT: *Moist woodlands, orchards, suburban shade trees.* NESTING: *Tree cavity or man-made box, abandoned woodpecker hole; 5–6 eggs.* UNUSUAL MANNERISMS: *Regularly partakes of sunflower seeds at feeding station.* IDENTIFYING HINTS: *Oft-repeated "peter, peter, peter" call. Crest and pale rust-colored sides.* STATUS IN INDIANA: *Common year-round resident and nesting bird, especially in the southern half of state.* RANGE: *Breeds south of Great Lakes to the Gulf of Mexico. Winters throughout its range.*

Black-throated Green Warbler

[DENDROICA VIRENS]

In the fall of each year a number of birds are killed as they migrate southward. Most of the birds that are killed are night migrants that become confused by city lights. Lighthouses, television towers, and tall buildings are especially hazardous to the birds that travel at night.

For many years, on some fall mornings, the sidewalks around the Empire State Building were littered with the bodies of dead birds that had hit the skyscraper during the night. The management of the building was prevailed upon to alter the lights on the building during the height of the fall migration, and the change greatly reduced the number of birds killed each year in this section of New York City.

No such major hazard exists in Indiana, to my knowledge; but each year a number of birds are killed here during their fall migration. One year in just a week's time, for instance, I heard of the following birds that were found in places where they would not ordinarily be found: an ovenbird by the Indianapolis Star-News Building, a bay-breasted warbler in front of the Ramada Inn at 16th and Meridian Streets, a Swainson's thrush on Monument Circle, a black-throated green warbler near the L. S. Ayres store on Washington Street, and a very confused least bittern with a broken wing at the Indiana University Medical Center on West Michigan Street. The least bittern convalesced at the Nature Center in Eagle Creek Park.

One of the more common migrating birds in Indiana is the black-throated green warbler. It can be expected here during the months of April and May and September and October, and like so many of our warblers, it winters outside the United States in Mexico and Central America. The male black-throated green warbler, as its name indicates, is a greenish bird with a black throat and bright yellow face patch. The females and young lack the black throat.

The voice of the black-throated green is one of the easiest of the warbler songs to learn. It is a rather low-pitched, minor-keyed "zoo-

SIZE: L. 4½–5¼″ (11–13 cm). COLORING: *Upper parts olive green, throat and sides of breast black, face yellow. Female similar but duller. In fall, females and young lack the black throat.* HABITAT: *Coniferous and mixed forests.* NESTING: *Cup of grass, moss, and plant fibers, lined with hair and feathers, most often placed in branch of conifer; 4–5 eggs.* UNUSUAL MANNERISMS: *Often found in suburban backyards. Surprisingly common visitor.* IDENTIFYING HINTS: *Black throat, yellow cheek patch, song—a buzzy "zoo-zoo-sue-see."* STATUS IN INDIANA: *Common spring and fall migrant, rare summer resident. Does not winter in Indiana.* RANGE: *Breeds from central Canada south to Great Lakes area. Winters southern United States south to South America.*

zoo-sue-see"; unfortunately, however, it doesn't sing in the fall. It does give a rather harsh "chip" sound that is somewhat different from the "chip" given by many of the other warblers.

The same day that I found a dead black-throated green warbler I watched a live one on the grounds of the Indianapolis Museum of Art. It was hard to believe that the two birds were of the same species.

I don't think that it is possible to gain an appreciation of birds by looking at pictures or seeing birds in a zoo or museum. They must be seen in their own environment—seen alive and animated, seen when they are hard at work, fulfilling their places in a complex world.

Pied-billed Grebe

[PODILYMBUS PODICEPS]

Grebes are duck-like birds especially well known for their diving abilities. The most common grebe in Indiana, and the only one that nests here, is the pied-billed grebe.

Although it is possible to see pied-billeds at any time of the year, it is during spring and fall that they are most evident. In the spring and fall the pied-billed can be readily found on most of our larger bodies of water and often even on small ponds and bogs.

During the most severe winter weather, when there is danger of the reservoirs and ponds freezing over, the pied-billed retreats south to find open water. As soon as this danger is past, the pied-billed returns.

It prefers to nest in ponds and marshes that have some open water and plenty of cattails and other aquatic plants. Four to eight eggs comprise the normal clutch, and immediately after the eggs hatch, the chicks are able to swim and dive and pretty much take care of themselves. How much easier it would be to raise a family if this were true of the human race!

The pied-billed, like the other members of the grebe family, has a marvelous diving ability; and when danger is imminent, it uses this talent,

rather than flying, to avoid trouble. Not only are grebes known for their diving abilities, but they are the only birds I know of that can slowly sink until they disappear under the water.

My son, Scott, and I were watching a pied-billed last year and making mental notes of how long it could stay submerged. The bird we were watching seemed to disappear completely, and, search as we would, we were unable to find that bird again.

When we got home that afternoon, I reread some of the literature on the pied-billed and found that this is a common defense ploy. The bird will submerge until only the tip of the bill is above water and then slowly swim until it feels that it is safe to surface again.

To identify the pied-billed grebe, look for a small, dark, almost tailless bird with a stubby bill. In the fall, the white area around the tail is a help in identifying this bird when it is swiming away from you. In the spring, look for the black throat patch and black ring around the bill.

One of the bonuses one receives from being a birder is having an excuse to be outside on a lovely fall day. A morning spent watching the antics of a pied-billed grebe, with the warm sun on your back and surrounded by the colorful foliage, is sure to stay in your memory long after most morning memories have faded.

SIZE: *L. 12–15" (30–38 cm).* COLORING: *Brown. In spring shows black neck patch and black around the bill. Winter plumage shows white neck patch.* HABITAT: *Marshes, ponds, and lakes.* NESTING: *Nest a floating mass of marsh vegetation fastened to water plants, often well concealed; 5–8 eggs.* UNUSUAL MANNERISMS: *Often sinks, rather than dives, into the water. Female covers nest when not incubating eggs.* IDENTIFYING HINTS: *White patch under tail and small size are good identifying marks from distance.* STATUS IN INDIANA: *Common spring and fall migrant. Breeds in northern part of Indiana. Winters in Indiana in small numbers where there is unfrozen water.* RANGE: *Breeds from northern Canada south to Florida. Winters as far north as there is unfrozen water and south to Argentina.*

RUBY-CROWNED KINGLET

SIZE: *L. 3¾–4½" (9–11 cm)*. COLORING: *Olive-gray above, with lighter gray front, white wing-bars, white eye-ring. Male's ruby crown seldom revealed.* HABITAT: *Coniferous forests; in winter can be found also in deciduous forests and thickets.* NESTING: *High above the ground, often in spruce, deep cup of mosses, small twigs, and plants, lined with fur and feathers. Very similar to golden-crowned's nest; 7–9 eggs.* UNUSUAL MANNERISMS: *Both kinglets have the habit of nervously flitting their wings almost continuously.* IDENTIFYING HINTS: *More often found in lower shrubbery. White eye-ring with unmarked head, most important field mark. In the spring has a surprisingly long, complicated, and penetrating song, especially for so small a bird.* STATUS IN INDIANA: *Common spring and fall migrant. Uncommon winter resident. Does not nest here.* RANGE: *Breeds from Alaska to southern Canada. Winters in small numbers in northern United States and in greater numbers in the southern states south to Central America.*

GOLDEN-CROWNED KINGLET

SIZE: *L. 3½–4" (9–10 cm)*. COLORING: *Olive-green above, with two white wing-bars. White line over eye. Males have orange crown bordered with yellow; females have a yellow crown.* HABITAT: *Coniferous forest; in winter can be found also in deciduous forests and thickets.* NESTING: *Nest often found high up in conifer, a hanging mass of moss open at the top; 8–9 eggs.* UNUSUAL MANNERISMS: *When here in the winter are among our busiest birds, seldom sitting still.* IDENTIFYING HINTS: *Once learned, the high, thin "see-see-see" call reveals this bird as surprisingly common. Prominent white eye stripe separates this species from the ruby-crowned. Next to the hummingbird, it is our smallest bird.* STATUS IN INDIANA: *Common winter resident from October to May. Does not nest here.* RANGE: *Breeds from central Canada to the Great Lakes area. Winters south United States as far as the Gulf of Mexico.*

Golden-crowned Kinglet

[REGULUS SATRAPA]

Ruby-crowned Kinglet

[REGULUS CALENDULA]

It is always surprising to me that so many people are unfamiliar with the kinglets. They are among the most numerous of birds that pass through Indiana; yet, while most persons have seen flocks of robins and blackbirds, few Hoosiers are aware of the huge numbers of kinglets that migrate through Indiana. It may be that their small size—only slightly larger than a hummingbird—is a factor in their going unnoticed; or maybe their unobtrusive ways lead to the kinglets' being unrecognized. In the spring and fall months, both the golden-crowned kinglet and the ruby-crowned kinglet can be found in virtually every woods and in most backyards in the state.

The *golden-crowned kinglet* is a tiny bird, about four inches long. Its back is greenish gray, and the breast is off-white. The best identifying mark is the white stripe over the eye. The female has a beautiful yellow crown. The male's yellow crown has an orange stripe running through the center. The golden-crowned does not normally nest in Indiana. It arrives here in October and leaves in April. It is seldom seen standing still and is usually associated with evergreen trees. In this environment it is generally busy feeding on the very small insects that seem to be ever present. Cold weather doesn't appear to bother the golden-crowneds at all, and even when the temperature gets down to the zero mark, I've seen these tiny mites happily pursuing their lifelong tasks.

The other member of the kinglet family seen in Indiana is the *ruby-crowned kinglet*. It, also, is colored greenish-gray above, with a light breast. The best field marks of the ruby-crowned are its white eye ring and the lack of color on the head. The red top, whence it got its name, is present only in the male, and is seldom seen. The ruby-crowned is here in the fall and again in the spring. Rarely will it winter in Indiana. Its song is outstanding and is surprisingly long for so small a bird. The song has been described as "the most song for the least bird." Words are inadequate, for it must be heard to be appreciated.

The ruby-crowned tends to feed lower than the golden-crowned and is not as restricted to evergreens as its compeer. Both the kinglets are quite tame and, if approached slowly and quietly, will continue their diligent endeavors, allowing you to observe them at close range.

It seems to me to be a commentary on our times and ways that some of the more obvious birds receive so much attention, while the kinglets go unheralded—rather like the non-productive, non-contributing people of the world who grab headlines, while those who do the work of the world and contribute to our society go largely unrecognized.

Vive les kinglets!

Canada Goose

[BRANTA CANADENSIS]

Along with our first killing frost and cold weather, we can expect to start seeing migrating Canada geese. The familiar V-shaped flying formation of these large birds is known to most everyone. Even people not interested in birds enjoy seeing these majestic geese as they make their way from their northern breeding grounds to their winter quarters in the southern parts of the United States.

Studies have shown that strong, healthy males generally are the lead birds in these V-formations, for it requires greater strength and abilities to be a windbreaker for the rest of the flock and to direct the flock on the best route south. The sight of these great birds, on a brisk October morning, can change an ordinary, mundane day into a day

SIZE: *L. 25–43" (63–107 cm). W. 50–68" (1.3–1.7 m).* COLORING: *Brown body, black head and neck, white cheek patch.* HABITAT: *Marshes, grassy fields, lakes, rivers. Often feeds in open grassland.* NESTING: *Large nest, usually on a grassy mound on the ground near water; 5–6 eggs.* UNUSUAL MANNERISMS: *Reputed to mate for life. Male staunch defender of nesting area. Birds often fly in "V" formation.*

filled with enthusiasm and excitement. How often have you heard a neighbor or co-worker say, "Winter must be on the way. I saw a flock of geese this morning!"

The status of Canada geese has changed, not only in Indiana, but also in most of our neighboring states. At one time, nesting Canada geese were almost unheard of, except in the northern areas of our most northern states. This is no longer true. In Eagle Creek Park, alone, at least six pairs of these geese successfully raised young in 1977. I suspect that the geese that are nesting in Indiana now are birds that are offspring of geese that, at one time, were part of a planned stocking program and thus are somewhat domesticated. Their behavior is different from the true wild geese: they don't seem to be as alert or as wary of man as the geese that nest in the far north.

Indiana has a generous supply of these fine birds, both as migrating birds in the fall and early spring and as nesting birds. A few winter here each year as long as they can find open water.

Next to the swan, the Canada goose, having a five-foot wingspan and weighing up to twelve pounds, is our largest waterfowl. It is a gray bird with a light-colored breast. The neck and head are black with a white patch that extends from the ear down around the throat. Often, these geese are heard before they are seen, and the well-known honking is the reason for their nickname, "the honkers."

The Canada goose has many qualities admired by man—strength, wariness, majestic bearing, fidelity (they mate for life, and some say that, if one of a pair is killed, the other will remain unmated), and tenacity (the male will defend the female and her brood at all costs). There have been many recorded instances of the male's giving his life in an attempt to protect the female and her chicks. So if some morning you see and hear a gaggle of geese, you might wish them a safe journey.

IDENTIFYING HINTS: *White neck and cheek patch on dark head. Honking calls are often heard before birds are seen.* STATUS IN INDIANA: *Fairly common nesting bird. Passes through Indiana in spring and fall in huge numbers. Will winter when there is open water. Occasionally become quite tame when fed by humans on a regular basis.* RANGE: *Breeds from Arctic Coast to North Carolina. Winters in Florida, Gulf Coast, and northern Mexico.*

Size: *L. 37–48" (93–122 cm). W. 80" (2 m).* Coloring: *Gray, with red forehead. Immatures, brown.* Habitat: *Freshwater marshes, prairie ponds.* Nesting: *Usually in an undisturbed marsh; 2 eggs.* Unusual Mannerisms: *Loud voice, having great carrying power.* Identifying Hints: *Huge size (one of our largest birds). Cross-like silhouette in flight.* Status in Indiana: *Largest gathering of this species found east of the Mississippi at Jasper-Pulaski State Fish and Wildlife area October to November, March to April.* Range: *Breeds in Siberia, Alaska, and scattered groups in Michigan, Minnesota. Winters in Texas, California, and Mexico.*

Sandhill Crane

[GRUS CANADENSIS]

If urged to express an opinion as to what the most outstanding ornithological happening in Indiana is, I would have to vote for the spring and fall gathering of sandhill cranes at Jasper-Pulaski State Fish and Wildlife Area. The sandhill crane is a close relative of the famed whooping crane, which has been studied so closely for the past twenty years. In spite of having received a great deal of assistance from the various fish and game agencies, the total population of the whooping crane is still under one hundred birds. When a bird that migrates great distances has such a small population, the prognosis for its ultimate survival is not good.

In contrast to the dismal outlook for the whooping crane, the sandhill cranes at Jasper-Pulaski seem to be flourishing. The third week of October 1977, for instance, a count of more than six thousand of these huge birds was obtained. This makes Jasper-Pulaski State Fish and Wildlife Area the site of the largest assemblage of sandhills east of the Mississippi River.

People come to the Jasper-Pulaski Area from great distances to add the sandhill crane to their life list. October is a fine time to see this awesome sight. The area is approximately one hundred miles northwest of Indianapolis. The most direct route from Indianapolis is to drive Interstate 65 north to Lafayette, then north on U.S. 421 to Medaryville. Signs will direct you from there to the refuge office.

As a rule, the sandhill does not put down in other parts of Indiana, although a few are occasionally sighted in places other than the Jasper area. A few are usually seen each year at Geist Reservoir and Eagle Creek Park, to mention two places. I've heard them calling, in past years, as they fly high above my home on their way to their wintering grounds on the Gulf Coast.

The sandhill is one of our largest birds; it stands up to four feet tall. Primarily gray in color except for its red forehead, the sandhill can be confused with few other birds. In flight it holds its head, neck, and legs fully extended. One of the field guides makes reference to the crane's flight silhouette as a "flying cross."

The sandhill's voice is truly remarkable and is one of the impressive sounds of nature—a loud, guttural trumpeting that has great carrying power. Many times a person will hear the call long before the bird is seen. It is a call that always conjures up visions of prehistoric times and images of what our land was like before man became the dominating force in our environment.

From all indications, the wonders of Brown County are viewed by many thousands of Hoosiers each year; but a trip northwest to the Jasper-Pulaski State Fish and Wildlife Area will provide you with a sight that is not duplicated anywhere east of the Mississippi. I'm sure the sight of these great birds, the sandhill cranes, will stay in your memory long after the beautifully colored foliage of Brown County has disappeared.

American Wigeon

[ANAS AMERICANA]

Ducks can be lumped into two major categories, the divers and the dabblers. The divers gather their food by diving beneath the surface of the water, and the dabblers feed by tipping just their heads beneath the water's surface.

One of the most attractive members of the dabbler group is the American wigeon, referred to in most bird books as the baldpate. In Indiana, the American wigeon is most often found in the spring and fall.

This bird winters in the southern states, and its normal breeding area is northwest of Indiana in Colorado, Nebraska, the Dakotas, and north to the Hudson Bay. Usually it is seen in small flocks of six to ten birds, and it often associates with some of the diving ducks.

SIZE: *L. 16–21" (40–53 cm). W. 34" (85 cm).* COLORING: *Male, white crown, chestnut body, black tail.* HABITAT: *Ponds, lakes, reservoirs, streams.* NESTING: *On the ground, sometimes away from water; 8–15 whitish eggs.* UNUSUAL MANNERISMS: *A dabbler (feeds by tipping).* IDENTIFYING HINTS: *Large, white patches on front part of wing.* STATUS IN INDIANA: *Migrant only. Most common from October to November, March to April.* RANGE: *Nests in western states. Winters primarily in southern states.*

The wigeon has acquired a taste for certain aquatic plants found in deep water and has learned that, by watching carefully when a diving duck surfaces, it is able to steal this material from the diver. Hence, one of its nicknames is "the poacher."

In return for this unearned meal, the wigeon often performs the valuable service of warning the other ducks when danger is imminent. Its nature is to be alert and skittish whenever an animal or person moves too close to the flock, and it is usually the wigeon that first gives the alarm call and takes to the air, much to the chagrin of the duck hunter!

A group of us watched some American wigeons feeding with a large flock of coots one day; and while the coots were busily feeding, largely unconcerned with our presence, the wigeons watched us closely. When we tried to get too close, the wigeons were the first to fly.

The male American wigeon in breeding plumage is one of our most handsome ducks. The body is a blend of soft browns, while the rump area is white with a black tail. The crown of the head is white (thus the reason for its nickname, "baldpate"), and the face has a green patch that extends from the eye to the back of the head. In flight the wigeon shows large, white shoulder patches which can be seen from a considerable distance.

There was a time when it was feared that this beautiful duck would join the ranks of other birds that man has caused to become extinct. This is no longer a problem; for with the elimination of spring duck hunting and more stringent hunting regulations, the wigeon has made a fine comeback.

Pine Siskin

[SPINUS PINUS]

If you are a birder, each season and each year offer a special challenge. As late fall approaches, an annual question is, "Will this year be a winter finch year?" The non-birder may ask the question, "What is a 'winter finch,' and why are they present some winters and not others?"

First, "winter finch" is a loose term encompassing a number of different species of birds. Basically, the following species are involved: pine siskin, red crossbill, white-winged crossbill, redpoll, evening grosbeak, and pine grosbeak. The prevailing theory is that when the food of the winter finches is scarce in Canada and Alaska, these birds move south in search of pine cones and various other seeds and berries that make up the bulk of their diet. Most of their food crops are cyclic; therefore, there are years when virtually no winter finches get as far south as Indiana.

Some years, reliable reports of winter finches in central Indiana are almost non-existent, as in 1976-77—although the previous year was a fair year, marked by numerous reports of good-sized flocks of evening grosbeaks from Lake County to southern Indiana. Occasionally, the crossbills, both red and white-winged, are found throughout the state. When red-breasted nuthatches come down early and in good numbers and purple finches make a showing, this report usually signals a winter finch year. Perhaps the best sign of all would be sightings of pine siskin before the first of November.

The pine siskin is a sparrow-sized bird that often associates with goldfinches. It can be separated from the winter plumage of the goldfinch by the heavy streaking on the breast which the goldfinch lacks. In flight the siskin often gives a characteristic flight song that is unique among birds—a loud, buzzing "z-i-i-i-p." When the pine siskins are here in any number, as they are some years, they will patronize a thistle feeder. Look for a heavily streaked bird with a splash of yellow in the wings and tail, possibly feeding with goldfinches.

SIZE: *L. 4½–5″ (11–13 cm).* COLORING: *Heavily streaked brown bird, with some yellow in wings and tail.* HABITAT: *Coniferous woods and mixed woods.* NESTING: *Shallow, saucer-shaped nest, about 20′ off the ground; usually 3–4 eggs.* UNUSUAL MANNERISMS: *Rather tame. A winter finch, makes erratic appearances in colder months.* IDENTIFYING HINTS: *Undulating flight. Voice, buzzy "z-i-i-i-p." Heavy streaking on the breast.* STATUS IN INDIANA: *Erratic winter visitor in fall, winter, and spring. Normally nests north of Indiana. First Indiana nesting record, 1978.* RANGE: *Breeds from Alaska to northernmost United States. Winters erratically all the way south to Gulf states.*

The normal breeding grounds for the siskin are in the evergreen forests of Canada. In the years that they migrate south to Indiana, they will stay from November until May. During the winter of 1975-76, more than two hundred pine siskins were banded by Charles and Tim Keller, federally licensed birdbanders working on the Indianapolis Museum of Art grounds. It is always interesting to see if any of the banded birds return in following years.

It is amazing to me to find how often a banded bird or a bird with an unusual marking or some special physical characteristic will return to a particular feeding station, a particular woods, or even a particular tree year after year. The odds against this happening at random are astronomical! It is almost as if some birds are on a huge rubber band, and each year the rubber band is stretched thousands of miles. Then, at a given signal, the rubber band is released, and the birds return to their original taking-off place.

NOVEMBER

THE ALMANAC MAY PROCLAIM that the end of the year is the last day of December, but the migrating birds give evidence that the last day of October ends their year in Indiana. Gone are the swallows, gone are the cuckoos. Most of the warblers, with the exception of a few yellow-rumps and yellowthroats, have moved to their winter home. The flycatchers have all left, except for a few phoebes. The vireos can no longer be seen in the Hoosier state. The tanagers and orioles are well on their way to the tropics. The calls of the house wrens and indigo buntings can no longer be heard here.

For those who love birds, there is a strong temptation to follow these lovely creatures to their winter homes; this would be not only a mistake but also a disappointment. A mistake because November will offer a new vista of birds in Indiana, a disappointment because the birds that have moved south will have changed personalities. Many will have put off their brightly colored garb and will have assumed a more modest and subdued behavior. For the most part, they will be silent, or nearly so. Gone will be much of the exuberance that is brought about by the instinct to procreate. I don't mean to imply that the southern states are devoid of exciting bird life, for this is certainly not true, as anyone who has viewed the nesting of the wood ibis and roseate spoonbills or the huge gatherings of shorebirds off the coast of the Carolinas, Texas, and Louisiana can attest. The South can lay claim to some wonderful ornithological happenings. And it is true, perhaps, that my view is prejudiced from many years' experience with birds of the northern states; but a black-throated green warbler flitting in a palm tree or an indigo bunting languishing in a palmetto appear strangely out of place—just as a magnificent frigate bird circling lazily over Lake Michigan or a laughing gull cackling and swimming on one of Indiana's reservoirs would seem absurd.

Granted, it is fun to travel and see the different birds that can be

258

found away from home. But naturalist John Burroughs cautioned that when one travels to see the birds of California or Florida, one goes as a visitor or formal traveler. The real personalities of the birds you have come far to see will not be apparent in a brief visit. He advised, further, that the place to observe nature is where you are—that the best place to observe birds today is the same place where you studied them yesterday.

November is the month when the "door" of winter is first opened, starting with the door slightly ajar in the first few days of the month and ending with the door open wide by the thirtieth of November. True, there are a greater number of birds that have departed Indiana than arrived, but those which do settle in preparation for a winter's term are as welcome as the first warblers which will arrive the following May.

The junco, now called the "dark-eyed junco," will make its appearance by the first week in November, soon to be followed by the tree sparrow. Sometime during the month, the diving ducks will move in, and many of them will stay here as long as there is open (unfrozen) water—the goldeneye, the lesser scaup, the canvasback, the bufflehead, and the redhead. All these can be seen in Indiana from November to April, usually (but not always) on the larger bodies of water. I'm always surprised to see these depth-loving birds swimming on the small, artificial lakes and ponds that are now so much a part of the landscaping plans for apartments and housing developments.

The end of November will "tell the tale" as to whether or not this will be the year for a winter finch invasion. Just as it is true that no two snowflakes, people, or days are exactly alike, so it is true that there are no two years identical with the appearance of winter finches in Indiana. Occasionally there will be a great invasion of these northern, seed-eating birds here, with the evening grosbeaks, pine siskin, red and white-winged crossbills, and redpolls arriving in good numbers and staying for the winter. The next year, maybe, an "echo" flight may occur, that is, the finches will be here only briefly, and in small numbers. The following year, perhaps, just one or two of these winter visitors will be present. Unfortunately, there are other years when few, or even none, of these interesting birds will get to Indiana, and then only a few lucky persons will see them.

I'm still looking for my first pine grosbeak and hoary redpoll in Indiana. One early winter morning, I thought I heard a pine grosbeak flying over a park near my home; but by the time I got to a clearing among the evergreen trees, the bird was gone, along with the opportunity to record my first pine grosbeak in Indiana. Sorry as I am for having failed to add this charming winter finch to my Indiana list, I feel cheered by the counsel offered by a philosopher who asserted, many years ago, that it is a good thing to have some mountains unscaled, some water uncharted, some jungles yet unexplored.

Maybe *this* year will be my pine grosbeak year. . . .

Fox Sparrow

[PASSERELLA ILIACA]

The fox sparrow is relatively little known in Indiana, which is surprising, since it is not a rare bird in this state. It was coming to Indiana each spring and fall long before the Indians were concerned with the invasions of the white man. True, the fox sparrow does not nest in our state; however, it is here for about six weeks each year—three weeks in the fall and again three weeks in the spring. It is one of the later fall migrants and one of the earlier spring migrants. It is usually seen the last week of October, staying several weeks before moving to the southern states to spend the winter. Come March, it will again move through Indiana to its nesting grounds in Canada and Alaska.

The fox sparrow gets its name from the similarity between its color and that of the red fox. It is the largest and reddest of the sparrows. The best field marks are its red tail and heavily streaked breast.

The fox sparrow is a rather shy bird and usually does not allow close approach or a long look. It is principally a ground feeder and often gives away its presence by its habit of kicking away fallen leaves as it searches for food. If the opportunity presents itself to observe closely the feeding of the fox sparrow, you will find that it frequently springs into the air and kicks with both feet off the ground.

The song of the fox sparrow is outstanding. It is a joyful sound and one that can be duplicated by whistling. Many bird songs are either so high-pitched or so complex that they are difficult for man to imitate.

Size: L. 6½–7½" (16–19 cm). Coloring: Reddish-brown back, rufous tail, white breast, very heavily streaked. Habitat: Dense woodland thickets, brushy roadsides, borders of woods, weedy pastures. Nesting: Nests on or near the ground; 4–5 pale green eggs. Unusual Mannerisms: Noisily kicks dead leaves aside in search of food. Identifying Hints: Large size, red tail, heavily streaked breast. Status in Indiana: Common spring and fall migrant. Does not nest here. Rare winterer. Range: Breeds from Alaska southeast to middle Canada. Winters primarily in southern states and Mexico.

Like most birds, the fox sparrow is the most vocal in the springtime, but occasionally it will give its full song in the fall.

The fox sparrow is a bird that seems to be subject to large population fluctuations. Most years, the fox sparrow is here in good numbers; but because of its tarrying in the north where severe weather can occur and also its compulsion to migrate north in late February and March, it is frequently a victim of heavy snow and ice storms. The fox sparrow can cope with snow; but snow followed by an ice storm, creating a hard crust on top of the snow, renders the fox sparrow helpless in its pursuit of food. When this happens, thousands of fox sparrows die, and it takes four or five years before it is able to regain its normal numbers.

The ability to recover from disaster seems to be a characteristic present in many species of birds. I wonder what sort of world we would have if, every few years, we had to regroup and start afresh?

Bobwhite

[COLINUS VIRGINIANUS]

I haven't investigated all the factors involved in determining whether recent winters have become more severe, but they certainly appear now to be longer and colder. A combination of low temperatures, lack of available water, and heavy snow cover is sure to have a negative effect upon some of our birds.

One bird that seems to me to have decreased in central Indiana the

SIZE: *8½–10½" (21–26 cm).* COLORING: *Reddish brown, dark tail, white throat, with prominent white stripe over eye.* HABITAT: *Uncultivated fields, hedgerows.* NESTING: *On ground, in grassy cover; 14–16 creamy white eggs.* UNUSUAL MANNERISMS: *Frequenty seen in large groups of 20 to 30 individuals which form a tight circle at night, with all heads pointed to the outside. When covey is flushed, they scatter in different directions. Noisy dispersal when this occurs is a defense*

mechanism used to startle enemies. IDENTIFYING HINTS: *Chunky shape, the black-and-white head pattern, and distinctive calling of its name.* STATUS IN INDIANA: *Fairly common nester in southern Indiana. Found here every month of the year. Susceptible to severe winters, and it is often necessary to reintroduce when population has declined.* RANGE: *Uncommon in the northernmost states, more common in the mid-United States and southern states.*

past ten years is the bobwhite—or quail, as it is sometimes called. It used to be that if you took a winter's hike at Geist Reservoir or Eagle Creek, you were sure to flush a covey of bobwhites. Now it's an unusual event to find bobwhites in either place. A few may be heard, but not nearly as many as there once were. In the early spring, the plaintive calling of the bobwhite was a sound that could be heard, not only in our parks, but throughout central and southern Indiana.

The last few years, I've heard bobwhites calling much less frequently than before. It may be that I'm overly sensitive to the activity of the bobwhites; for in my home area in upstate New York they could not survive the long, cold winters. Every few years the State Conservation Department would attempt to get bobwhites established; but along would come an especially bad winter, and the quail would again disappear.

The bobwhite is a robin-sized, chicken-like bird. Except for the breeding season, the bobwhite is most often found in a group, or covey.

The male has a white throat and white stripe over the eye. In the female the throat and eye stripe are buffy. When flushed, the short, dark tail is a reliable field mark.

The bobwhite nests here, most commonly, in the central and southern portions of the state. It is a ground nester and prefers clumps of dead grass along a fence row or weedy pastures and open meadows. Twelve or more eggs would be a normal clutch. The young chicks are able to fly within a few days after hatching. Both adult birds are very protective of the young birds and will suffer great personal threats to protect them.

Perhaps the most outstanding characteristic of the bobwhite is its manner of communicating. The familiar call, "Bob white" or "Bob, bob, white!" (hence its name) is most often given by the male in the spring and summer. Less known is the call given by a receptive female, as well as the gathering call, usually heard in the fall, when the flock has become scattered and the birds are trying to get together again. The quail also has an alarm call and a conversational chatter uttered when feeding.

Let's hope that either our winters moderate or that the bobwhite will find a way to survive the colder winters here, for Indiana wouldn't be the same without the welcome calling of the bobwhite.

Red-bellied Woodpecker

[CENTURUS CAROLINUS]

Birds' names are often no help in identifying birds. The Cape May warbler is seldom found in Cape May, New Jersey. The Philadephia vireo is a bird not normally found in the City of Brotherly Love. The common teal is a rare bird east of the Mississippi River. The short-billed dowitcher has a bill that is longer than ninety-five percent of all birds' bills.

A common Indiana bird that has a misleading name is the red-bellied woodpecker. The prevailing theory as to how this bird got its name is that many early ornithologists did a great deal of collecting of birds to insure correct identification; and this bird, when closely examined as a museum skin, does show a tinge of pink on the belly in some plumages. In the field this wash of pink on the underside is seldom seen. So if you see a woodpecker with a large amount of red on its head visiting your feeding station, chances are that you are seeing a red-bellied woodpecker.

This well-groomed appearing woodpecker is a common, year-round resident of Indiana. It nests throughout the state, perhaps more commonly in the southern third of the state than in the northern third. Like all our woodpeckers, the red-bellied excavates a hole in a tree for its nest. There it will lay four or five white eggs. Evidently the Equal Rights Amendment has been ratified by the red-bellied woodpeckers, for both the male and the female incubate the eggs and share in feeding the young birds.

One of the favorite foods of the red-bellied is the nuts from beech, oak, and other nut-bearing trees. Frequently these birds are seen in the fall hiding nuts and acorns which they will use for food when hard weather sets in. As those of you who have a feeding station can attest, the red-bellied will readily come to your backyard to eat wild bird seed and suet, as well.

The male red-bellied has a black-and-white back, a light-colored breast, and a red crown. The female and young birds are similarly colored but lack the red crown. The bird that is frequently confused with the red-bellied is the red-headed woodpecker, which has an *all*-red head.

The red-bellied is a rather noisy bird, especially in winter. Although it doesn't have a song in the normal sense of bird songs, it does give a variety of sounds that call our attention to the presence of this bird.

During one mid-winter freeze a small band of us ventured out to see how the birds were faring in the severe weather. At nine o'clock in the morning the temperature was 19 degrees below zero and the wind chill factor was 62 degrees below zero. In spite of this, the chickadees, titmice, juncos, and red-bellied woodpeckers seemed to be going about their business of surviving cheerfully. Not once was there heard any grumbling about the high cost of keeping warm, transportation problems, or the possibility of a natural gas shortage!

Size: *L. 9–10½" (23–26 cm)*. Coloring: *Red top of the head and nape, black-and-white horizontal stripes on the back and wings. Pale buffy breast.* Habitat: *Orchards, coniferous and deciduous forests.* Nesting: *Nests in cavity in tree or stump; 4–5 white eggs.* Unusual Mannerisms: *Often is seen trying to store acorns and other nuts.* Identifying Hints: *Black-and-white horizontal stripes on the back and red nape of the neck and head best field marks. Name, "red-bellied," a misnomer. Red belly only evident on museum skins.* Status in Indiana: *Fairly common year-round resident and nesting bird.* Range: *Breeds south of Great Lakes area to Gulf states and Florida. Winter resident throughout its range.*

Hooded Merganser

[L O P H O D Y T E S   C U C U L L A T U S]

Mergansers are fish-eating ducks best told from other ducks by long, narrow bills, the saw-toothed edges of which enable them to seize and eat fish efficiently. All three members of the merganser family found in the United States—the red-breasted, the common, and the hooded— occur in Indiana and sometimes are found here in considerable numbers. They are not held in high esteem by the epicurean or the hunter because a fish diet causes the merganser's flesh to take on an unpleasant flavor. What the mergansers lack as table birds, they make up aesthetically, for in their breeding plumage, all three are strikingly handsome. In fact, many people consider the hooded merganser equal to the wood duck in attractiveness.

The hooded merganser is the smallest of the mergansers. The male has a large crest that he can raise or lower, like a fan, and when fully extended, the crest shows a large triangle of white. The breast is also white. The back is black and the sides, chestnut. The female and young males appear as dull, gray-crested birds without the white in the crest. In flight, the hooded shows small, white wing patches in the base of the wing.

Normally, the hooded is with us in some numbers during the months of October, November, March, and April. If the winter is mild and the ponds and reservoirs are not frozen, a few of these showy birds will winter in Indiana.

The major breeding grounds of the hooded merganser are in southern Canada and in our most northern states. There, the hooded merganser will select a secluded-wooded area near water to begin its housekeeping chores. It is often in the same type of habitat that the wood duck prefers, and like the wood duck, the hooded will find a cavity in a tree to lay her 10 to 12 eggs. Soon after the chicks hatch, the female will try to persuade her young that the real world is a wonderful place, and that they will be much happier once they leave the comforts of the snug tree house.

SIZE: *L. 16–19" (40–48 cm). W. 26" (65 cm).* COLORING: *Male, black back, black head, with prominent white crest and crown. White belly, chestnut sides. Female, gray-brown throughout, reddish-brown head and crest.* HABITAT: *Rivers, lakes, woodland ponds.* NESTING: *Nests in natural tree cavity, usually near water; 10–12 white eggs.* UNUSUAL MANNERISMS: *Usually seen in small groups. In spring the white crest on the head of the male is used for courtship display.* IDENTIFYING HINTS: *In flight, small white wing patch, on the water, white crest— together with dark sides—separate this small merganser from similar-appearing bufflehead.* STATUS IN INDIANA: *Fairy common spring and fall migrant. Rare winter visitor when there is open water. Rare nester in Indiana.* RANGE: *Breeds from central Canada, south to the northern-most part of the United States. Occasional rare nester in some of the southern states. Winters from northern United States, south to Mexico and the Gulf Coast.*

Canvasback

[AYTHYA VALISINERIA]

Traditionally, the first extended cold wave of late autumn will bring to Indiana the diving ducks. Perhaps the most esteemed of the diving ducks is the canvasback—valued by the gourmet and by those who appreciate looking at beautiful forms of nature.

The canvasback, which is exclusive to North America, nests primarily in the Great Plains area of the United States, west of the Mississippi River, and in western Canada. When the weather turns cold and the ponds and marshes of its breeding grounds start to freeze, the canvasback begins to move south.

Not normally a very common bird in Indiana, the canvasback is usually seen in relatively small numbers in the fall and again in the early spring. Although it is sometimes seen on gravel pits and ponds, the best places to look for this duck are on the larger bodies of water.

The canvasback is usually accompanied by other species of diving ducks. It is a powerful diver and can dive to depths of twenty to twenty-five feet in search of its favorite food, wild celery roots. When it surfaces with its prize, other ducks try to steal this aquatic goody from the canvasback. It is said that the wild celery gives the canvasback the flavor that makes it so prized as a table bird.

"Stately" is a word that always comes to mind when the canvasback is first seen. It is a large duck and, when sitting on the water, seems to be dark at both ends and white in the middle. When viewed in good light, the male canvasback has a chestnut-colored head, a black breast, white back and sides, and a black tail.

The female is a slate-brown bird with a darker-gray chest and tail. I've always felt the best identifying marks of the canvasback are the comparatively long bill (as long as the head) and the shape of the head. Rather than round, as are the heads of most ducks, the canvasback has a long, sloping profile. These two field marks, the bill and the head, are aids in identifying the canvasback at considerably long distances.

270

SIZE: *L. 18–22″ (46–56 cm). W. 34″ (85 cm).* COLORING: *Male, red head and neck, black breast, white sides and back. Female, gray back, brown head, neck, and breast.* HABITAT: *Prefers the larger bodies of water.* NESTING: *Builds bulky nest near water, usually close to cattails or similar vegetation; 7–10 olive-colored eggs.* UNUSUAL MANNERISMS: *Deep diver.* IDENTIFYING HINTS: *Erect posture, sloping profile of head, white body, rusty head of male.* STATUS IN INDIANA: *Uncommon migrant: late October to November, early December; March and early April.* RANGE: *Breeds in several western states north to western Canada and Alaska. Winters in Finger Lakes of New York, south to the Gulf of Mexico.*

More Americans will be thinking of one particular bird during the last week of November than at any other time of the year. I, for one, hope that the turkey, rather than the canvasback, will grace your table on Thanksgiving Day.

Dark-eyed Junco

[JUNCO HYEMALIS]

Snow and the junco seem to go hand in hand in Indiana, for it is usually about the time of our first snowfall that the junco becomes evident. In early spring, when the snow is disappearing, the juncos also will leave Indiana.

The juncos that occur in Indiana are now called "dark-eyed juncos." Most field guides refer to the junco found east of the Mississippi as the "slate-colored junco" and the junco found west of the Mississippi as the "Oregon junco." It has rather recently been determined that these two juncos interbreed and hence can no longer be considered as two separate species; so now they are both officially named the dark-eyed junco.

Early ornithologists called these birds, "snowbirds." Somehow, snowbird seems a more appropriate name than the junco's new official name, for not only is the junco found in Indiana when there is snow on the ground, but juncos appear to take special delight in snow. They have no qualms about kicking away in the snow in search of their favorite winter food, weed seeds. They can also be seen taking a snow bath or cozily burrowing into a snow bank to sleep.

The dark-eyed junco is a sparrow-sized bird with a dark gray head and body and a white belly. It has white outer tail feathers that are much in evidence in flight. In the winter, if you see a small bird which shows white tail feathers as it moves about, feeding on the ground, the odds are 99 out of 100 that you are seeing a dark-eyed junco.

Another help in identifying the junco is learning to recognize the sound it makes in the winter. It can best be described as a soft "smack" which can be duplicated by kissing the back of your hand.

SIZE: *L. 5–6½" (13–16 cm).* COLORING: *Slate-gray back and cowl, white belly, two white outer tail feathers.* HABITAT: *Coniferous and mixed forests, gardens, city parks, roadside thickets.* NESTING: *Nest placed on or near the ground, concealed by weeds and grasses. Compact structure made up of grasses, bark shreds, mosses—lined with fine grasses; 4–5 white eggs.* UNUSUAL MANNERISMS: *Frequent visitor to winter feeding station; normally feeds on the ground.* IDENTIFYING HINTS: *Flashing of the two white outer feathers identify this bird in any plumage.* STATUS IN INDIANA: *Common winter visitor from October through April. Does not nest here.* RANGE: *Breeds from southern Canada north. Winters from Alaska to the Gulf States.*

Juncos are seldom seen singly; more often they group together in small flocks. Occasionally, when conditions are favorable, hundreds of juncos can be found busily feeding in fields where weeds are prolific.

To attract juncos to your feeding station, try throwing some wild bird mix on the ground, for these birds prefer feeding on the ground, rather than on an elevated shelf. By doing this, you should be able to entice a small group of snowbirds to your yard—good company in the winter months.

Common Goldeneye

[BUCEPHALA CLANGULA]

It is almost impossible to go on a winter's bird hike without being rewarded by an unusual sight or pleasant experience. Granted, there are days that don't produce a large number of birds, but frequently these days are compensated for by other thought-provoking sights. One might be a red fox, gingerly working his way across a lake that is thinly covered with ice. Another could be a raccoon or possum that has prematurely awakened from his winter's nap and, after slowly assessing the season's handiwork, decides to resume his snooze.

One bird that seems to delight in the most severe weather is the common goldeneye. This beautiful diving duck is found throughout Indiana from October until May. The common goldeneye prefers large, rather deep bodies of water, but is frequently found on small ponds, gravel pit quarries, or wherever there is open water. Look where water isn't frozen solid.

Watch for a duck that shows a lot of white on the sides, and on close examination you will see that it has a dark back and head. The male has a round white spot between the bill and the eye. The female doesn't show as much white and appears to be a gray bird with a brown head. The female also lacks the white face mark. In flight, both the male and female goldeneye look to be dark-headed with prominent white wing patches. Another good field mark is the whistling sound made by the wings. Hunters refer to the goldeneye as "the whistler" because of this characteristic.

SIZE: *L. 16–20" (40–51 cm). W. 31" (77 cm).* COLORING: *Male, black backed, white body, greenish head, white spot in front of eye. Female, gray body, brown head, white neck-ring.* HABITAT: *Lakes and ponds.* NESTING: *Uses natural tree cavity near water; 8–12 eggs.* UNUSUAL MANNERISMS: *Elaborate courtship display in spring. Tree nester.* IDENTIFYING HINTS: *Whistling of the wings in flight a good aid, also white face mark of the male when on the water.* STATUS IN INDIANA: *Seen throughout the state from November to April, usually on the larger bodies of water. Sometimes a raft of as many as 30 to 40 birds may be seen.* RANGE: *Breeds from Alaska to northern Canada, south to northernmost United States. Winters south to northern Mexico, the Gulf Coast, and Florida.*

The common goldeneye nests in the most northern parts of the states that border Canada and north to Hudson Bay. An unusual feature of the goldeneye is that it is one of the few ducks that will nest above ground level. It will utilize a cavity in a tree and there incubate eight to twelve eggs for about a month.

It is always surprising to me that more people don't enjoy the out-of-doors in the winter. There is a tranquillity then that is not found in any other season. There is a subtle feeling that the trees and plants are enjoying a rejuvenating rest and that soon they will awaken and face the world with renewed energies. A revealing experiment that I have conducted is to ask someone to close his eyes and think of something pleasant which is associated with winter. Strangely enough, these comforting memories are almost always reminiscent of times gone by spent in the out-of-doors. Never has anyone told me that the thought that emerged was enjoyment received from watching the crowning of a new super bowl victor!

Purple Finch

[CARPODACUS PURPUREUS]

The purple finch is usually considered to be a member of the winter finch tribe—that is, a part of a variety of different kinds of birds that may or may not be seen in the United States in wintertime. The winter finch members seem to be subject to irregular behavior patterns, but the

SIZE: *L. 5½–6½″ (14–16 cm)*. COLORING: *Male, raspberry red with color more prominent on head and rump. Female, brownish bird, heavily streaked breast, with white line over the eye.* HABITAT: *Coniferous forests; Christmas tree farms.* NESTING: *Nest placed on horizontal branch of evergreen tree at varying heights above the ground; usually 4 eggs.* UNUSUAL MANNERISMS: *Erratically present throughout range.*

When present will patronize feeding station offering sunflower seed.
IDENTIFYING HINTS: *Learn the flight song—a distinctive "tick."* STATUS
IN INDIANA: *Fairly common spring and fall migrant. Present in good
numbers in some winters.* RANGE: *Breeds from Canada to northernmost
states. Winters as far south as Florida, Texas, and the Gulf Coast.*

purple finch even more so than the rest of the group. It refuses to conform.

Supposedly, it breeds in southern Canada and northern United States, but occasionally it will breed in the middle states, another evidence of its nonconformity. Most birds sing in the spring, just prior to the breeding season, but the purple finch has a lovely song in the fall. The purpose of this fall song is unknown, since it is obviously not establishing a territory or seeking out a mate. The fall song is quite different from the spring song, and, as far as I know, it serves no practical purpose.

The purple finch will come to a feeding station, for it is fond of sunflower seeds. It will come to trees in your backyard, especially if you have sweet gum, tulip, or sycamore trees. As with many birds, the males and females look very different. The males are very colorful, while the females are more subdued in coloration. The basic reason for this is that the less gaudy color of the female serves as camouflage, thus enabling her to bring off a good percentage of fledglings in her nesting cycle.

The male purple finch is a very pretty bird, but I feel that "purple" is not the proper color description. It is more raspberry than purple in color, with a deeper red on the head and rump. The female looks like a heavily streaked, brown sparrow. Inasmuch as the purple finch raises three or four young a year and the immatures all look like the female, the odds are that you will see four birds in the female plumage for every raspberry-colored male. The best way to detect the purple finch, at any time of the year, is to learn the flight note—a hard, metallic "tick." The purple finch gives this call while in flight, and when learned, will help you discern its presence very quickly.

Winter is really the best time to learn the birds. There are fewer of them, and those that will stay will allow a closer, longer look. Discipline yourself to learn the birds that you see in your backyard or at your feeder this winter. If you do, you will find that the winter will pass more swiftly and will seem much brighter than in previous years.

DECEMBER

THE COMPETITION FOR LEISURE time during the month of December is intense, and the hours free to spend out-of-doors for most Hoosiers are few. Interest in the Old Oaken Bucket contest has now shifted to debate over who has the better basketball team—the Big Red or the Boilermakers. And, will the Fighting Irish earn top honors again in the national ratings? Indeed, a good part of Sundays is taken up with trying to determine what teams will meet in this year's "super bowl." Holiday shopping and preparing the house for the holidays also detract from time that could possibly be spent outside. By succumbing to these time stealers or by being intimidated by a weather forecast of cold snow or bone-chilling sleet, what a treat is missed! There are few greater pleasures in life than taking an early morning hike in December, when the air is cold and brisk, the evergreen trees laden with a fresh coat of snow, and when the woods are so quiet every faint sound is magnified.

By now our wintering birds are firmly entrenched and will remain here until it is their time to leave. Golden-crowned kinglets are present in good numbers, and the tree sparrows are busy devouring their quota of weed seeds, oblivious of frigid temperatures. The goldfinches, although no longer wearing their bright yellow-and-black summer plumages, continue to add to the beauty of the scene by calling a cheerful "kur chick-a-dee" as they seek out thistle seeds previously overlooked.

Now is the time to look for the rough-legged hawk, that great northern bird of prey that moves south in the winter to try its hunting skill in warmer climes. Maybe this will be a good year for the goshawk, that aggressive accipiter that seems to get to Indiana only every three or four years.

Ralph Waldo Emerson delighted in the "punctuality of birds," but the presence of many of our winter birds is actually dependent upon the availability of food, rather than a date on a calendar. If there is an ample crop of suitable food in the north, the finches won't find it necessary to move this far south. If the rodent and rabbit populations are abundant in Canada, the rough-legged and goshawk will remain there, and we will have to wait until next year to see them.

Now is the time to implement a winter feeding program. It needn't be elaborate. Beef suet placed in a mesh onion or potato bag and hung in a tree will entice hairy and downy woodpeckers. For Carolina chicka-dees (or, in northern Indiana, the similar-looking black-capped chicka-dees) and tufted titmice, put sunflower seeds in a hanging feeder or on a flat shelf. These seeds are also appreciated by cardinals, blue jays, and white-breasted nuthatches. Mixed seed tossed on the ground will be welcomed by the ground feeders: song sparrow, junco, tree sparrow, and—if you are lucky—the towhee and brown thrasher.

A relatively new addition to a winter feeding program is the thistle feeder. Used primarily to attract goldfinches, it comes in two forms— a clear, plastic cylinder or a bag of fine mesh. Either one should, of course, be filled with thistle seed, now available in most garden and feed stores. These feeders are amazingly successful and will frequently attract winter finches, as well as goldfinches, even in the heart of a city.

Another activity in which you may wish to participate is the annual Christmas Bird Census. This event takes place in just about every city in the United States. The date varies from year to year and from one place to another, but it is generally held a week before—or a week after— Christmas Day. (Readers may check with the nearest Audubon Society for specific information about their localities.) In recent years groups in Indianapolis, Ft. Wayne, South Bend, Bloomington, Terre Haute, Evansville, Gary, Lafayette, and Michigan City (Indiana Dunes), among others, have each taken a Christmas Bird Census.

The first Christmas count ever held in the United States took place in 1905. In 1976, a total of 1,121 communities and 27,000 persons spent part of a day taking a census of the birds in their area. They reported seeing 650 different species, and the overall census totalled more than 79 million birds. As the years have gone by, the information acquired has become more and more important. Population fluctuations and trends can now be ascertained by scrutinizing the data accumulated.

There are many beneficial aspects of birding that I haven't dwelled upon, as I hope that you will discover them for yourself—like the thrill to be found seeing a rare bird or in finding a bird nesting in an uncommon locale or like the satisfaction to be found in identifying, by yourself, a difficult species. Perhaps you'll find a new dimension that just being out-of-doors can add to your life, to say nothing of the healthfulness that being in the sunshine and clean air offers.

I hope this year's journey hasn't been an arduous one for you. It needn't be, for birding can be enjoyed at your own tempo. You may wish to become familiar with the birds of Indiana gradually over the years, or you may choose to embark on a "crash" course and learn them in a few years. I know that your life, regardless of which course you choose, will be enriched by enjoying Indiana birds.

American Kestrel

[FALCO SPARVERIUS]

Late fall is the time of year when our commonest hawk is most often seen. The American kestrel, or sparrow hawk, is often not recognized as a hawk because of its small size (not much bigger than a robin); but its behavior is truly hawk-like. It is the only member of the falcon family that the average person can expect to see in Indiana. Falcons are large-headed birds with long, pointed wings and are noted for their swift flight, aggressive behavior, and hunting ability. In spite of its diminutive size, the kestrel has all of these falcon characteristics.

In the winter it is most often seen sitting on top of a telephone pole, surveying the surrounding terrain, waiting for an unsuspecting mouse or sparrow to come into view. When sure of its prey, the kestrel will swoop swiftly from its perch, strike the bird or mouse in the back with its talons, insert its powerful bill into the base of the skull, then, with a quick forward motion, tear off the top of the skull. The kill is quick and sure. It happens so fast that neither the victim nor the observer is aware of what has happened.

The kestrel doesn't seem to be discouraged by human activity. Within one week I saw this bird at a shopping center near my home,

at the Scottish Rite Cathedral on Meridian Street, and on the telephone lines that run parallel to Route 65, near 38th Street and Lafayette Road. The kestrel will accept a man-made nesting box if placed in the right area, but it prefers to nest in a deserted woodpecker's nest. I've also found it nesting on the ledge of a fourteen-story hotel and on the top of a tall, metal utility post.

Hawks are not known for their beautiful coloring, but the kestrel is an exception. The male is a very handsome bird. It has a chestnut-colored back and tail, blue wings, and light-colored breast with just a wash of rose near the neck area. The head has a distinct black-and-white pattern with a chestnut crown. The female's colors are similar, but she lacks the blue wing. Another good field mark is its ability to hover. There are only a few birds that do this, and none resembling the kestrel. So, if you see a robin-sized bird hovering over an open field or golf course, you are seeing America's smallest falcon, the kestrel.

SIZE: *L. 9–12" (23–30 cm). W. 21" (.5 m).* COLORING: *Rusty black, reddish tail, black-and-white face pattern. Males have bluish wings, which the females lack.* HABITAT: *Found in both large cities and small towns, parks, farmlands, open country.* NESTING: *Nests found in eaves of buildings, natural tree cavities, old woodpecker holes, man-made nesting boxes. Rarely use nesting materials; 4–5 eggs.* UNUSUAL MANNERISMS: *In summer, diet consists primarily of grasshoppers and other insects; in winter, rodents and small birds, like sparrows. Is one of few birds having the ability to hover in one place.* IDENTIFYING HINTS: *Pointed wings. Loud "killy, killy, killy" call. Often seen perched on telephone lines.* STATUS IN INDIANA: *Year-round resident; fairly common nesting bird.* RANGE: *Breeds from Alaska south to Florida. Winters from the Great Lakes area south to northern tip of South America.*

Barred Owl

[STRIX VARIA]

Toward winter, as the hours of daylight decrease and the hours of darkness increase, the likelihood of hearing an owl increases. The owl most likely to be heard is the barred owl, for the barred owl is our most vocal owl. Although it has a variety of rather frightening sounds, its typical call is a loud "Who cooks for you—who cooks for you all?" Both the male and the female give this call, and, when the courtship procedure begins in December and January, the woods can ring with the love song of the barred owls. For those not familiar with this sound, it can be an unsettling experience to hear it on a cold, still winter's night.

The barred owl is a common owl in Indiana. It is found throughout the state in each month of the year. It prefers the larger, deciduous, swampy woods; and once a suitable woods is found, the barred owl has a great reluctance to abandon the area. Often a pair of these owls or their progeny will occupy a favorite woods for up to twenty years. They nest in a tree cavity or in an abandoned nest of a hawk, crow, or squirrel. They hesitate to build their own nests. They are early nesters, and frequently the female is sitting on eggs in the midst of a snowstorm. One brood of two or three young per year is normal.

The barred owl is a large, bulky, brown bird without ear tufts. The

SIZE: *L. 18–22" (46–56 cm). W. 44" (1.1 m).* COLORING: *Gray brown, with vertical streaking on the breast, and brown eyes.* HABITAT: *Swampy woodlands or wooded areas near water.* NESTING: *Nests in natural tree cavity, occasionally an abandoned crow's or hawk's nest; 2–4 white eggs.* UNUSUAL MANNERISMS: *Exhibits great loyalty to same nesting site year after year.* IDENTIFYING HINTS: *No ear tufts. Call, "Who cooks for you—who cooks for you all?"* STATUS IN INDIANA: *Fairly common year-round resident and nesting bird. More common in the southern half of Indiana.* RANGE: *Breeds from central Canada to southern United States. Winters throughout its range.*

prominent, large eyes are brown, rather than the yellow of most owls. The streaking on the body is vertical.

The barred owl is nocturnal, but on dark, cloudy days it sometimes can be heard or seen searching for its favorite food, mice and rats. There seems to be a correlation between the red-shouldered hawk and the barred owl; they like the same kind of habitat, they have very similar feeding habits, and they often nest near one another. The red-shouldered hawk is busy during the day pursuing rodents—and the barred owl takes up the chase at night. It is interesting to speculate on what the rodent population would be if there weren't hawks and owls.

The next time you hear the woods resounding with an emphatic "Who cooks for you—who cooks for you all?" don't be alarmed, as you are hearing the call of one of nature's most efficient rodent-control agents. And just think—there are no city, state, or federal funds involved!

Field Sparrow

[SPIZELLA PUSILLA]

It comes as a surprise to most people that so many birds spend the winter in Indiana and other northern states. Anyone who has a winter bird feeding program eventually becomes aware that certain sparrows, woodpeckers, blue jays, chickadees, cardinals, nuthatches, goldfinches, and a few other birds prefer braving the elements rather than going south for the winter. A winter hike into areas that have a body of water and diversified habitat would reveal that a good many other birds winter in the North on a regular basis. Birds like bluebirds and robins, which are almost synonymous with spring and summer, regularly winter here in good numbers. As a rule, you won't have these birds coming to your feeder. They prefer finding their own food and a degree of shelter.

Both of the kinglets, the ruby-crowned and the golden-crowned (not birds you are likely to have at a feeder), seem to have no difficulty wintering here, especially the golden-crowned. I've found them many times when the temperature was zero or below. Cedar waxwings are also

SIZE: *L. 5–6" (13–15 cm).* COLORING: *Clear breast, brown back, chestnut cap, white eye-ring.* HABITAT: *Pastures, abandoned farmlands, fields.* NESTING: *Cup-shaped nest on or near the ground; 3–4 eggs.* UNUSUAL MANNERISMS: *Persistent singer.* IDENTIFYING HINTS: *Pink bill and white eye-ring.* STATUS IN INDIANA: *Common in spring, summer, and fall. Common nester; uncommon winter resident.* RANGE: *Breeds southern Canada south to northern part of the Gulf states. Winters primarily in southern states.*

present in the winter, sometimes in flocks of as many as thirty to forty birds.

I recall a day one winter—when neither mad dogs nor Englishmen would venture forth—when a small group of us crossed the frozen waters of Eagle Creek Reservoir. There were snowdrifts two and three feet high. A brisk, bone-chilling north wind was blowing a rather heavy snow, producing a wind chill factor of —20 degrees and making visibility about zero. After crossing the frozen reservoir, we searched out a patch of woods to break the wind. As we caught our breath and collected our thoughts, the high, thin whistles of cedar waxwings were heard. In a tangled multiflora hedge was a flock of about a dozen waxwings busily eating berries, seemingly unmindful of us and the harsh realities of winter. Other than the waxwings, there were very few birds in evidence that morning.

Under normal winter conditions, Indiana retains a good number of ducks as long as the lakes and reservoirs have unfrozen water. Mallards and blacks, along with diving ducks—goldeneyes, buffleheads, lesser scaups, redheads, and canvasbacks—can be found all winter, primarily on the larger bodies of water.

While the majority of the sparrow tribe leaves Indiana as autumn begins to wane, a few stay over. It sems to me that we have more field sparrows wintering here now than ever before. Field sparrows are a common bird in the spring, summer, and fall; and they now winter, at least in central Indiana, in fair numbers. The field sparrow can be identified by its unstreaked breast, chestnut cap, and pink bill. In the spring and summer its plaintive notes, ending in a trill, are among the most common sounds heard in the pastures and fields where this bird spends most of its time.

The birds that winter here are not any less mobile than those that migrate south in the winter. Quite the contrary. All of our wintering birds are very capable of a long migration. It almost seems as though there is an atmosphere of challenge prevalent in winter not found during the rest of the year, as though our wintering birds elect to accept the challenge even when they have the option of a winter in Florida.

Winter Wren

[TROGLODYTES TROGLODYTES]

When observing most birds, a good rule of thumb would be to look up; but to see a winter wren, the opposite is true—you must look down, for the winter wren is almost always seen on or near the ground. An ideal habitat for the winter wren would be an area featuring fern-covered fallen trees and a fast-moving brook. Inasmuch as few back-yards have such a ravine, it is necessary to leave the comforts of home to seek out the haunts of the winter wren. It is an effort well worth making, for this little mite is an intriguing bird. He is not much bigger than a hummingbird, and his secretive nature makes it a real challenge to observe him at close range.

It has been my experience that the best way to study this wren, once you have caught a glimpse of the bird, is to make yourself comfortable and let him come to you. If you try to track him down, he will lead you a merry chase. If you remain quiet and still, the inquisitive nature of the winter wren will force him to investigate the huge stranger who has invaded his domain. You will then be able to see his mouse-like coloring and the tail that is always in a perpendicular position. The winter wren is always active and seems to have an amazing ability to disappear under some fallen log and then reappear many feet from where you first saw him.

In Indiana the winter wren is present from October through April and, to my knowledge, does not nest in the state. He prefers the cool northern woodlands and swamps of the most northern states and Canada. It is a more common bird here than is generally known, however. In March and April, when the winter wrens are moving north to their breeding grounds, they can be found in virtually any woods that has a ravine and running water. Occasionally they can be seen in suburban backyards, especially around brushpiles.

I have had the pleasure of hearing the winter wren's full song only a few times and never in Indiana, but it is one of the great sounds of

SIZE: *L. 4–4½" (10–11 cm)*. COLORING: *Dark brown throughout with barred lower belly and rump area. Stubby tail.* HABITAT: *Dense tangles and ravines, woodpiles, fallen logs along water's edge.* NESTING: *Spherical nest, often concealed among roots of upturned, fallen trees or under stumps; 5–6 eggs.* UNUSUAL MANNERISMS: *Always busy, seldom seen standing still.* IDENTIFYING HINTS: *Stubby tail, small size, darker coloring.* STATUS IN INDIANA: *Uncommon fall, winter, and spring migrant. Does not nest in Indiana.* RANGE: *Breeds from Alaska to northern border of United States. Winters south of the Great Lakes to the Gulf states and north Florida.*

nature. It is a surprisingly long, intricate, and loud song for so small a bird. The first time I ever heard this song, one April morning in upstate New York, I couldn't believe it was coming from this four-inch bird. Someone aptly described the song of the winter wren as "the spirit of the brook." If a Hoosier wishes to enjoy this marvelous sound, he should disregard Horace Greeley's advice—and head north!

Tree Sparrow

[SPIZELLA ARBOREA]

Frigid winds, snow, and below-freezing temperatures are not the conditions that would seem to set the stage for the arrival of one of the most attractive members of the sparrow family, but, 'tis true! The tree sparrow is present with us only during the winter months.

How this sparrow acquired the name, "tree sparrow," I don't know. A more appropriate name would be "ground sparrow" or maybe "weed sparrow," for looking down, rather than up, is the way to see the tree sparrow.

The tree sparrow nests in the far north—as far north as any of our land birds—up to the very timberline of Canada and Alaska. There, in the brief summer, it has time to raise but one brood before it is time to start its two-thousand-mile journey south. It will spend the winter months in mid-America, usually not any farther south than Tennessee, Virginia, or North Carolina. The tree sparrow is a rather common bird in Indiana and should start to patronize your feeding stations in early December. Look for a clear-breasted sparrow with one dark spot in the center of the breast. The dark spot, together with the rusty cap and two white wing-bars are all that is needed to identify this sparrow.

Although the tree sparrow doesn't normally sing its true song until late February or March, it does have a very pretty warble that it sings all winter long. Singly, it is not much of a song, but collectively, when a flock of twenty or thirty of these birds are busy feeding in a field of weed seed, they sound like a miniature orchestra tuning up for a

Size: *L. 5½–6½" (14–16 cm)*. Coloring: *Brown back, two white wing-bars, chestnut cap, clear breast with one dark spot in center.* Habitat: *Weedy fields, edges of woods, bushy thickets.* Nesting: *Bulky nest on or near the ground. Lined with hair and feathers; 4–5 eggs.* Unusual Mannerisms: *Often seen in good-sized flocks collectively giving their sweet, tinkling notes.* Identifying Hints: *Rusty cap and clear breast with central mark.* Status in Indiana: *Winter resident from the middle of October to middle of April. Does not nest here.* Range: *Breeds from Alaska throughout northern Canada. Winters from the Great Lakes area south to northern portions of Gulf states.*

concert. Thoreau, in his journals, refers to this sound as the "tinkle of icicles."

Two characteristics of the tree sparrow that endear it to all nature lovers are its cheerfulness and friendliness; but in addition to these assets, the tree sparrow is of great value economically, for it eats harmful weed seeds prodigiously. In the winter ninety percent of the diet of this friendly sparrow consists of weed seeds. It is not unusual for one of these birds to eat more than one thousand weed seeds in a day. During its stay here, the tree sparrow rids Indiana of literally tons of detrimental weed seeds.

Birders have always had a special affection for this bird. The fact that most of the other sparrows have moved on while the tree sparrow chooses to share the discomforts of winter with us is, I'm sure, a reason why it is held in such high esteem. It's rather like a friend who continues to be a friend during adverse times, when other "fair-weather" acquaintances have moved on.

Evening Grosbeak

[HESPERIPHONA VESPERTINA]

The term "winter finch" refers to a group of birds that is composed primarily of birds of the far north that visit the United States in the winter on an irregular basis. In some years, they are not seen at all in Indiana. In other years, there will be an invasion of these birds, and they will be quite abundant, even showing up at residential feeding stations. Recent years in Indiana have been poor for winter finches, but occasionally we are blessed with a banner winter finch year. There are a number of theories offered as to why these birds are so irregular in their movement south from Canada. The most widely accepted theory is that they move south when they have an inadequate food supply on their breeding grounds. When there is a bumper cone crop in Canada and Alaska, most of the winter finches stay close to their breeding grounds.

SIZE: *L. 7½–8½″ (19–21 cm).* COLORING: *Male, yellow, with black wings and prominent white wing patches. Large, whitish bill. Female, silver gray with a wash of yellow, black wings with white patches.* HABITAT: *Nests in northern coniferous forests. During "winter finch" years can be found in suburban backyards and parks.* NESTING: *Frail, loosely constructed nest, most often placed in evergreens; 3–4 eggs.* UNUSUAL MANNERISMS: *Shows preference for seeds of the box elder tree. Readily partakes of sunflower seeds at a winter feeder. Some years nearly absent from the United States.* IDENTIFYING HINTS: *Large white wing patches evident in flight. Flight notes distinctive, suggestive of robust house sparrow call. Large finch-type bill.* STATUS IN INDIANA: *Erratic winter visitor. Present about every three years in good numbers, from November to April.* RANGE: *Breeds from northern Canada to northernmost United States. Winters occasionally as far south as South Carolina.*

Of the eight species that make up the group of winter finches, the most common, I would say, is the pine siskin, and the rarest, the pine grosbeak. Somewhere between these two extremes is the evening grosbeak.

Normally, evening grosbeaks are found in Indiana in fairly small groups, fifteen to twenty birds, but relatives of mine in Canada tell me of seeing flocks of two or three hundred of these beautiful birds. When it is a banner year for the evening grosbeaks, they can be found throughout the state, occasionally even at feeding stations in urban areas. This occurs when cold weather has set in and snow is on the ground.

The status of the evening grosbeak has changed greatly since it was first discovered in the 1800s. At that time, it was considered to be a very rare bird that could only be seen in the most northern regions of the United States. The first Indiana records were reported by Amos W. Butler about one hundred years ago. During the last twenty-five years evening grosbeaks have increased their population in Indiana to the point that now they are seen every three or four years, even in the southern parts of the state. In years of a great influx of these birds, they have been reported as far south as Georgia and Louisiana.

Evening grosbeaks are very fond of the winged seed of the box elder, a member of the maple tree family, and they will go to great lengths to find this tree. If you have one of these trees in your neighborhood, watch it closely for these birds.

The field marks of this beautiful winter finch are the golden yellow of the males contrasted with black wings showing prominent white wing patches that are evident even in flight. The female is similar, but the coloring is much subdued. Both the male and female possess a large, whitish bill, from which its name is derived.

If you wish to attract this bird to your backyard, try putting out sunflower seeds, a food the evening grosbeaks dearly love. They will also make use of a birdbath. The sight of evening grosbeaks feeding on sunflower seeds, then happily splashing in a birdbath—when the ground is covered with snow—is a sight not soon forgotten.

SIZE: *L. 5–5¾″ (13–14 cm)*. COLORING: *Brown streaked back, white belly*. HABITAT: *Primarily deciduous woods*. NESTING: *Nest frequently built behind peeling bark of a tree; 6–7 eggs*. UNUSUAL MANNERISMS: *Usually seen flying to the base of a tree and spiraling upwards, searching the bark for food*. IDENTIFYING HINTS: *Learn to recognize the one thin, high-pitched note*. STATUS IN INDIANA: *Seen in Indiana during the months September through April. A common winter resident*. RANGE: *Nests from Alaska to southern Canada. Winters as far south as Florida*.

Brown Creeper

[CERTHIA FAMILIARIS]

Winter offers a marvelous opportunity to watch clearly the behavior of a number of birds that tend to be overlooked at other times of the year. One bird that is deserving of a closer look is the brown creeper. It's a fairly common bird in Indiana, and the period from October until May is the time to look for it here. It normally nests from the most northern parts of the United States to northern Canada and even southern Alaska.

It always amazes me that so little of nature goes to waste. The sparrows eat the weed seed, bluebirds and many other birds utilize cavities in dead trees for nesting, and the brown creeper uses loose bark, still clinging to the tree, for a nesting site. The female may spend as long as a month building a hammock-shaped nest of leaves, shredded bark bits, grasses, and moss. She fits it behind a piece of bark hanging off a tree!

Unfortunately, the creeper frequently goes undetected even when it is in close proximity to human activity. The brown creeper is a very unobtrusive bird and a very small one—just five or six inches long—with much of its length taken up by the tail. Its call note in winter is a rather soft pronunciation of the letters "ts," given in one syllable.

I can't recall ever having seen a brown creeper sitting still! It is always busy performing its lifework, looking for very small insects that have been overlooked or ignored by other birds.

The best way to see this mite of a bird is to sit very quietly in a wooded area and watch for what, at first, seems to be a dead leaf lazily floating to the ground. If this alleged leaf stops at the base of the tree and starts to spiral its way back up, examining every crevice in the bark, it's a brown creeper, not a leaf! The best field marks of the brown creeper are its small size, brown back with white belly, and the needle-like, decurved bill.

Often, the brown creeper is a visitor to your yard when you're not aware of his presence, but I am sure that if you put out a little beef suet during the winter season, the creeper will appreciate it. The suet needn't be gift wrapped nor have a name tag on it—he'll find it!

Mourning Dove

[ZENAIDURA MACROURA]

Doves have always been a symbol of peace and goodwill. At the opening ceremonies of the Montreal Olympiad, it was the releasing of large numbers of white doves that expressed the hope that all nations could live together harmoniously until the next Olympiad, to be held in Moscow in 1980.

During Christmas and Easter celebrations, the dove is prominently displayed in our stores, schools, homes, and places of business as an expression of love and hope. Yet, paradoxically, the dove is one of the most hunted birds in the United States. Thanks to the efforts of concerned citizens and various conservation-minded groups including national, state, and local Audubon Societies, our only remaining wild dove, the mourning dove, is protected by law in Indiana.

The mourning dove is a year-round resident in Indiana and is seen here each month of the year. It is one of our most common nesting birds. It prefers to build its rather flimsy nest in evergreens, but will accept any number of other trees or large shrubs as a substitute for evergreens. The mourning doves, which frequently will raise two or three broods of two birds each year, are very dutiful parents. The female incubates the eggs all day and is replaced by the male at night. The young are first fed a semi-liquid called "pigeon milk," which they get by regurgitation from the crop of the parent bird.

The mourning dove is a medium-sized, taupe-colored bird with a black spot behind the eye and a pointed tail. In flight the wings produce a whistling sound. Many people mistake the call of the mourning dove for that of an owl, mainly because it is most often heard in the early

SIZE: *L. 11–12" (28–30 cm).* COLORING: *Soft brown, showing white on edges of sharply pointed tail.* HABITAT: *Open fields, fringe areas around woods, suburban yards.* NESTING: *Loosely made nest of sticks, placed anywhere from low shrubs to tall trees, but frequently in evergreens. Two or more broods per year; 2 eggs.* UNUSUAL MANNERISMS: *Very tame, frequent visitor to the ground under feeders. May be seen in large flocks in fall and winter.* IDENTIFYING HINTS: *Voice, a low, mournful "coo-ah, coo, coo, coo." Long, pointed tail. Whistling of wings is evident in flight.* STATUS IN INDIANA: *Common year-round resident and nester.* RANGE: *Breeds and winters from southern Canada throughout the United States.*

morning hours and again as night is descending. It is a low, rather sorrowful "coo-ah, coo, coo, coo." This melancholy song, familiar to most of us, is the reason for this lovely dove's name.

The main diet of the mourning dove is weed seeds, and they are often seen feeding by the edge of a field and along the sides of the road. During a harsh winter, they will readily come to a feeder and appreciate wild bird seed scattered on the ground.

Happily, the mourning dove is doing well in Indiana, and during the holiday seasons this symbol of peace can be seen, not only in our artificial decorations, but—more significantly—alive and flying free.

White-winged Crossbill

[LOXIA LEUCOPTERA]

Red Crossbill

[LOXIA CURVIROSTRA]

My suggestion for a family of birds symbolic of the Christmas season is the crossbills. December is the month that the crossbills usually become evident in Indiana, and they are seldom found far from their favorite food, the cones of the evergreens. Unfortunately, the crossbills are not common birds in Indiana, and during many years they do not get down to Indiana at all. The most generally accepted theory is that when the cone crop in Canada is poor, the crossbills move south in search of a good supply of cones. For the first time in a number of years, both of the crossbills were seen in the Indianapolis area in 1975. The white-winged crossbill was seen in Eagle Creek Park for several weeks in late December, and the red crossbill was seen on the grounds of the Indianapolis Museum of Art, as well as at Eagle Creek.

It is unfortunate that the *white-winged crossbill* is so uncommon in Indiana, for it has so many appealing qualities. It is normally very tame, especially when feeding. There have been recorded instances of the white-winged actually being captured by hand. The male is among the most beautiful of birds; it has a soft pink body with contrasting black wings that have two broad white patches. The female and young males are brown-streaked birds with darker wings that also show the white wing-bars.

The male *red crossbill* is a brick-red bird with dark wings which, unless seen in fairly good light, could pass for a dark, unstreaked sparrow. The female is a tawny-brown bird with darker unstreaked wings. Both the white-winged and the red crossbills are parrot-like in their actions, and they frequently use their bills and feet for climbing from branch to branch.

The crossbills have an unusual breeding cycle. While most birds mate and raise their young in the spring and summer, the crossbills have been documented as having bred in early fall and in January, February, and March. Although, as a rule, they nest only in the northernmost parts of the United States, the red crossbills have nested as far south as North Carolina.

The crossbills are the only Indiana birds that have crossed upper and lower mandibles or bills. There are two theories as to why the crossbills have this unusual formation. One is that by inserting its bill into a pine cone and cracking it open, it can most efficiently extract the scales and seeds that are a staple in its diet.

The other theory has its origin in a German legend which claims that when Jesus was hanging on the cross, a group of birds tried desperately to remove the nails from the feet and hands of Jesus of Nazareth. It is said that God was so impressed by their efforts that He deemed that they should always have crossed bills to commemorate their courageous behavior.

RED CROSSBILL

Size: *L. 5¼–6½" (13–16 cm)*. Coloring: *Male, dark red with blackish wings. Female, olive gray, showing yellowish on the rump and underparts.* Habitat: *Evergreens, primarily those with a good crop of cones.* Nesting: *In coniferous trees, sometimes an early nester; 3–4 eggs.* Unusual Mannerisms: *Parrot-like, unusually tame,* Identifying Hints: *Lack of white wing-bars, crossed bills, and voice, a sharp and loud "kip, kip, kip."* Status in Indiana: *Not known to nest in Indiana. Most winters is not present. When present here, arrives after end of November and may stay until the middle of April. Found in Indiana about every three years.* Range: *Normally nests north of the Great Lakes to Alaska, with scattered nesting records south of its normal range. Has been found nesting in every month of the year.*

WHITE-WINGED CROSSBILL

Size: *L. 6–6½" (15–16 cm)*. Coloring: *Male, pink-red back and breast, black-winged with two white prominent wing-bars. Females lack the red but show the white wing-bars.* Habitat: *Coniferous forests.* Nesting: *In evergreen trees; 2–4 eggs.* Unusual Mannerisms: *Parrot-like in mannerisms. Allows close approach.* Identifying Hints: *White wing-bars, crossed bills, voice similar to red crossbill but not as harsh.* Status in Indiana: *Rare winter visitor, reported every four to five years. When present in Indiana is usually seen after the middle of November until the middle of April.* Range: *Breeds from Alaska north to the Canadian timberline and south to the northernmost border of the United States.*

SELECTED BIBLIOGRAPHY

BEARDSLEE, CLARK S., and HAROLD D. MITCHELL. *Birds of the Niagara Frontier Region*, Bulletin of the Buffalo Society of Natural Sciences, Volume 22. Buffalo, N. Y., 1965.

BENT, ARTHUR CLEVELAND. *Life Histories of North American Birds* (entire series of 25 volumes). New York: Dover Publications, Inc., 1919–1958.

BULL, JOHN, and JOHN FARRAND, JR. *The Audubon Society Field Guide to North American Birds: Eastern Region*, The American Museum of Natural History. New York: Alfred A. Knopf, 1977.

BUTLER, AMOS W. *The Birds of Indiana*, Report of the Indiana Department of Geology and Natural Resources. Indianapolis, 1897.

CHAPMAN, FRANK M. *The Warblers of North America*. New York: D. Appleton & Company, 1907.

GREENEWALT, CRAWFORD. *Hummingbirds*, American Museum of Natural History. New York: Doubleday & Co., 1960.

HARRISON, HAL H. *A Field Guide to Birds' Nests*. Boston: Houghton Mifflin Company, 1975

JOHNSGARD, PAUL A. *Waterfowl of North America*. Bloomington: Indiana University Press, 1975.

KLIGERMAN, JACK, ED. *The Birds of John Burroughs*. New York: Hawthorn Books, Inc., 1976.

KORTRIGHT, FRANCIS H. *The Ducks, Geese, and Swans of North America*. Washington, D.C.: Stackpole Co. & Wildlife Management Institute, 1942.

PEARSON, T. GILBERT, ED. *Birds of America*. New York: Doubleday & Co., 1936.

PETERSON, ROGER TORY. *A Field Guide to the Birds*. Boston: Houghton Mifflin Company, 1934.

POUGH, RICHARD H. *Audubon Bird Guide: Small Land Birds of Eastern and Central North America*. Garden City, N.Y.: Doubleday & Co., 1946.

———. *Audubon Water Bird Guide*. Garden City, N.Y.: Doubleday & Co., 1951.

REILLY, EDGAR M., JR. *The Audubon Illustrated Handbook of American Birds*. New York: McGraw-Hill, Inc., 1968.

ROBBINS, CHANDLER, BERTEL BRUNN, and HERBERT S. ZIM. *Birds of North America: A Guide to Field Identification*. New York: Golden Press, 1966.

TORREY, BRADFORD, and FRANCIS E. ALLEN, EDS. *The Journal of Henry David Thoreau*. New York: Dover Publications, 1962.

INDEX